Investor Relations Strategy

Anne Guimard

Investor Relations Strategy

Best Practices and Proven Techniques for Maximizing Shareholder Value

Third Edition

palgrave
macmillan

Anne Guimard
FINEO Investor Relations Advisors
Paris, France

ISBN 978-3-032-21678-6   ISBN 978-3-032-21679-3 (eBook)
https://doi.org/10.1007/978-3-032-21679-3

This Palgrave Macmillan imprint is published by the registered company Springer Nature Switzerland AG
The registered company address is: Gewerbestrasse 11, 6330 Cham, Switzerland

Preface

Investor Relations has always been about trust—and trust is built by people. No matter how sophisticated technology becomes, how complex markets grow, or how fast information circulates, Investor Relations ("IR") remains, at its core, a human discipline. It relies on dialogue rather than transmission, understanding rather than spin.

When the first edition of *Investor Relations: Principles and International Best Practices of Financial Communications* was published in 2008, the profession was already evolving, but its destination was not yet clear. Investor Relations was still widely perceived as a support function, primarily responsible for results announcements, regulatory compliance, and the mechanics of investor engagement. Strategic influence existed, but it was often informal, unevenly recognized, and heavily dependent on individual management practices rather than on established frameworks or governance.

The second edition, published in 2012, reflected the first major external shock to the modern capital markets environment. In the aftermath of the global financial crisis of 2008, collapsing confidence, heightened regulatory scrutiny, and prolonged macroeconomic uncertainty reshaped expectations around financial communication and disclosure. At the same time, social media began to accelerate information flows and broaden investor access, while Debt Investor Relations and Environmental, Social, and Governance ("ESG") considerations moved decisively from peripheral concerns to mainstream investor dialogue. This edition was therefore substantially expanded to address these changes, with greater emphasis on career development in

Investor Relations, the transition to International Financial Reporting Standards, and the growing need for practical tools, guidelines, checklists, and templates to support practitioners operating under heightened scrutiny.

In the decade that followed, the role of Investor Relations was further reshaped by successive external disruptions. The 2020 COVID-19 pandemic compressed decision-making cycles and intensified demands for clarity, leadership, and empathy under extreme uncertainty. Geopolitical fragmentation, trade tensions, and armed conflicts introduced new layers of risk, volatility, and cross-border complexity. At the same time, capital markets became more concentrated and more activist, ownership structures shifted further toward large institutional and passive investors, and proxy advisors gained decisive influence over governance outcomes. Technology accelerated both the speed and the persistence of market narratives, while non-financial factors—ranging from ESG performance to resilience and crisis preparedness—became inseparable from valuation and credibility.

This evolution has further accelerated as capital markets themselves have globalized. As emerging and frontier markets gain visibility and weight in global portfolios, the quality of Investor Relations has become a critical enabler—not only for individual issuers, but for the credibility and effectiveness of entire markets. Well-run IR functions help capital markets fulfill their fundamental purpose: attracting long-term capital, allocating it efficiently, and withstanding macroeconomic shocks and geopolitical disruptions of a scale never seen since the profession emerged in the 1960s. Ultimately, they support sustainable economic development.

Together, these forces have changed not only what Investor Relations does, but what it is expected to deliver.

The role of the Investor Relations Officer has expanded from organizer and spokesperson to trusted adviser—expected to anticipate market reactions, help frame decisions before they are taken by the management team and the board of directors, and ensure that strategy, performance, and risk are understood in context, not merely disclosed.

I have been writing about and training on Investor Relations for more than three decades—first as an Investor Relations Officer at multi-listed conglomerates, and later as the founder of FINEO Investor Relations Advisors, an international strategic IR advisory and training firm. What has kept me returning to the subject is its structural evolution: the elevation of Investor Relations from a technical, compliance-driven function to a strategic discipline that now sits at the heart of leadership and capital allocation.

It is against this accumulation of structural change and external shocks that the third edition has been developed.

This third edition remains intentionally practitioner-focused. It is not an academic analysis of capital markets, nor a regulatory or technical manual on ESG, artificial intelligence, or disclosure standards. Its purpose is to help corporate leaders and practitioners understand how Investor Relations works as a strategic discipline across different markets, ownership structures, and cycles, and how it can be executed with credibility, discipline, and judgment. Topics such as ESG, digitalization, activism, perception analysis, private capital, debt markets, and sovereign investors are therefore addressed not as specialist silos, but through the lens of Investor Relations strategy and execution, reflecting how these forces shape investor expectations and capital-allocation decisions in practice.

It continues the original mission of this book: to offer a practical, globally relevant guide to Investor Relations grounded in real-world experience, not theory. But it reflects a world in which IR is broader, more exposed, and more consequential than ever before. Today, Investor Relations must integrate financial analysis with governance insight, sustainability with strategy, and narrative with data—under constant scrutiny from investors, regulators, boards, and the public.

In markets that are saturated with information, the task of Investor Relations is no longer to say more, but to ensure that what is said makes sense—over time, across channels, and under pressure. This is why Investor Relations today is not simply a communications function, but a leadership discipline.

This book describes Investor Relations accordingly. It is designed to elevate the understanding of what effective Investor Relations truly requires beyond tactics: judgment, authority, discipline, and strategic intent. The practices and frameworks presented here all flow from that premise. They are all based on events that I have seen companies and clients navigate.

Across markets, cycles, and technologies, one truth endures: the quality of Investor Relations is a competitive differentiator that can lead to higher valuation. It has been my firm's motto since founding in 1998. Critically, it reflects the quality of leadership a company brings to its relationship with capital markets. Trust is never a given—it is built, deliberately and over time.

The time has come to acknowledge that Investor Relations is ultimately about managing meaning, not just information.

Paris, France Anne Guimard

Competing Interests The author has no competing interests to declare that are relevant to the content of this manuscript.

About This Book

This book is intended as a practical guide to Investor Relations for practitioners, senior executives, students, and anyone involved in the interaction between companies and the capital markets. No single structure can perfectly reflect the diversity of situations encountered in practice. The organization of this book therefore aims to provide a logical progression for readers who wish to follow the discipline step by step, while also serving as a structured learning path for those focusing on specific contexts or as a flexible reference tool for those who need guidance on specific topics.

Because the book is designed for readers with different levels of experience and different objectives, it can be read in more than one way. Some readers may prefer to read it from beginning to end in order to follow the full logic of the discipline. Others may wish to consult specific chapters or sections depending on the issues they face in their professional responsibilities. The structure of the book is therefore deliberately modular, allowing individual topics to be approached independently while still forming part of a coherent overall framework:

Chapter 1 defines the function, explains its role within the company, and clarifies its regulatory and strategic foundations.

Chapter 2 examines how superior Investor Relations creates competitive advantage and how companies can differentiate themselves through IR excellence.

Chapter 3 discusses Investor Relations across different capital structures and situations: going public, cross-border listings, private companies, private equity, sovereign wealth funds, debt investor relations, and the role of IR in major corporate-finance decisions. It also examines related topics that increasingly influence the capital story, including ESG considerations and shareholder activism.

Chapter 4 focuses on the foundations of Investor Relations strategy, including organizational positioning, mandate definition, reporting lines, resources, board oversight, and the governance processes that enable effective IR.

Chapter 5 presents the strategic choices available to IR practitioners: crafting the narrative, managing expectations and guidance, periodic reporting and disclosure, attracting analyst coverage, shareholder identification and diversification, board engagement, and integrated communications.

Chapter 6 addresses the operational execution of Investor Relations: the IR calendar, day-to-day operations, investor engagement programs, infrastructure decisions, budgets, technology, and the continuous improvement processes that strengthen IR effectiveness over time. The chapter also covers Initial Public Offering ("IPO") execution, the Investor Relations operating cycle, targeting practices, communication tools, and the assessment of market perception.

Chapter 7 provides a framework for measuring the value that Investor Relations delivers, moving beyond the share price and activity metrics to capital markets outcomes and competitive differentiation.

Chapter 8 looks ahead to what will change, what will endure, and the capabilities IR professionals will need in an evolving market environment.

Chapter 9 provides practical tools and checklists covering shareholder-base management, investor engagement programs, global IR management, and technology implementation.

Within each chapter, the content is organized into short sections focusing on specific questions or practical situations. This format reflects the way Investor Relations is often practiced, where professionals need to address concrete issues under time pressure rather than follow a purely theoretical approach. Readers should therefore not be surprised to find concise subsections, bullet-point summaries, and practical checklists throughout the book. These are intended to make the material easier to use in real-life situations.

The book does not assume that all companies face the same challenges. Examples and discussions refer to listed companies, companies preparing for an initial public offering, privately held groups, and organizations operating in both developed and emerging markets. Readers are encouraged to focus on the sections that correspond most closely to their own situation.

At the end of each chapter, **Practical Implications** translate each chapter's concepts into actionable guidance to help readers quickly identify the key points when using the book as a reference: what to prioritize, what to avoid, and how to apply the frameworks in real situations. The content of this book is intended for informational purposes only and reflects general observations and professional experience rather than legal, regulatory, or investment advice. Readers should consult appropriate professional advisers before taking decisions or actions based on the concepts discussed herein.

Contents

List of Figures

List of Tables

1

Introduction to Investor Relations

This chapter establishes the fundamental principles of Investor Relations and explains why the discipline has evolved from a compliance-driven activity into a strategic management function that directly affects capital access, valuation, and competitive positioning. It sets out the conceptual foundations that underpin the rest of the book, proposes a working definition suited to today's market realities, and examines the relationship between valuation, capital allocation, and market perception. The chapter then maps the scope of Investor Relations—its functional responsibilities, core mission, and expanding perimeter—before positioning IR as a form of strategic dialogue in the competition for capital.

A clear understanding of these principles is essential for building a coherent and effective Investor Relations strategy. The chapter also shows how the absence of a structured IR approach can create measurable disadvantages, including a higher cost of capital and reduced strategic flexibility, and explains why Investor Relations has become a global discipline characterized by common principles applied in different market contexts.

1.1 What Is Investor Relations: Foundations and Definitions

Long gone are the days when Investor Relations was a support function, a burdensome reporting exercise, or a reactive interface with financial markets. What began as the domain of ex-bankers, stockbrokers, or financial analysts who could read a balance sheet and speak to the CFO has evolved into a

A. Guimard, *Investor Relations Strategy*, https://doi.org/10.1007/978-3-032-21679-3_1

sophisticated management discipline operating at the intersection of finance, communication, corporate strategy, and governance. Today, Investor Relations shapes how companies are understood, valued, and trusted by capital markets over time—and there is no going back. As global competition for capital intensifies, transparency expectations rise, and scrutiny of governance and long-term value creation deepens, the quality of Investor Relations has become a decisive source of sustainable competitive advantage in capital markets. This book positions Investor Relations as an investment in credibility, resilience, and strategic optionality—one that directly influences valuation, cost of capital, and ownership quality. It clarifies what Investor Relations truly is—and just as importantly, what it is not—establishing a modern, globally relevant understanding of IR.

Investor Relations emerged as a distinct corporate function in the United States in the 1960s, when equity ownership was expanding rapidly among both institutions and individuals. General Electric is often cited as pioneering the creation of Investor Relations.

Sixty years later, this distinction between passive shareholder relations and proactive capital market strategy remains the fundamental dividing line between IR as a cost center and IR as an investment whose return can be measured and a competitive advantage that can make a difference.

Today, IR is a sophisticated strategic function sitting at the intersection of finance, communication, corporate strategy, and governance. No longer confined to regulatory compliance, it has become a discipline that directly influences enterprise value through its impact on cost of capital, market positioning, and corporate reputation. In some markets, stock exchanges now require issuers, as listed companies are often referred to, to have an identifiable Investor Relations function as a condition for listing.

A frequent source of misunderstanding is whether Investor Relations has a marketing role. The answer is both precise and nuanced.

Investor Relations is not product marketing, brand, or share-price promotion. It does not seek to "sell" securities in the way commercial functions sell goods or services. It operates within strict legal, regulatory, and ethical boundaries that fundamentally distinguish it from promotional communication.

That said, Investor Relations does have a marketing dimension in the economic sense of the term: it operates in a competitive market for capital. Capital is scarce, investor attention is finite, and companies compete continuously—not only on fundamentals, but on how clearly, credibly, and consistently those fundamentals are understood.

In this context, IR is responsible for the marketing of value: articulating the company's investment proposition, competitive positioning, and long-term value-creation logic in a way that enables the market to make an informed judgment about fair value and appropriate ownership.

This form of marketing is not promotional. It is analytical, fact-based, and cumulative. It relies on disciplined narrative, consistency over time, and the alignment of words with decisions and outcomes. When done well, it reduces uncertainty, information asymmetry between management and investors, and misinterpretation without inflating expectations.

The Legal and Regulatory Foundations of Investor Relations

Investor Relations is a strategic management function that operates within a strict legal and regulatory framework. This framework is built on widely accepted principles that govern how financial information is prepared, disclosed, and used by market participants. These principles are the backbone of trust between issuers and investors and directly shape the day-to-day practice of IR.

The core disclosure principles can be summarized as follows:

- Transparency—Clear, accurate, and sufficiently complete disclosure of all material information.
- Equal access to information—All shareholders and potential investors, regardless of their location or the size of their holding, should have access to the same information at the same time.
- Timeliness—Material developments must be disclosed promptly, not when it is convenient for the company.
- Accuracy—Information must be truthful, not misleading, supported by verifiable facts and robust internal processes.
- Consistency and comparability of data—Information should be presented in a way that allows investors to compare performance over time and against peers. Changes in metrics, definitions, or presentation must be justified. Unexplained changes invite investor suspicion that the company is trying to hide something, which erodes credibility—a costly reputational damage for any issuer.
- Accountability—Those responsible for preparing, approving, and disseminating disclosure (board, management, IR, finance, legal) can be held liable for breaches of laws and regulations.

Lawmakers and market authorities (regulators, stock exchanges) translate these principles into concrete obligations for issuers and for certain recipients of information as well. These include rules on inside information, selective disclosure, market abuse, periodic reporting, ad hoc announcements, and securities trading policies. Failure to comply can lead to administrative sanctions, civil liability, and, in some cases, criminal prosecution.

Since the second edition of this book was published, the regulatory landscape has evolved dramatically. New and more detailed disclosure requirements around climate risk, Environmental, Social, and Governance ("ESG"), cybersecurity, human capital management, and board diversity have expanded the IR remit far beyond traditional financial reporting. Investor Relations must now orchestrate and explain a much broader set of information—financial and non-financial—so investors can assess risk, resilience, and long-term value creation. This enables informed decisions to invest, hold, sell (in full or in part), or avoid investing in the company altogether.

It is important to remember that these rules are not simply constraints: they provide the foundation for fair, efficient markets in which effective Investor Relations can create lasting value. For those who understand how to use them strategically, they also create communications opportunities when disclosing beyond requirements can drive a higher valuation. This is typically the case when in the same sector, one company discloses more operational metrics than its nearest competitor.

Three Widely Used Definitions of Investor Relations

Over time, professional bodies and regulators have proposed formal definitions of Investor Relations. Although they use different wording, they converge on a common core.

- National Investor Relations Institute (NIRI, United States)

"Investor Relations is a strategic management responsibility that integrates finance, communication, marketing and securities law compliance to enable the most effective two-way communication between a company, the financial community, and other constituencies, which ultimately contributes to a company's securities achieving fair valuation."

Several elements are worth highlighting:

- Strategic management responsibility—IR is not an isolated communication activity buried somewhere in the organization; it belongs at senior management level.

- Integration of finance, communication, marketing, and securities law compliance—IR is multidisciplinary by design.
- Two-way communication—IR is all about fostering dialogue, not one-way disclosure where only the investors get to ask questions, and management to provide the answers.
- Fair valuation—the objective is not a "high" share price at any cost, but one that fairly reflects the company's fundamentals and prospects.
- Other constituencies—long before the term "stakeholders" became commonplace, this definition acknowledged that IR sits within a broader ecosystem than just shareholders or financial analysts.

- The Investor Relations Society (IRS, United Kingdom)

"Investor Relations is the communication of information and insight between a company and the investment community. This process enables a full appreciation of the company's business activities, strategy and prospects and allows the market to make an informed judgement about the fair value and appropriate ownership of a company."

The UK definition reinforces and nuances some points:

- Information and insight—IR goes beyond raw data; it must provide interpretation and context. This is exactly what the preface of this book referred to: managing meaning.
- Business activities, strategy, and prospects—the focus is explicitly forward-looking and strategic, not only historical performance.
- Informed judgment about fair value and appropriate ownership—IR is not only about valuation but also about attracting the shareholders that will stay for the long run and support the company's long-term ambitions.

- Gulf Cooperation Council ("GCC") Financial Markets Committee (2025)

"Investor Relations (IR) is the effective two-way communication of the relevant and necessary information required between an issuer and the financial markets. It enables the investment community to consistently make an informed judgement about the fair value of an issuer's shares and securities. The aim of an IR team is to communicate and provide the financial markets with accurate, sufficient, and timely information about the issuer's objectives, strategy, activities, operating environment, and financial situation, in a manner that provides the most accurate snapshot of the issuer as an investment target.

The principal role of the IR function is to manage interest from these audiences. IR needs to establish a framework of communications activities to ensure the investment community is fully informed about the performance of the business, as well as identifying potential issues that may influence the issuer's reputation. Further, IR serves to emphasize the quality of the relationship between the issuer and its stakeholders through credibility and trust. Together, all this improves the understanding of the issuer's investment proposition. In turn, over time, this can increase the valuation of the issuer's equity by attracting capital, reducing share-price volatility, and potentially lowering funding costs.

From an IR point of view, the IR function needs to be seen to keep the market informed at all times with timely disclosure, in accordance with statutory reporting requirements. The overall objective of the regulatory environment is to ensure confidence in the financial markets, and the most important task for regulators is to maintain the utmost confidence in their markets."

In 2025, the stock exchanges of the Gulf Cooperation Council (GCC), namely, Bahrain, Kuwait, Oman, Qatar, Saudi Arabia, and the United Arab Emirates, put together a definition that is more operational and emphasizes:

- Explicit linkage between IR and volatility reduction and lower funding costs.
- The framework of communications activities—IR as a structured program, not only ad hoc, compliance-driven interactions.
- The role of IR in reputation and trust-building.
- The importance of understanding local regulatory context and obligations.
- It is interesting that the GCC markets, building on US and UK practice, chose to craft their own definition, reflecting the need to professionalize the practice of IR across their emerging and fast-developing capital markets.

Across geographies and levels of market maturity, we can identify a shared "IR core":

- Two-way communication

IR is not a one-way disclosure exercise. It is a dialogue in which the company both explains and listens. A well-run IR function asks investors, analysts, and journalists questions, seeks feedback, and leverages it to enhance IR engagement and strategy formulation.

- Fair valuation as the ultimate objective

All three definitions link IR to the market's ability to reach an informed judgment about fair value. The role of IR is not to "talk up the share price" at any cost, but to reduce information asymmetry so that buyers and sellers can meet on common ground, which will, in turn, contribute to share-price formation.

- The bridge role between company and investment community

IR is the conduit between corporate decision-making and capital markets. It translates corporate strategy, performance, and risk into language and formats that the investment community can use.

- Information quality: accurate, sufficient, timely, relevant, and necessary

The recurring emphasis is on information that is not only compliant but also decision-useful: accurate, complete enough to be meaningful, and delivered on time and responsive to investors' real information needs—not just minimum legal requirements. Issuers and investors do not always share the same view of what "relevant" means. Investors may treat most information as relevant, while companies tend to be more selective. For instance, a company may assume that investors may not be interested in a product launch announcement, when they actually are. Ongoing, candid dialogue helps establish common ground and reduces frustration on both sides.

There are however strategic nuances worth highlighting.

Different emphasis in each of the above definitions of Investor Relations has practical implications for how IR should be organized and measured:

- NIRI's "strategic management responsibility": IR should report at senior level (typically CFO or CEO), not be treated as a subset of communications. It is part of strategy execution and capital allocation, not just messaging.
- IR Society's focus on "information and insight": IR must explain the business model, strategy, and prospects, not just historical numbers. It is a market education function, helping the investment community truly

understand how the company creates value. More often than not, companies don't realize and therefore underutilize the power of educating the market on their businesses and competitive environment. This is a true differentiator that works well, especially for smaller companies which struggle getting to (and staying on) the investors' and analysts' radar screen, when large companies are much better researched and don't need to make much of an effort in this area.
- GCC's emphasis on volatility and funding costs: Reducing share-price volatility, increasing liquidity, and lowering cost of capital are legitimate IR key performance indicators ("KPIs"). IR performance can and should be tied to measurable business outcomes over time, beyond the share price which can be largely impacted by external factors out of the control of the company.
- GCC's regulatory and reputation focus: In emerging and international markets in particular, understanding local rules, disclosure expectations, and the trust-building role of IR is critical. IR is both a compliance and a confidence-building function.

All three definitions focus on "stakeholders/other constituencies": IR increasingly operates within a wider stakeholder ecosystem: debt investors, ESG investors, employees, rating agencies, media, and, in many markets, a growing base of retail investors, all current and prospective alike.

A New Working Definition of Investor Relations

While these definitions remain robust, they do not yet fully capture several structural shifts at play:

- ESG integration as core to IR strategy

Environmental, Social, and Governance considerations have moved from a separate Corporate Social Responsibility ("CSR") report to central elements of the investment case and risk assessment, from "nice-to-have" to "must-have."

- Technology and data

While technology has always been an accelerator of the evolution of IR, the practice is being reshaped by IR platforms, virtual and hybrid engagement formats, AI-powered analytics, real-time ownership data, and sentiment tracking. The speed and granularity of information flows have changed expectations. Worth noting is that investors used to have less information about a sector or a company than the issuer. This is no longer the case as they have developed a critical edge over most IR departments that have not been afforded similar resources to invest in technology and tend to be largely underinvested.

- Retail investor surge and market democratization

In many markets, retail investors have become more visible and vocal, through digital platforms, apps, and social media and representing a large, sometimes the largest contributors to trading volumes. IR must build in the capabilities to effectively address the needs of this stakeholder group.

- The activist and stewardship landscape

Shareholder activism, as well as more assertive corporate governance stewardship by large passive and active asset managers, has made IR a frontline function in defensive preparedness and ongoing governance dialogue. Boards, too, are developing the practice of having a designated non-executive director for shareholder engagement.

- Corporate access beyond earnings

Perception studies, investor targeting, capital markets days, thematic deep dives, and continuous investor outreach events (a service offered by brokerage firms and investment banks that is known as "corporate access") are now part of standard IR practice, far beyond the traditional "results roadshow" or "Non-Deal Roadshow" (NDR).

The resilience over several decades of the three definitions above reflects the maturity and continued evolution of the IR profession: the core purpose of IR—building trust-based dialogue that enables fair valuation—has remained constant, even as the tools, stakeholders, and competitive landscape have transformed dramatically. This chapter's working definition below builds on this foundation while explicitly incorporating these contemporary realities and recognizing Investor Relations' strategic influence:

- First, information asymmetry has become the primary source of mispricing. Investors can analyze financial statements as competently as management; what they lack is reliable understanding of strategic choice, risk perception, and management credibility. IR's role has shifted from "reporting what happened" to "explaining why management chose this path and what could go wrong."

- Second, compliance with disclosure rules is necessary but no longer sufficient. The competitive advantage in IR comes from the practice that exceeds compliance—the dialogue, context, and consistency that build trust and reduce mispricing.
- Third, trust has become quantifiable. Companies with strong IR practices—characterized by predictability, transparency, and consistency—trade at premiums to intrinsic value. This premium reflects how the market is pricing the reduced risk of information-driven surprises and management credibility problems.

Bringing these strands together, and taking into account the evolution of markets and practice, we would like to offer a new definition of Investor Relations to reflect these shifts:

> Investor Relations (IR) is a strategic management function that directly builds and maintains long-term, trust-based relationships between a company and its financial stakeholders – primarily shareholders, potential investors and the wider capital markets ecosystem, including financial analysts and the financial media, in compliance with regulatory disclosure requirements. At the same time, it contributes to the balanced understanding of the company's track record, culture, strategic directions and potential by employees, customers, business partners, competitors and the communities where the company is operating.
> Sitting at the intersection of finance, strategy, communication and regulation, IR translates the company's performance, risk profile and future ambitions into clear, decision-useful information that investors can understand, analyze and act upon when deciding to buy, sell or hold the company's securities. Adequately resourced and strategically executed, IR serves as a competitive differentiator that supports fair price formation and long-term value creation.

This definition applies to equity and debt, to public and—where they engage with capital providers—private companies.

In the next section, we will move from definition to scope: which stakeholders IR is responsible for, what activities and channels it covers in practice, and how its remit has expanded from a narrow focus on listed equity to a broader role in the competition for capital.

1.2 The Scope of Investor Relations

Once we know what Investor Relations is, we need to be clear about what it actually does. For boards and executives, this is not an abstract question. How you define IR's scope determines staffing, budget, reporting lines, involvement in decisions, and ultimately the value IR can create. In practice, the scope of IR can be described in terms of its functional responsibilities (what IR does day to day) and its strategic mission (what IR seeks to influence in capital markets).

Three Functional Responsibilities: Information, Interpretation, Interaction

IR has three functional responsibilities which form the operational backbone of IR:

1. ***Information***—ensuring that accurate, timely, and relevant information is provided to the market in line with regulatory requirements and best practice. Without this, you increase the risk of misunderstandings, rumors, regulatory issues, and a permanent "uncertainty discount" on the share price.
2. ***Interpretation***—helping investors understand not just the numbers, but the strategy, business model, risk profile, and governance that underpin those numbers. Without interpretation, investors fill the gaps themselves—often using peer assumptions or worst-case scenarios. Investor education always pays off and can actually be a powerful competitive differentiator.
3. ***Interaction***—creating structured, ongoing dialogue between management and the investment community, and feeding investor perspectives back into the organization. Without this feedback loop, management and boards make decisions in a vacuum and miss early-warning signs—raising the risk of value-destructive decisions.

Without any one of them, you invite distinct risks:

- information gaps trigger regulatory and reputational problems
- lack of interpretation forces investors to fill knowledge gaps with worst-case assumptions;
- missing feedback loops leave management strategically blind to emerging market concerns.

Most importantly, these three responsibilities are interdependent—high-quality information is useless without interpretation, and dialogue without actionable data is merely conversation.

In practice, this means that the scope of IR spans, at a minimum:

- Financial reporting and disclosure
- Equity and, in many cases, debt investor communication
- Analyst and rating agency relationships
- Capital markets days, conferences, roadshows, and investor meetings (including one-on-one meetings and other outreach events)
- Perception analysis, market intelligence, and systematic feedback to management and the board
- Governance- and ESG-related dialogue with shareholders and proxy advisers on the resolutions to be submitted to shareholders' approval.

Each of these activities has direct strategic consequences. For example:

- the quality of financial disclosure affects analyst models and valuation multiples;
- the way you manage rating agency relationships influences your cost of debt;
- systematic perception analysis helps you avoid "surprises" in investor reactions;
- Taken together, they are the operational expression of IR's strategic role.

IR is therefore not simply "doing the results presentation" or "sending out press releases." Nor is it only a sub-branch of public relations, corporate communications, or compliance. Effective IR supports the company's access to capital and the long-term alignment between management, the Board, and owners.

IR's Core Mission: Identity, Valuation, Reputation

Beyond its day-to-day responsibilities, Investor Relations seeks to deliver three strategic outcomes:

1. Convey the firm's identity—articulating what makes the company unique: its business model, competitive advantages, strategic direction, corporate culture, and value-creation criteria. When identity is clear, investors can quickly understand "who you are" and whether you fit their mandate.

2. Establish its market position toward adequate valuation—ensuring that markets understand the company's true worth, the metrics that matter, and the peers against which it should reasonably be compared. When this is done well, you reduce the risk of inappropriate peer comparisons and hasty valuation shortcuts.
3. Contribute to building corporate reputation—shaping how stakeholders perceive the company's credibility, reliability, and long-term viability, particularly the quality of its management and governance.

These three strategic outcomes work together to create what we might call the IR value proposition: helping markets understand not just what a company is today, but what it can become—and why investors should believe in that future. As later chapters will show, this value proposition can be observed in concrete metrics: the stability and composition of the shareholder base, trading liquidity, analyst coverage, valuation multiples, and even the company's ability to use its shares as acquisition currency or ward off hostile attacks.

The Expanding Perimeter: From Shareholders to Stakeholders

In a world of globalized capital and heightened transparency, the boundaries between "Investor Relations" and "stakeholder relations" have become increasingly permeable. Employees are often shareholders through equity schemes. Customers factor corporate values and ESG performance into purchasing decisions. Suppliers and business partners assess a company's long-term viability and ethical standards. Communities grant—or withdraw—the social license to operate.

Each of these stakeholder groups can materially influence the company's ability to create long-term value and therefore matters to investors. For example, a strike, a customer boycott, a supply-chain controversy, a data breach, a social media crisis, or an authorization withdrawal can all destroy value quickly—even if last quarter's financial statements were strong.

The modern IR function must navigate this expanded stakeholder universe while maintaining its core focus on capital providers. This requires:

- Message consistency across stakeholders, while tailoring delivery and emphasis to each audience's priorities (and languages)
- Breaking down communication silos between IR, corporate communications, sustainability, HR, and other internal functions

- Understanding stakeholder interdependencies and how serving broader stakeholders ultimately creates shareholder value
- Balancing transparency with competitive confidentiality and legal constraints.
- Managing the tension among competing demands is not just good governance—it directly affects valuation, liquidity, and cost of capital.

IR as Strategic Dialogue

Against this backdrop, Investor Relations can best be described as a two-way communications stream, a strategic dialogue. In this respect, it has much in common with marketing and customer–supplier relationship management. This bidirectional dimension distinguishes modern IR from simple information dissemination or one-way reporting (Fig. 1.1).

Indeed, the dialogue flows in both directions, not unlike a customer–supplier relationship framework in the sense that it is structured, reciprocal, and grounded in clearly articulated expectations:

- Company to markets—communicating strategy, performance, competitive positioning, management quality, governance standards, risk management, and long-term value-creation plans.
- Markets to company—providing feedback on market perceptions, peer comparisons, valuation concerns, strategic questions, competitive threats, and emerging investor priorities.

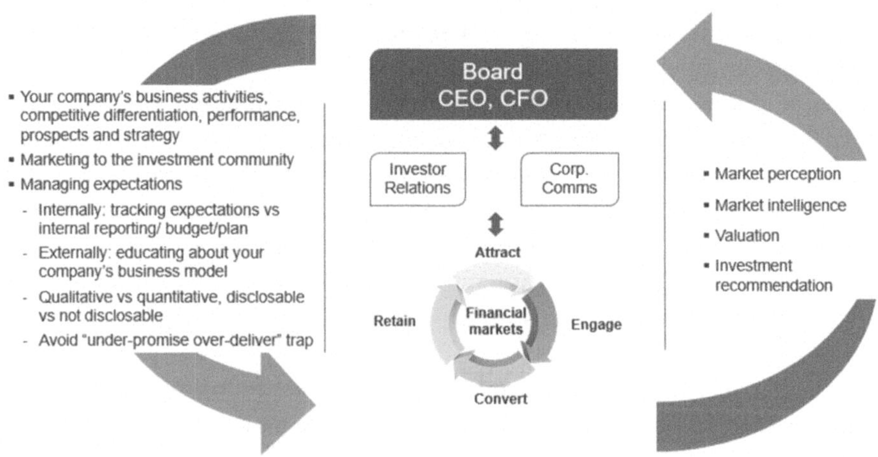

Fig. 1.1 Investor Relations is a two-way communication stream

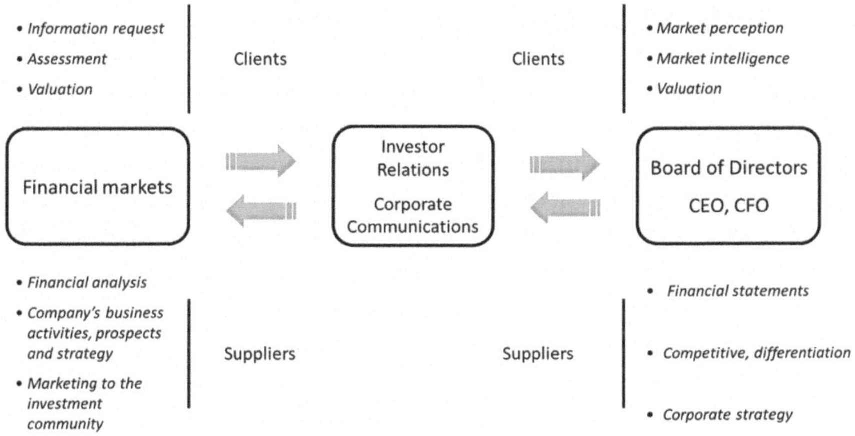

Fig. 1.2 Investor Relations: the customer–supplier relationship model

What once occurred primarily through quarterly earnings calls and annual investor days now happens continuously across multiple channels: formal filings, press releases, investor presentations, virtual roadshows, ESG disclosures, digital platforms, webcasts, direct retail investor engagement, and even social media (Fig. 1.2).

Technology accelerates the dialogue, increasing both its speed and its consequences. It also raises the cost of poor coordination and inconsistency—making disciplined message governance and IR's positioning more important than ever.

This creates real operational challenges. For example, if the CFO emphasizes "pricing discipline and margin protection" on the earnings call while marketing simultaneously launches "aggressive discount campaigns" on social media, the market will catch the contradiction immediately—and may punish the stock before IR has a chance to clarify. This is why many companies implement strict pre-announcement quiet periods or messaging lockdowns requiring IR clearance for any material external communication. Internal alignment is critical.

Understanding the scope of IR leads naturally to a more fundamental question: why does it matter strategically? The answer lies in the way IR shapes access to capital, valuation, resilience, and reputation in an increasingly competitive marketplace. Technology has made IR transparency both easier (distribution) and riskier (instant detection of inconsistencies, lack of control over the information recipients).

1.3 IR in the Competition for Capital

Going public means entering a new competitive environment: an IPO adds another layer of competitive pressures. From listing onward, an issuer competes not only in its industry, but also for investor attention and capital—against tens of thousands of other listed companies worldwide. Whether a company seeks to raise equity, debt, or hybrid financing, it competes against every other investment opportunity available to capital providers, at least theoretically.

This competition plays out through multiple dimensions, including:

- Risk-adjusted return expectations—investors allocate capital where they expect the best returns for a given level of risk.
- Information quality and transparency—superior disclosure reduces perceived risk, narrows the information gap, and can lower the cost of capital.
- Management credibility and track record—investors pay a premium for teams they trust to deliver on their commitments.
- Growth prospects and market positioning—compelling growth narratives and defensible competitive advantages, including the ability to attract and retain talent, be a supplier of choice, command higher valuations.
- Governance and risk management—strong governance and robust risk frameworks signal lower execution risk.
- ESG performance—environmental, social, and governance factors increasingly influence capital allocation decisions.

Various industry studies and buy-side surveys often suggest that companies recognized for the exemplarity of their IR programs often enjoy tangible advantages over peers with similar fundamentals, for example:

- Valuation—higher trading multiples and, in some markets, measurable valuation premiums compared to peers with weaker IR.
- Liquidity—tighter bid-ask spreads and higher average daily trading volumes, making it easier for investors to build or exit positions.
- Analyst coverage—broader and better-quality analyst coverage, which improves visibility and reduces the risk of being "forgotten" by the market, thereby negatively affecting liquidity.
- Volatility—lower event-driven share-price volatility around results or major announcements, because expectations are better managed.

These are tangible benefits. They directly impact your ability to raise capital, finance acquisitions, retain talent through equity-based compensation, and withstand periods of turbulence.

1.4 From Communication to Strategic Influence

Because it operates at the intersection of finance, strategy, communication, and governance, IR has a direct influence on several drivers of enterprise value. To unlock this potential, IR must be positioned as a strategic lever, not just an information channel, and certainly not a box-ticking compliance exercise. In practice, this requires three organizational prerequisites:

1. Direct CEO/CFO access—the head of IR needs direct, regular access to the CEO and CFO. Weekly touchpoints should be the norm, not the exception. IR engagement with the Board is becoming the norm, too.
2. Pre-decision input—IR should provide market perspective before major strategic decisions (M&A, capital allocation shifts, listing changes, significant ESG commitments) are finalized, not after the press release has been drafted.
3. Message control—IR must have final authority over investor-facing communications, even when this means challenging or refining messages prepared by other departments.

Without these prerequisites, you have investor communications, not strategic Investor Relations—and the difference can cost millions in valuation.

1.5 A Global Discipline

While the principles described in this chapter apply globally, implementation details vary by market. Local regulation, market structure, liquidity, free-float structures, macroeconomics, and investor culture all influence how IR is organized and executed. IR professionals should understand these differences intimately, since they advise management and boards on market-specific capital strategy—working in tandem with internal and external legal counsel.

For internationally active companies, or companies with an internationally diversified shareholder base—or the objective to have one—this means two things. First, your IR strategy must be coherent globally—the core story, numbers, and governance must align across all markets. Second, execution needs to be locally flexible—the communication approach, the degree of idiomatic articulation, the topics emphasized, and the conduct of meetings may differ between, for example, London, New York, Tokyo, Riyadh, and Johannesburg.

1.6 The Consequences of Operating Without Strategic IR

Companies that underinvest in IR or treat it purely as a compliance function typically face some combination of:

- Persistent valuation discount—the market "prices in" uncertainty, opacity, or perceived governance risk.
- Limited investor diversification—a narrow, often short-term-oriented shareholder base that can amplify volatility.
- Sparse or low-quality analyst coverage—if analysts do not understand the story, or if there is no knowledgeable point of contact within the company, they will either ignore it or oversimplify it.
- Greater vulnerability in crises—without pre-existing trust and transparent communication habits, bad news can trigger disproportionate market reactions.
- Higher cost of capital—through lower valuation, higher credit spreads, or more restrictive terms from lenders and investors.

In other words, the cost of poor IR is real and measurable, reflected in a share price discount rather than the premium observed earlier.

In summary, the strategic importance of Investor Relations can be seen in three areas:

- Value and capital—influencing valuation, liquidity, cost of capital, and access to funding.
- Risk and resilience—reducing the risk of mispricing, rumors, and over-reactions, and strengthening the company's ability to navigate crises.
- Alignment and execution—aligning internal stakeholders around a clear story and bringing external market insight back into strategic decision-making.

The full strategic framework for winning the competition for capital is explored in Chapter 2. Here, at the end of this chapter, the key message is that Investor Relations is both a clearly defined scope of responsibilities and a strategic function with direct impact on value creation, risk, and long-term corporate success. Companies that recognize this and organize accordingly will treat IR not as a cost center, but as an investment in a lasting competitive advantage.

Practical Implications

- Treat Investor Relations as a management discipline that informs corporate strategy decision-making in capital markets
- Clarify internally what IR is responsible for—and what it is not—before adding tools, channels, or reporting layers
- Anchor IR activity in three core responsibilities: information, interpretation, and interaction
- Ensure senior management understands that IR shapes identity, valuation, and reputation over time
- Recognize that operating without strategic IR is a choice—with predictable consequences for credibility, valuation resilience, and access to capital

Having established the principles and scope of Investor Relations, the next chapter examines how the function creates competitive advantage across four distinct arenas: stock market competition, business competition, aspiration competition, and geographic competition. It explains how this advantage translates into lower cost of capital, better access to funding, and enhanced strategic flexibility.

2

Investor Relations as a Competitive Advantage

Having defined Investor Relations, this chapter examines how Investor Relations creates competitive advantage in the competition for capital and identifies the specific benefits that companies can expect from investing in a professional IR function.

The strategic importance of Investor Relations, outlined in the previous chapter, leads to a practical question: what specific competitive advantages can companies expect from investing in world-class IR?

From the moment a company becomes publicly traded, it enters a global competition for capital—not only against direct competitors in its industry, but against thousands of companies across jurisdictions, geographies, business models, and sizes. To win, a company must differentiate itself positively to attract, engage, and retain the investors best aligned with its strategy and stage of development. Financial performance alone, assuming it is made easily available to the public, just won't do it.

When executed to perfection, Investor Relations creates tangible competitive advantages that extend far beyond share-price performance. While these advantages are most visible in public markets, many of the underlying principles—clarity, transparency, consistency, and credibility—also apply, to a significant extent, to private companies that deliberately leverage disclosure and investor-style communication.

At its core, superior IR contributes to:

- A better diversified and more resilient shareholder base.
- A stronger corporate reputation.
- More favorable valuation and risk perception.

A. Guimard, *Investor Relations Strategy*, https://doi.org/10.1007/978-3-032-21679-3_2

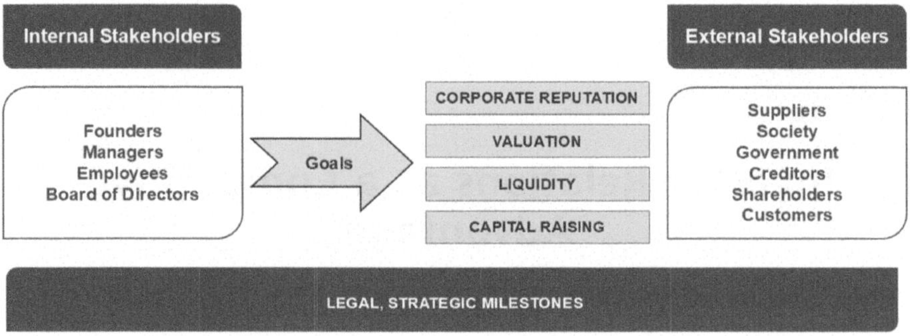

Fig. 2.1 The role of Investor Relations through the company's life cycle

- Greater brand awareness and strategic visibility.
- Enhanced ability to attract and retain talent.

Management's determination to make Investor Relations a competitive advantage is the decisive factor in realizing these outcomes. This requires more than simply "having an IR function." It means building a professional, adequately resourced, and appropriately positioned IR capability—one that is embedded in decision-making, closely connected to senior management, and trusted as a strategic adviser rather than treated as a reporting or compliance function.

Beyond organizational commitment, leadership must also understand which competitive advantages matter most at different stages of the company's life cycle, and how these advantages can be developed deliberately and consistently over time (Fig. 2.1).

This chapter examines seven distinct competitive advantages that superior Investor Relations can deliver. These advantages are often closely intertwined and mutually reinforcing. Together, they explain how IR enables companies not only to compete more effectively for capital, but also to support long-term growth, strategic flexibility, and value creation.

2.1 Understanding Your Competitive Landscape Through Benchmarking

Competition in capital markets operates across multiple, overlapping dimensions. Companies are assessed simultaneously against peers defined by analysts, investors, indices, geographies, and business models—often in ways that extend beyond management's traditional view of business competition.

Understanding this competitive landscape is a prerequisite for using Investor Relations as a strategic lever. Without a clear view of *who you are being compared to, and on what basis*, it is impossible to define which competitive advantages matter most, or how IR should be positioned to support them.

Stock Market Competition

Stock market competition refers to the universe of companies that investors and analysts group together when making portfolio allocation decisions—regardless of whether management considers them to be direct business competitors.

This peer group typically includes companies that:

- Appear in the same analyst sector or thematic reports
- Are included in the same indices or index sub-segments
- Exhibit similar market capitalisation, trading liquidity, and free float
- Share comparable business model characteristics, such as capital intensity, cyclicality, end-markets, dividend policy, or growth profile
- Are categorised similarly by investors (for example, growth vs. value, income, ESG-focused, quality or momentum stocks).

These criteria are not mutually exclusive, and benchmarking may be based on only a subset of them rather than applied to all simultaneously.

The result is a list of the companies against which your stock is *implicitly arbitraged* when investors rebalance portfolios or analysts consider their universe of coverage. Relative positioning within this group influences visibility, attractivity, capital flows, valuation multiples, and risk perception—often independently of absolute performance.

From an Investor Relations perspective, understanding this competitive set is essential because it defines the reference points investors use when assessing your company's appeal.

Business Competition

Business competition refers to your direct competitors for customers, market share, and industry positioning. While this group may overlap with the stock market peer set, it often does not fully coincide.

Your business competitors matter in IR for several reasons:

- Their disclosure practices establish informal benchmarks for what investors perceive as "good" or "standard" disclosure within your industry, thereby highlighting potential areas for improvement for other issuers.
- Their guidance and strategic communication shape sector-level expectations that influence how your own performance is interpreted.
- Their equity stories can either sharpen or blur your differentiation in the minds of investors and analysts.

In many sectors, portfolio managers explicitly construct relative trade ideas—"Buy Company A, sell Company B." When this happens, the quality and clarity of IR becomes a decisive differentiator. A weaker narrative, less transparent disclosure, or inconsistent communication can tilt the balance, even when fundamentals are comparable.

Moreover, the performance of direct competitors often creates spillover effects—positive or negative—on your own valuation, regardless of company-specific fundamentals. This makes it essential to proactively educate analysts and investors about *who your true business competitors are* and *why your competitive positioning differs.*

Avoiding discussion of competitors does not eliminate comparisons; it merely leaves them to be defined by others. Your company may not be the largest in its sector, but it may be the most profitable, the fastest-growing, or the most resilient. These distinctions should be articulated with the same discipline and clarity used in commercial pitches to customers—letting facts, not assertions, speak.

Aspiration Competition

Aspiration competition consists of the companies you aim to be compared with over time, and, where appropriate, to outperform—the "peer set of tomorrow" rather than today.

These are typically companies whose:

- Valuation multiples set reference points for long-term ambition.
- Shareholder base reflects the quality and stability you seek to attract. For instance prestigious institutional investors holding a meaningful stake in your competitor's capital.
- Research coverage signals visibility and credibility with the investment community.
- Reputation rankings and awards reinforce leadership, trust, and employer appeal.

- Governance standards and ESG positioning are perceived as best-in-class in external ratings.

Company size is never a defining criterion when assessing IR excellence. What matters is perceived quality, credibility, and strategic positioning.

Aspiration peers play a critical role in shaping:

- Long-term valuation ambitions and market capitalisation targets
- The type of investors the company seeks to attract and retain
- The roadmap for improving IR quality, disclosure standards, and market engagement.

Used judiciously, aspiration benchmarking provides direction without encouraging imitation. It helps management and IR teams articulate *where they want to be valued*, not merely where they are today.

Geographic Competition

As capital markets have become increasingly global and integrated, competitive positioning is no longer confined to domestic markets.

Geographic competition includes:

- Local peers competing for domestic investor attention and index inclusion
- International companies in the same sector attracting the same global capital
- Issuers competing for inclusion or weighting in major global indices (MSCI, FTSE, STOXX)
- Market leaders in capital markets the company aspires to access, such as European companies seeking greater US investor coverage
- Frontier or emerging-market companies competing for capital against peers in more developed markets.

Global investors routinely compare companies across borders, adjusting for perceived differences in regulation, governance, liquidity, and risk. As a result, geographic benchmarking directly influences liquidity, valuation, investor access, and expectations regarding disclosure quality and governance standards.

Only once this multi-layered competitive context is clearly defined can management and IR teams answer the strategic question that follows:

– What competitive advantages do we need to win the competition for capital?

The answer lies in the seven competitive advantages of superior Investor Relations examined in the next section.

2.2 The Seven Competitive Advantages of Superior Investor Relations

Superior Investor Relations does not create value through a single mechanism. Its impact unfolds through a set of interrelated competitive advantages that, taken together, strengthen a company's position in capital markets and beyond.

These advantages are not automatic. They result from deliberate choices made by management regarding transparency, investment in IR capabilities, engagement, consistency, and strategic intent. While they reinforce one another over time, each advantage addresses a distinct dimension of the competition for capital.

Advantage 1—A more diversified and resilient shareholder base

A diversified shareholder base is one of the most valuable strategic assets a listed company can build. Like a diversified customer base in business, it reduces dependency risk and enhances resilience across market cycles.

Superior Investor Relations supports diversification across:

- Investor types (such as long-only institutions, active managers, ESG-focused funds, retail investors)
- Geographies
- Investment horizons and styles recognizing that companies overwhelmingly seek long-term investors rather than short-term capital—thereby reinforcing the importance of IR excellence.

A well-balanced shareholder structure contributes to:

- Greater share-price stability, as investors with different objectives are less likely to act in unison
- Reduced vulnerability to sudden capital outflows linked to style rotations or macro shocks
- Greater strategic freedom for management, particularly during periods of transformation or market stress.

Companies with a concentrated or mostly short-term-oriented shareholder base or with an excessively high proportion of foreign investors, often discover their fragility precisely when conditions deteriorate. By contrast, a diversified and engaged register provides both stability and optionality.

Advantage 2—A stronger corporate reputation through transparency and governance

Reputation has become a measurable and material driver of valuation, risk perception, and investor behavior. In this context, transparency and governance are no longer viewed as compliance obligations alone, but as competitive differentiators.

Companies perceived as transparent and well-governed benefit from:

- Higher trust from investors and analysts
- Greater tolerance during periods of underperformance or uncertainty
- Faster recovery from adverse events, activism, or reputational challenges.

Superior Investor Relations reinforces reputation by ensuring that disclosure is consistent, intelligible, and credible over time. It signals management quality, discipline, and alignment with shareholders' interests.

In an environment of heightened scrutiny—driven by regulation, ESG integration, and social expectations—companies that are perceived as open, predictable, and well governed enjoy a structural advantage over those that communicate defensively or reactively.

Advantage 3—More favorable valuation and risk perception

Between companies with comparable fundamentals, valuation differences are rarely accidental. They reflect how well the market understands the business, trusts management, and believes in the sustainability of the strategy.

Excellence in Investor Relations contributes to valuation differentiation by:

- Reducing information asymmetry and perceived uncertainty
- Supporting lower risk premiums and more stable valuation multiples
- Improving the quality and consistency of analyst expectations.

Valuation is not merely a reflection of today's share price. It directly influences:

- The cost of equity and the company's required rate of return
- The effectiveness of shares as acquisition currency
- Exposure to activism or hostile bids

- The attractiveness of equity-based compensation.

In this sense, valuation is both an outcome of Investor Relations and a strategic resource. Companies that consistently explain their business model, risks, and value drivers are better positioned to achieve a valuation that reflects their intrinsic potential rather than short-term sentiment.

Advantage 4—Stronger external credibility

Investor Relations is often the most visible and credible communication platform a listed company has. Its reach extends well beyond investors and analysts to customers, suppliers, partners, regulators, employees, and potential recruits.

Through continuous share-price disclosure and publicly available company information, the market provides daily, free access to information for all audiences.

This in turn enhances strategic and commercial visibility by:

- Increasing presence in financial and business media
- Reinforcing perceptions of scale, credibility, and stability
- Signaling long-term commitment to markets, innovation, and governance.

For many companies—particularly B2B, industrial, infrastructure, or technology firms—this visibility provides commercial leverage that traditional marketing cannot replicate. Financial transparency and public-market discipline act as trust signals in procurement processes, partnership discussions, and long-term contractual relationships.

As a result, IR contributes not only to capital-market positioning, but also to broader strategic credibility.

Advantage 5—Improved access to high-quality partners and suppliers

Investor Relations also functions as a window into the company for its broader ecosystem. Through public disclosure, market engagement, and visibility, companies become more attractive to potential partners, suppliers, and advisors.

This advantage leads to:

- Higher-quality inbound interest from strategic partners
- Greater selectivity in choosing suppliers, advisors, and partners
- Improved positioning for alliances, joint ventures, or ecosystem involvement.

Companies that articulate their strategy clearly and credibly through IR are more likely to attract counterparties aligned with their long-term objectives. In this way, IR indirectly shapes the quality of the company's operating environment.

Advantage 6—Enhanced ability to attract and retain executive talent

Top executives assess potential employers through a capital markets lens, even when they are not investors themselves. They'll read the company's annual reports, browse its website, and may even listen in earnings calls. Reputation, valuation trajectory, governance quality, and strategic clarity all influence talent decisions.

Superior Investor Relations supports executive attraction and retention by:

- Reinforcing the credibility and ambition of the company's strategy
- Signaling a professionally managed, transparent, and well-governed environment
- And in certain cases, supporting meaningful equity compensation.

Companies recognized for IR superiority are often perceived as well run and future-oriented. This is also made possible by richer content on the company's social policies. This perception matters in competitive talent markets, particularly for leaders who value visibility and accountability and is reinforced by richer ESG disclosure, particularly on social policies and career advancement opportunities.

Advantage 7—Sustained access to capital across market cycles

Ultimately, one of the most powerful advantages of best-in-class Investor Relations is the ability to maintain access to capital—equity and debt—on optimal terms, even during periods of stress.

Companies with strong IR benefit from:

- Greater investor willingness to engage during challenging periods
- More flexibility in timing capital market transactions
- Improved credibility with debt investors and credit stakeholders.

Investor Relations does not execute capital raising, it keeps the option open. That optionality—often invisible during periods of market stability—becomes decisive when conditions deteriorate or strategic opportunities arise unexpectedly.

Together, these competitive advantages explain why Investor Relations, when treated as a strategic discipline, becomes a source of durable differentiation.

They do not materialize spontaneously. They are built, tested, and reinforced in specific capital-market contexts and at different stages of a company's lifecycle.

Chapter 3 therefore shifts the focus from competitive advantage to strategic application. It examines how Investor Relations is used deliberately to win the competition for capital—from going public and accessing international markets to managing private capital, debt investors, and major corporate-finance decisions—and how valuation, liquidity, and cost of capital become practical levers for translating IR strategy into measurable outcomes.

Practical Implications

- Define explicitly and prioritize which competitive advantages IR is expected to deliver, based on company maturity and capital markets objectives.
- Map your true competitive landscape, including stock market peers, aspiration peers, and geographic competitors.
- Use IR to reinforce visibility, shareholder-base quality, governance credibility, valuation resilience, reputation.
- Reassess competitive positioning periodically as ownership structure, strategy, or market context evolves.

Competitive advantages do not materialize spontaneously; they are developed within specific capital-market contexts and at different stages of a company's lifecycle. The next chapter examines how Investor Relations is applied in practice as companies compete for capital across a range of situations, including public offerings, cross-border listings, private capital raising, debt financing, and major corporate-finance transactions.

3

Competing for Capital: The Role of Investor Relations Across Market Contexts

The competitive advantages created by effective Investor Relations must be applied across very different capital structures, market situations, and phases of the corporate lifecycle. This chapter examines how the role of IR evolves depending on whether a company is preparing for an IPO, already listed, privately held, or operating in complex ownership environments.

Investor Relations strategy defines how a company positions itself in the competition for capital. Capital providers allocate resources comparatively, across jurisdictions, asset classes, and business models, assessing not only financial performance but credibility, consistency, and confidence in management's ability to deliver on their stated ambitions over time. IR strategy determines how consistently those assessments are shaped, reinforced, and protected across market cycles.

Investor Relations strategy sits at the intersection of corporate strategy and capital markets expectations. It is neither a communications plan nor a collection of tactical best practices. It is the structured articulation of how a company engages current and prospective providers of capital—equity and debt alike—over time, through both favorable and adverse conditions. A well-designed IR strategy aligns what the company seeks to achieve strategically with how capital providers assess value, risk, governance, and credibility.

A central premise of this chapter is that credibility and trust are cumulative—and fragile. They are built through consistency between words and actions, disciplined disclosure (including financial reporting formats) over time, and management's ability to engage constructively with market expectations without becoming captive to short-term sentiment. Investor Relations

A. Guimard, *Investor Relations Strategy*, https://doi.org/10.1007/978-3-032-21679-3_3

strategy must therefore be resilient, capable of supporting the company through growth phases, strategic transitions, and periods of volatility.

This chapter maps how Investor Relations strategy operates across distinct capital-market situations. It addresses IPOs, cross-border listings, private companies, private equity, sovereign wealth funds, debt markets, corporate-finance decisions, ESG integration, and shareholder activism—demonstrating how a single strategic objective is pursued across very different contexts. While the chapter focuses on strategic context, it also prepares the ground for execution. The organizational, governance, and informational foundations required to deliver these strategies consistently are addressed in subsequent chapters.

3.1 Going Public

The decision to go public and become a publicly traded company is among the most consequential strategic choices a company can make. It is not merely a financing transaction or a liquidity event; it is a structural transformation that permanently reshapes how the company is governed, evaluated, and held accountable. An initial public offering or "IPO" marks the company's entry into a global, continuous, and highly competitive market for capital, in which tens of thousands of listed issuers compete simultaneously for investor attention, confidence, and long-term commitment.

From the moment of listing, the company no longer competes only in its product and service markets. It also competes in capital markets—against companies of different sizes, sectors, geographies, and business models—whose only common feature is that they offer alternative uses of capital, investment opportunities. This competition is relentless and unforgiving of inconsistency. Investor Relations becomes the strategic function through which a company positions itself within this environment and sustains its attractiveness as a destination for capital, aligned with its desired share-ownership structure and free float.

The Rationale for Going Public

An IPO fundamentally alters the company's relationship with its stakeholders. Private ownership allows for discretion, selective transparency, and a relatively low degree of accountability. Public ownership replaces this with continuous scrutiny, formalized disclosure obligations (and the associated risk of legal penalties), and exposure to diverse—and often competing—investor expectations. Strategy, performance, governance, and communication become inseparable in the eyes of the market.

In this context, the IPO should not be understood as a transaction that concludes a phase of corporate development. Rather, it marks the transition into a new operating model in which management accepts that strategic decisions will be assessed not only on their intrinsic merits, but also on how they compare with peers and how consistently these merits are executed over time. Investor Relations plays a central role in helping management navigate this shift, ensuring that the company is not merely listed, but understood, trusted, and investable.

Many IPO disappointments do not stem from weak businesses, but from a mismatch between what companies believe they are offering and how capital markets actually evaluate them. The discipline imposed by public markets is not primarily financial; it is behavioral. Consistency, transparency, and credibility become strategic assets.

In this corporate life-changing context, an IPO requires establishing governance discipline that extends beyond compliance to become a visible signal of sound management stewardship. Public investors assess governance not only through org charts or board independence, but also through observable behavior: how capital is allocated, how setbacks are communicated, and how consistently stated principles are applied, even under pressure.

Companies typically consider going public when private sources of capital are no longer sufficient to support their ambitions, when scale or speed of growth requires broader funding, or when existing shareholders seek partial liquidity and diversification. In practice, IPO rationales are rarely singular. They reflect a combination of strategic motives, each with implications for Investor Relations.

Access to capital at scale is often the most visible driver. Public equity markets offer depth, diversity, and repeatability of funding that private markets cannot always provide. When supported by a credible strategy and a well-constructed shareholder base—combining an optimal mix of large shareholders with a balanced, diversified free float—public equity can become a structurally efficient source of long-term capital. Investor Relations is instrumental in explaining how the business model, growth trajectory, and risk profile justify sustained investor support.

Valuation considerations are equally central. Public markets often ascribe higher valuation multiples to listed companies than to private peers, not simply because of liquidity, but because transparency, governance discipline, and strategic clarity reduce perceived risk. Valuation is therefore not an outcome of listing per se; it is the result of how convincingly the company articulates its long-term value creation logic. Investor Relations ensures that the company's strategy, segment economics, capital allocation priorities, and performance drivers are understood in a way that allows the market to value the business appropriately. This is precisely what "fair valuation," as referenced in the definitions of Investor Relations in Chapter 1, means.

Liquidity is another core objective. An IPO creates an organized market for the company's shares, enabling founders, financial sponsors, and employees to monetize holdings over time without disrupting corporate continuity. Liquidity also enhances strategic flexibility by providing acquisition currency, supporting equity-based compensation, and enabling future capital raises. The size of the free float and the composition of the shareholder base are therefore strategic design variables, not technical by-products of the transaction. By leveraging investor targeting techniques—now increasingly powered by AI—Investor Relations plays a role in shaping ownership dynamics that support stability rather than volatility.

Reputation and visibility also change fundamentally. A listing increases public profile and credibility with customers, suppliers, regulators, and potential employees. It often elevates the company's standing within its industry. At the same time, it heightens scrutiny and expectations around governance, disclosure quality, and responsible corporate behavior. Investor Relations becomes both the external interface with capital markets and an internal benchmark for what listed-company discipline requires.

These benefits are inseparable from obligations. Going public forces the company into regular and timely disclosure, the strict handling of price-sensitive inside information, and an information rhythm dictated by capital markets rather than internal convenience. It requires management to operate under continuous comparison (against peers, indices) and to balance short-term market reactions with their long-term strategic objectives. In this sense, an IPO adds a new dimension to the competitive landscape in which companies compete for capital on a daily basis.

Investor Relations Across the IPO Lifecycle

From an Investor Relations perspective, going public is best understood as a multi-year lifecycle rather than a one-time event. IPO outcomes are determined as much by what happens before and after listing as by the transaction itself. The IPO lifecycle can be viewed across four strategic phases: preparation, execution, early public ownership, and long-term stabilization.

It is highly advisable—and in certain jurisdictions mandatory actually—that some form of Investor Relations function be in place before the IPO. It contributes to preparing the organization for public-market reality. This phase is fundamentally about readiness rather than promotion, with the latter role largely undertaken by investment banks and advisors. The objective is to ensure that strategy, governance, reporting, and internal behaviors do not only comply with a whole new set of regulations but are also aligned with the expectations of public investors. Investor Relations helps management anticipate how the company will be analyzed, compared, and valued once listed, and highlights gaps between internal narratives and external perception as the IPO unfolds. Companies that underestimate this phase often find that weaknesses exposed during the IPO process persist long after listing.

During the IPO execution phase, the company is simultaneously exposed to investors, analysts, media, and regulators—often across multiple jurisdictions (for example, the listing venue, the country of incorporation, and its operational footprint). At this stage, Investor Relations safeguards consistency between strategy, disclosure, and expectations. The investment case must be compelling, but it must also be sustainable. Decisions taken at this stage—particularly around positioning, guidance policy, and shareholder targeting—create expectations that persist long after listing. Over-promising or poorly calibrated guidance is especially damaging because it shapes analyst models and investor expectations for years to come. It is essential that management takes ownership of this and does not outsource or surrender objective-setting to the financial intermediaries executing the IPO. These will be long gone by the time the company reports earnings for the first time and faces market reaction to how actual results compare with stated targets at the IPO.

The first phase of the IPO is also when the foundations of the IR function are put in place and a minimal set of tools is implemented, including an investor and analyst contact database and an IR section on the corporate website.

Once trading begins, the emphasis shifts to credibility. "Life as a listed company" marks this new beginning. The aftermarket is where the market tests whether management delivers in line with what was communicated. Early reporting cycles, the quality of disclosure, and responsiveness to investor questions establish behavioral patterns that often persist for years. Investor Relations acts as the interface through which expectations are managed, misunderstandings corrected, and trust built. Markets are generally tolerant of operational learning curves, provided behavior remains consistent and transparent.

Over time, as the company moves beyond its initial period as a newly listed issuer, Investor Relations assumes a long-term stewardship role. The focus moves from explaining the IPO story to articulating the financial and operational performance resulting from strategy execution, while sustaining access to capital, maintaining valuation credibility, and managing the evolution of the shareholder base. At this stage, Investor Relations contributes directly to resilience across market cycles and supports strategic optionality.

Seen through this lifecycle lens, the IPO initiates a permanent engagement with capital markets. Investor Relations is the function that ensures continuity across these phases, aligning long-term corporate strategy with the disciplines and expectations of public ownership. In other words, Investor Relations serves as a gatekeeper, a salesperson, an intelligence gatherer, and the owner of the all-important feedback loop, without which strategy formulation would be at risk of failure.

The specific organizational capabilities, timelines, and tools required to execute this lifecycle effectively—from pre-IPO information systems to roadshow logistics to analyst engagement—are addressed later in the book.

From Transaction to Listed-Company Strategy

The most successful IPOs are often those in which the share price never falls below the issue price. Companies that view the IPO as a finishing line frequently struggle with volatility, reactive communication, and erosion of credibility once listed. By contrast, companies that approach the IPO as the entry point to a long-term capital markets strategy—one in which Investor Relations is treated as a strategic capability rather than a transactional support function—are better positioned to build enduring investor relationships and maintain strategic flexibility.

Between two companies with comparable financial performance, capital markets tend to favor the one that communicates more consistently and clearly, with greater coherence and strategic intent. Investor Relations is therefore not an accessory to the IPO process. It is one of its principal determinants of long-term success—and one of the few levers management can proactively design as it enters public markets.

Furthermore, markets reward the discipline and transparency with which challenges are addressed and communicated. Over time, this matters more to valuation outcomes than any single financial metric.

The decision to go public also implicitly accepts the possibility of its reversal. Delisting may occur through a take-private transaction, following an acquisition in which the new owner chooses not to maintain a public listing, or as a strategic withdrawal from public markets. In all cases, delisting is not a symmetrical alternative to an IPO, but the outcome of a reassessment of whether the benefits of public ownership continue to justify its obligations. Persistent valuation discounts, insufficient liquidity, rising costs of capital, constraints on strategic flexibility, or a change in ownership priorities can ultimately prompt companies and shareholders to reconsider the merits of remaining listed. From an Investor Relations perspective, this underscores a central premise of public ownership: access to capital must be earned continuously. When credibility, governance, or market confidence erodes—or when ownership objectives fundamentally change—the rationale for remaining listed itself comes into question.

3.2 Cross-Border Listings

Competition for capital is global. For many companies, access to domestic capital markets alone is no longer sufficient to support growth ambitions, visibility and recognition needs, valuation objectives, or the desired shareholder base. In this context, a cross-border listing is not a question of prestige, but a strategic decision to reposition the company within a broader capital markets ecosystem.

From an Investor Relations perspective, the implications are significant. A cross-border listing does not simply add a trading venue; it expands the company's competitive set for capital and subjects it to new standards of comparison, disclosure, governance, and scrutiny. Investor Relations becomes responsible for ensuring that this broader exposure translates into sustainable access to capital rather than merely incremental costs and organizational complexity.

The Rationale for Cross-Border Listings

Companies typically consider cross-border listings when structural constraints limit their ability to attract sufficient capital in their home market. This is particularly relevant for issuers from smaller or emerging markets, where investor depth, liquidity, or research coverage may be insufficient to support long-term growth strategies. In such cases, an international listing can be transformative, providing access to institutional capital pools, specialized investors, and financial ecosystems that do not exist domestically.

For companies from large and liquid developed markets, the rationale is more nuanced. Secondary listings that once delivered incremental liquidity, broader coverage, or valuation uplift increasingly fail to do so, often generating negative returns once ongoing costs and organizational burden are taken into account. The strategic question is therefore not whether a cross-border listing is possible, but whether it creates value relative to its complexity.

Currency and market alignment also influence listing decisions. Listing in the same currency or time zone as a company's principal investors or revenue base can reduce perceived risk, improve comparability, and concentrate trading activity during core market hours. However, these benefits materialize only if Investor Relations can manage the resulting complexity in disclosure, comparability, and communication discipline across markets.

Another frequently cited motivation is the pursuit of valuation advantages. Companies may seek exposure to markets where their sector is better understood, more actively researched, or structurally valued at higher multiples. A cross-border listing, however, does not automatically close valuation gaps; it merely places the company in a new comparative framework. Without adequately resourced ongoing maintenance, sustained investor education, credible delivery, and alignment with local research and reporting conventions, any perceived valuation arbitrage remains theoretical.

Finally, cross-border listings may support broader strategic objectives. Presence on a major international exchange can enhance corporate reputation, signal commitment to higher governance standards, and support the attraction of global talent as well as customers. Where companies have significant operations abroad, foreign listings may also facilitate local employee share ownership, strengthening alignment and engagement.

> A compelling example is that of a French software company that initially went public on Nasdaq and, a few years later, listed its shares on Euronext Paris at the strong urging of European institutional investors already on its share register. These investors were holding shares traded in US dollars and exposed to a different time zone, creating both currency and operational frictions. The subsequent dual listing—supported by coordinated transatlantic Investor Relations teams—helped rebalance the shareholder base and analyst coverage in line with the company's revenue profile, which was evenly split between the United States and Europe. The resulting free-float composition proved not only optimal, but also significantly more effective and less costly than any advertising campaign for the company's services could have been. For a simple reason: being listed means being present in the media every day.

In all cases, Investor Relations sits at the intersection of capital markets, reputation, and internal stakeholder alignment.

Implications for Investor Relations Strategy

A cross-border listing transforms Investor Relations into a fully international discipline. The company must engage with investors who differ in culture, investment style, regulatory expectations, and time horizon, while maintaining a single, coherent equity story. Investor Relations is responsible for ensuring that this story remains accessible and consistent across markets, including in different languages.

Two of the most critical challenges are differences in legal systems and financial comparability:

- A cross-border listing may subject the company to the extraterritorial application of the second market's legal and regulatory framework, introducing litigation, enforcement, and liability risks that do not exist in the company's home jurisdiction.
- Cross-listed companies are assessed against international competitors with different scale, business models, disclosure practices, and even accounting standards (for example, US Generally Accepted Accounting Principles (US GAAP) versus International Financial Reporting Standards (IFRS)). Investor Relations must actively frame how the company should be analyzed and valued, rather than leaving the market to draw its own comparisons. In this instance, as in many others throughout this book helping the market better understand the company is a powerful differentiator.

Shareholder base dynamics also change. Cross-border listings typically increase the proportion of international institutional investors, which can enhance liquidity and visibility but may also increase volatility and sensitivity to macroeconomic or geopolitical shifts. This reflects the persistence of home bias in investment behavior, whereby investors tend to favor markets where they feel equally informed as local investors. Overcoming this bias requires sustained market education and a credible Investor Relations presence capable of translating the company's equity story across regulatory, cultural, and geographic boundaries.

Ultimately, managing this trade-off between diversification and stability is a strategic IR responsibility, closely linked to targeting priorities and engagement focus.

Governance and disclosure expectations invariably rise when shares are listed on several different exchanges. International investors tend to apply the highest standards observed in their global portfolios, regardless of local regulatory minima. The IR department must therefore intensify peer benchmarking, including an assessment of how peers execute Investor Relations. In doing so, it acts as an internal catalyst for governance clarity, transparency, and disciplined communication, working closely with management and the board to ensure credibility across jurisdictions.

From Domestic Issuer to Global Capital Markets Participant

A cross-border listing represents a shift in identity. The company moves from being primarily a domestic issuer to becoming a participant in global capital markets, where comparison is constant and capital is highly mobile. Success in this environment depends not only on the choice of exchange, but also on the company's ability to articulate a differentiated investment case, deliver against it consistently over time, and commit sufficient resources to its ongoing maintenance.

Investor Relations is central to this transition. It provides the continuity that allows a cross-border listing to function as a strategic asset rather than a costly legacy decision. In an environment where international investors can increasingly access companies without formal secondary listings, superior Investor Relations—rather than the listing itself—often becomes the decisive factor in converting global visibility into sustainable valuation and access to capital.

3.3 Investor Relations for Private Companies

Investor Relations is often perceived as a discipline that begins on listing day. In reality, the competition for capital starts much earlier, and many companies will never become publicly listed yet still need to compete repeatedly for financing, credibility, and attention. Venture capital funds, growth equity investors, family offices, private credit providers, and strategic investors all allocate capital selectively and comparatively. From their perspective, private and public companies are not separated by principle or disclosure requirements, but by degree of transparency, structure, and discipline.

More fundamentally, Investor Relations in private companies is not limited to fundraising. The same discipline that underpins effective dialogue with investors—clarity of strategy, consistency of reporting, credibility of governance, and openness about performance—also influences how customers, suppliers, partners, and potential employees assess the company. Private companies that apply Investor Relations strategically can therefore strengthen their competitive position even when they are not actively raising capital.

Ongoing Investor Relations Discipline and Opportunities

Private companies benefit from Investor Relations capabilities for reasons that extend well beyond the mechanics of capital raising. While access to funding is often the catalyst for realizing the need for professional financial communication, the underlying advantages are broader and more durable.

Companies that develop Investor Relations capabilities early—often beginning with media engagements—are better able to articulate their business model, performance, strategy, and value-creation logic with clarity. This, in turn, allows them to target investors whose mandates and time horizons align with their objectives and to progress through due diligence with greater efficiency and confidence. This discipline reduces perceived risk and strengthens negotiating positions, regardless of whether the capital provider is a venture fund, a growth equity investor, or a private lender.

Beyond fundraising, Investor Relations supports strategic visibility, market positioning, and internal reporting discipline. Although private companies are not subject to public disclosure obligations, they may choose to communicate selectively when it serves clear strategic objectives, such as during major acquisitions or other transformational moves. Publishing selected milestones, performance indicators, or evidence of strategic progress can help establish leadership in emerging categories, attract inbound interest from investors or partners, and shape how the company is perceived within its broader ecosystem. Over time, selective transparency allows companies to set market reference points and to anticipate stakeholder reactions before disclosure becomes unavoidable.

Commercial credibility represents another important dimension. In many business-to-business environments, customers and partners increasingly expect transparency regarding financial stability, governance, and long-term viability. The ability to present coherent financial information, a clear strategy, and a credible governance narrative reassures counterparties and can improve commercial terms. What is prepared for investors can often be repurposed—judiciously—to support customer due diligence and supplier negotiations.

Talent attraction and retention further reinforce the case. Senior executives, particularly those with experience in listed companies, evaluate private employers through a public-market lens. They look for transparency and professionalism of governance. They observe public signals—media coverage, digital presence, and management communication—to assess credibility. Investor Relations, through its analytical and narrative skills, enables private companies to engage credibly on these topics and to present equity participation and stock-based compensation in a coherent manner.

Finally, Investor Relations contributes to readiness for strategic transitions. Whether a company is considering an IPO, a sale, a refinancing, or a generational change in ownership, the infrastructure required for credible communication cannot be built overnight. Companies that embed Investor Relations capabilities as an ongoing discipline are better positioned to respond opportunistically to market windows and strategic options.

This dynamic is illustrated by the following example:

A privately held, leveraged buyout-backed company was required to present in June its full-year results for the twelve months ended 31 December to its workers' council. Those historical results were negative and failed to reflect the effectiveness of a turnaround that was already well underway and visible in the company's first-quarter financial reporting. At the same time, pandemic-related disruptions had prompted suppliers to impose highly restrictive payment terms, placing the company under significant cash strain.

Management therefore considered issuing a press release as early as April, highlighting the turnaround and supported by selected first-quarter (March-ended) performance indicators compared with the prior year. The objective was to counter the negative perception created by weak prior-year results and to signal that the turnaround was taking effect. While the information was accurate and strategically relevant, shareholders ultimately decided against public disclosure, concerned that it could establish a precedent they would neither wish—nor need—to repeat.

The preparatory work was however not wasted. The draft press release was repurposed into a structured letter addressed directly to key suppliers, and the supporting presentation became the basis for follow-up discussions. Within a short period, supplier payment terms normalized and the company's insurance risk ratings returned to pre-pandemic levels.

What made the difference was not public disclosure, but disciplined narrative construction and credible financial evidence. A determined CEO, unwilling to leave any lever untouched in support of the turnaround, combined with a robust reporting framework overseen by a CFO with strong strategic-finance expertise, enabled the company to reset stakeholder perceptions and restore commercial confidence.

The Private Capital Audience and Its Implications

Unlike public markets, where investor universes are broad and relatively standardized, private capital is both more concentrated and more heterogeneous. Different categories of private investors optimize different outcomes, apply different risk lenses, and engage with companies in different ways. From an Investor Relations perspective, this diversity reinforces the need for clarity and intentionality.

Venture capital investors focus on market potential, execution speed, and the quality of the founding team, often within the constraints of finite fund lives and defined exit expectations. Growth equity investors place greater emphasis on scalability, unit economics, governance maturity, and downside protection. Family offices and long-term investors may prioritize capital preservation, values alignment, and reputational considerations, while sovereign funds and strategic investors often combine financial objectives with broader strategic or developmental goals. Private credit providers, in turn, concentrate on cash generation, liquidity, and risk management.

Treating these constituencies as interchangeable is a common and costly mistake. Effective Investor Relations requires private companies to recognize these differences and to adapt their communication accordingly, while maintaining a consistent narrative at all times. Thinking like an Investor Relations officer—who must also think like an analyst or an investor—means understanding not only what the company wants to communicate, but how different capital providers are likely to interpret it and relaying those insights to the Board and senior management.

Benefits of Transparency

Private companies enjoy a degree of discretion that public companies do not: they can decide when, what, and how to disclose. Used thoughtfully, this discretion becomes a strategic asset. Voluntary transparency can create value when it reinforces positioning, builds trust, or supports strategic objectives, while excessive or poorly judged disclosure can undermine competitive advantage.

As we have seen, voluntary, selective publication of performance indicators, strategic progress, or governance practices can help demonstrate leadership, reassure customers, and support recruitment of senior talent. At the same time, confidentiality and competitive sensitivity remain essential. The strategic question is not whether to disclose, but whether disclosure builds stakeholder confidence without revealing information that would primarily serve competitors—who are often better informed than companies may wish to acknowledge.

Importantly, the benefits of Investor Relations disciplines often extend beyond the investor base. Companies that can explain their strategy and performance clearly to investors (and to the public) are typically better equipped to communicate with customers, suppliers, and employees. This spillover effect strengthens perceived reliability, improves negotiating positions, and enhances resilience during periods of uncertainty or crises. In this sense, Investor Relations becomes a broader reputation-management and trust-building capability. It contributes to the corporate culture and also helps foster a sense of belonging, cohesiveness internally.

Building Credibility Over Time

For private companies, credibility is not conferred by a listing or a regulatory framework; it is earned through consistent behavior. What management promises, how it performs against those promises, and how openly it communicates along the way collectively shape investor and stakeholder confidence.

During fundraising or financing exercises, credibility is reinforced when narrative and evidence align, when management demonstrates mastery of the business's economics, and when risks are addressed candidly rather than downplayed. After capital has been committed, expectations often converge with those of institutional shareholders in public markets: regular reporting, contextual insight, and early communication of challenges are valued more highly than polished messaging—or silence.

Investor Relations helps institutionalize this behavior. Structured communication, disciplined reporting, and systematic capture of investor feedback support professionalization and prepare the organization for a broader and more demanding stakeholder base over time.

Embedding Investor Relations as a Management Discipline

Few, if any, private companies will have a formally designated Investor Relations Officer ("IRO"), yet the activities associated with Investor Relations still require clear ownership and accountability. Whether led by founders, the CEO, the CFO, or supported by external advisers, Investor Relations in private companies should be treated as a permanent capability rather than an episodic response to financing needs.

Common pitfalls arise when companies view this as a one-off event, delegate all investor communication to advisers, financial intermediaries, or confuse confidentiality with opacity. The most effective private companies avoid these traps by embedding Investor Relations into their management processes and by recognizing its relevance beyond capital raising alone.

Private companies compete not only for capital, but also for customers, partners, and talent. Investor Relations disciplines—transparent, consistent, and strategic communication—support all of these objectives. The fundamental principles of Investor Relations therefore apply as much to private companies as to listed ones, even if the form and intensity of application differ.

For ambitious private companies, Investor Relations is no longer optional, even if an IPO is not on the horizon. It is a strategic capability that enhances visibility, credibility, and optionality, and that separates those companies that effectively attract capital and opportunity from those that fail to do so.

3.4 Investor Relations for Private Equity

Private equity Investor Relations operates within the same overarching competition for capital as corporate Investor Relations, but in a structurally different environment. Instead of addressing a broad, anonymous shareholder base and an ecosystem of analysts, private equity Investor Relations manages relationships with a concentrated group of highly sophisticated capital providers. These limited partners—pension funds, sovereign wealth funds, insurance companies, family offices, and similar institutions—commit capital contractually for long periods and evaluate managers across successive fund cycles.

The strategic purpose of private equity Investor Relations is therefore not limited to a single fundraising exercise. It is to build, maintain, and compound trust over time, so that investors remain confident throughout the life of a fund and are willing to recommit capital to future vehicles.

As the asset class has matured, Investor Relations in private equity has evolved from a largely transactional support function into a strategic discipline spanning the entire fund lifecycle. Its remit now extends beyond fundraising into fund positioning, relationship management, performance communication, and increasingly the articulation of governance and ESG practices. While the regulatory framework, tools and metrics differ from those used in public markets, the underlying objective remains the same: to secure attractive, durable access to capital.

The Specificities of Private Equity Investor Relations

The similarities between private equity and corporate Investor Relations are evident. Both disciplines aim to explain strategy and performance, manage expectations, and support an attractive cost of capital. The differences arise from the structure of the relationship with investors and the regulatory environment.

Private equity capital is committed, contractual, and long term. Limited partners cannot simply exit a position in response to disappointment or uncertainty; instead, dissatisfaction is expressed through reduced engagement, strained relationships, or the decision not to participate in future funds. This makes the quality of communication and relationship management even more consequential.

The investor base is also far more concentrated. While public companies may engage with hundreds or thousands of shareholders, private equity firms typically manage deep, bespoke relationships with a limited number of investors. Communication is correspondingly more tailored, more intensive, and more continuous. There is no daily share price to serve as a proxy for market sentiment.

The language of performance differs, too. Private equity investors focus on value creation over time, capital deployment, and realized outcomes rather than quarterly earnings. Investor Relations must therefore frame performance in a way that reflects the economics, the returns of closed-end funds, and long investment horizons, while maintaining consistency and credibility across reporting periods.

Investor Relations Across the Fund Lifecycle

In private equity, fundraising is not an occasional activity but the central commercial engine of the firm. Investor Relations plays a critical role in shaping how each fund is positioned within the firm's fund offering and broader track record and how it relates to previous and future vehicles. Consistency matters as much as in corporate Investor Relations: investors assess not only the attractiveness of a single fund, but the coherence of the firm's strategy, team, and value-creation approach over time. Investor expectations are no less demanding.

Once capital is raised, the Investor Relations function becomes the steward of the ongoing relationship. Communication is governed by contractual obligations, but expectations often go beyond minimum requirements. Investors seek transparency around portfolio development, capital deployment, and distributions, as well as timely context when market conditions or portfolio events change. Over time, disciplined communication supports confidence through inevitable periods of underperformance or volatility.

A defining feature of effective private equity Investor Relations is that material developments—positive or negative—are best addressed proactively, reinforcing the perception that the manager is in control and aligned with investor interests.

The Link Between Fund-Level IR and Portfolio Outcomes

Although private equity Investor Relations operates primarily at the fund level, its influence extends directly to outcomes at the portfolio-company level. High-quality, consistent communication builds a credible sponsor track record—one that documents value creation, governance discipline, and risk management across investments.

This track record becomes particularly important when portfolio companies seek refinancing or approach an exit. Lenders, buyers, and public-market investors scrutinize not only the company's standalone performance, but also the sponsor's history and the quality of information provided over time. Investor Relations helps ensure that the narrative presented to limited partners aligns with what is communicated to external counterparties, reducing friction in due diligence and supporting valuation.

When a portfolio company prepares for an IPO, the distinction between private equity Investor Relations and corporate Investor Relations narrows. At that point, the sponsor's Investor Relations capability may contribute directly to shaping the equity story, preparing management for public-market scrutiny, and leveraging institutional relationships built over years of fund-level engagement.

In a private-equity-backed IPO, the sponsor's narrative establishes credibility before the transaction, supports readiness during execution, and deliberately withdraws thereafter to allow the company's market positioning to stand on its own.

Professionalization and Strategic Importance

As private equity firms grow in scale and complexity, Investor Relations has increasingly become a professionalized, strategic function rather than an peripheral responsibility. Leading firms recognize that sustained success depends not only on investment performance, but also on the quality of relationships with capital providers, current and prospective, and the credibility of communication over time.

Compared with corporate Investor Relations, private equity Investor Relations places less emphasis on public disclosure discipline and more on deep, repeat relationships with a small number of influential investors. Yet the strategic imperative is identical. Capital is allocated competitively, trust is earned incrementally, and reputation compounds over successive cycles.

Private equity Investor Relations is therefore best understood not as a subset of corporate Investor Relations, but as its sister discipline. The legal frameworks, metrics, and communication formats differ, but the core purpose is the same: to win and retain capital through transparency, consistency, and strategic alignment.

3.5 Investor Relations at Sovereign Wealth Funds

Investor Relations at sovereign wealth funds (SWFs) remains far less codified and far less visible than corporate IR, despite the growing scale, sophistication, and international footprint of these investors. This relative opacity reflects the unique mandates, ownership structures and political contexts in which SWFs operate. As a result, Investor Relations at sovereign wealth funds can take markedly different forms, depending in particular on whether the fund is based in a developed economy or an emerging one.

A Fundamentally Different Starting Point

Unlike listed companies, sovereign wealth funds do not compete for capital in the traditional sense. They are capital allocators, much less frequent capital raisers. Their "investors" are typically citizens (given the role in pension funding of large SWFs), governments, and future generations, rather than shareholders seeking more or less short-term returns. Yet SWFs are subject to growing scrutiny from a wide range of stakeholders: domestic constituencies, international regulators, investee companies, co-investors, rating agencies, and, increasingly, civil society.

In this context, Investor Relations at SWFs is less about valuation support and more about:

- Legitimacy and trust-building

- Transparency around mandate, governance, and risk appetite
- Reputational risk management across borders
- Clarifying the fund's role as a long-term, responsible capital provider, with ESG considerations increasingly prominent on its agenda
- Representing national interests internationally and facilitating Foreign Direct Investment, often through partnerships or joint ventures with state-owned entities.

IR therefore sits at the intersection of financial communication, public accountability, and geopolitical sensitivity.

Investor Relations as a Pillar of Sovereign Credibility

Sovereign wealth funds from developed economies typically operate in environments with strong democratic institutions, independent media, and high expectations of transparency. As a result, their IR practices tend to be relatively formalized and closely aligned with international best practices.

These SWFs publish extensive annual and quarterly reports, disclose asset allocation frameworks, risk management principles, and ESG policies, and maintain sophisticated websites accessible to a global audience.

In these cases, Investor Relations typically focuses on:

- Clear articulation of the fund's mandate and investment horizon
- Detailed disclosure on governance, proxy voting policies, internal controls, and corporate accountability mechanisms
- Transparent reporting on returns relative to long-term benchmarks, rather than short-term performance
- Proactive engagement on ESG integration and stewardship activities
- Regular dialogue with parliaments, supervisory bodies, and the public.

In emerging economies, sovereign wealth funds often face a very different set of challenges. Governance frameworks may be evolving, political influence may be more pronounced, and public trust in institutions less firmly established. At the same time, these funds may be viewed with suspicion by foreign governments and regulators when investing abroad.

These have progressively strengthened their communication efforts over time, but information on how they are structured is harder to come by. Investor Relations in such contexts often remains selective and strategic rather than fully transparent. Its priority and main mandate is often to promote the country as a destination for global investment inflows.

IR priorities in these environments typically include:

- Reassuring host countries and regulators about the fund's commercial, non-political objectives
- Clarifying decision-making autonomy and governance safeguards
- Managing country risk perceptions attached to the fund's country of origin
- Supporting access to international deal flow through credibility and relationship-building
- Controlling information asymmetry to avoid domestic political sensitivities.

In this setting, Investor Relations is frequently blended with public affairs and diplomatic communication, requiring careful calibration of messages across jurisdictions.

Investor Relations must therefore manage parallel narratives: one focused on public accountability at home, another on professionalism and predictability abroad. Consistency of principles matters more than uniformity of disclosure.

As sovereign wealth funds continue to grow in size, visibility, and influence, Investor Relations is gradually evolving from an ad hoc communication function into a strategic capability.

While the form and depth of Investor Relations will continue to vary widely across sovereign wealth funds, the underlying direction of travel is clear: opacity is increasingly costly, and credibility increasingly valuable.

3.6 Debt Investor Relations

Debt capital is a core component of the capital structure for many companies, whether publicly listed, privately held, or state-owned. In certain market conditions, debt may represent a structurally more attractive source of financing than equity. As a result, companies increasingly find themselves competing for debt capital in much the same way they compete for equity capital: on credibility, transparency, and confidence in management's ability to manage risk over time. Simply put, debt investors want confidence they will be repaid, while equity investors are betting on future capital gains.

Debt Investor Relations addresses this competitive dynamic. Its purpose is to ensure that lenders and fixed-income investors understand the company's strategy, financial profile, and risk management approach, and are able to assess creditworthiness with confidence. While the instruments and metrics differ from equity markets, the strategic objective is identical: securing reliable, flexible, and attractively priced access to capital.

The Perspective of Debt Investors

Debt investors approach companies through a fundamentally different lens from equity investors. Their primary concern is not upside potential, but the preservation of capital and the predictability of cash flows and repayment. They focus on downside risk, liquidity, covenant headroom, and management's ability to navigate adverse conditions. As a result, the credibility of a company's risk management framework often matters as much as its growth strategy. In debt Investor Relations, as in equity Investor Relations, clear, consistent disclosure is a core requirement across all disciplines and priorities.

From an Investor Relations standpoint, Debt Investor Relations requires a shift in emphasis rather than a different story. Like equity investors, debt investors value timely, clear communication—particularly during periods of market stress or company-specific disruption. Confidence is built when management communicates proactively, explains developments in context, and demonstrates consistency between stated policies and actual behavior over time.

Certain debt instruments—such as Islamic finance sukuk and ESG-labeled bonds—remain fully embedded within the debt IR framework but introduce additional, non-financial layers of disclosure, governance, and reputational accountability.

Islamic finance IR requires specialized expertise in Shariah-compliant structures and investor expectations that differ materially from conventional credit markets. While sukuk are integrated into the broader debt capital structure alongside public bonds, private debt, ESG instruments, and bank facilities, post-issuance IR involves ongoing Shariah compliance oversight, including annual certification and disclosure of any changes affecting Shariah status. In addition to issuer-level creditworthiness, sukuk investors expect transparency on the underlying assets and engagement with dedicated governance bodies such as sukuk trustees and Shariah boards. As a result, "Islamic finance IR" introduces a continuous ethical and eligibility dimension that extends beyond traditional financial covenants.

ESG-labeled bonds likewise introduce specific ongoing disclosure and credibility requirements. Green, social, and sustainability bonds are fully integrated into the broader debt IR framework, yet they too require specialized capabilities in allocation and impact reporting, as well as engagement with a wider set of stakeholders. Beyond issuer credit fundamentals, ESG bond investors expect regular, detailed reporting on the use of proceeds, underlying projects, and associated environmental or social outcomes, typically supported by external verification. As a result, ESG bond IR introduces a continuous transparency and credibility dimension to debt IR, where shortcomings in reporting quality, timeliness, or ESG consistency can raise greenwashing concerns, undermine investor confidence, and create reputational and regulatory risks beyond traditional financial covenant monitoring.

Investor Relations Across the Debt Lifecycle

Debt Investor Relations is not confined to issuance events. While bond offerings, private placements, or refinancing transactions create moments of intense engagement, the relationship with debt investors and lenders extends throughout the life of the instrument.

Between transactions, ongoing communication supports market confidence and preserves access to capital. Investors and analysts assess not only headline financial performance, but also how management responds to changing market conditions, adjusts capital allocation, and prioritizes financial resilience. Companies that invest in continuous dialogue are better positioned to refinance efficiently, negotiate terms from a position of strength, and maintain flexibility when conditions deteriorate.

This lifecycle perspective reinforces the strategic nature of Debt Investor Relations. Companies that treat communication with debt investors as a one-off exercise around issuance risk higher funding costs and reduced optionality. Those that approach it as a continuous discipline strengthen their standing as credible and resilient borrowers.

Debt and Equity: Two Instruments, One Story

Debt and equity are closely interconnected. Decisions relating to leverage, capital allocation, dividends, and investment priorities affect both shareholder returns and creditor risk. From the perspective of capital providers, it therefore makes little sense to analyze these dimensions in isolation. Investors increasingly expect companies to articulate a single, coherent capital story that explains how equity value creation and balance-sheet discipline coexist.

Developments affecting credit quality often have immediate equity implications. A rating agency downgrade, for example, will typically weigh on the share price. Best practice in investor communications therefore requires that financial metrics most frequently used by debt investors—such as net debt to EBITDA, liquidity ratios, and refinancing schedules—are also clearly communicated to equity investors. Maintaining investment-grade status is, in this context, frequently presented as a strategic objective to both audiences.

This has important implications for Investor Relations. Equity and debt narratives must be consistent, mutually reinforcing, and grounded in the same strategic assumptions. Growth ambitions presented to equity investors must be compatible with the leverage levels, cash-flow stability, and downside protection expected by debt investors. For instance, issuers should not hesitate to state their intention to remain investment grade, or to confirm that their balance sheet remains comfortably within covenant thresholds, in presentations to equity investors when addressing concerns raised by debt investors. Where inconsistencies arise, confidence erodes quickly.

For this reason, internal organizational separation between Investor Relations and treasury functions must not translate into fragmented message development and external communication. Whether responsibility for Debt Investor Relations sits within IR, treasury, or a hybrid structure, the message delivered to capital markets must be aligned. In practice, this argues for closer integration between equity and fixed-income audiences, including coordinated engagement with analysts, investors, and rating agencies who assess the company across its full capital structure—for example, by inviting both equity and fixed-income teams to earnings calls or roadshows.

3.7 Investor Relations and Corporate Finance

In many organizations, corporate finance and Investor Relations remain siloed functions: strategy and transactions are decided first, and communication follows. This separation is increasingly untenable. Every significant financial decision—whether related to capital allocation, leverage, shareholder returns, refinancing, or transformational transactions—reshapes how the company is perceived, valued, and financed, and therefore requires early integration of investor insight.

Corporate finance determines the economic value a company seeks to create. Investor Relations influences whether that value is recognized, trusted, and whether it will supported by capital providers through the good, the bad, and the ugly. When the two operate in isolation, even sound financial decisions risk destroying value through misalignment with market expectations. When they operate as a single strategic system (one that transcends reporting lines), companies materially reduce uncertainty, protect access to capital, and improve long-term valuation outcomes. They raise their investor appeal, not only in absolute but also against their competitors.

From a capital markets perspective, corporate finance is experienced through a set of recurring decision domains that shape investor confidence and risk assessment. Investor Relations acts as the strategic interface across the four such domains below.

Capital Allocation Decisions

Capital allocation is one of the most powerful expressions of strategy. It reveals management's priorities more clearly than any mission statement. How a company balances investment, shareholder returns, cash buffers, and balance-sheet strength signals its view on growth, risk, and long-term value creation.

Investor Relations plays a critical role in ensuring that these decisions are understood in context. Capital markets are less concerned with the specific mix of uses of cash than with the consistency of that mix over time and its alignment with stated objectives. When capital allocation decisions visibly reinforce the company's strategic narrative, credibility accumulates. When they appear reactive or inconsistent, market trust can erode dissipate quickly.

Disciplined communication around capital allocation allows investors to anticipate how management will respond as conditions change. This predictability of behavior—more than predictability of outcomes—is a major contributor to valuation stability and cost-of-capital efficiency.

Table 3.1 is a capital allocation narrative framework to translate capital-allocation decisions into clear, credible, investor-focused messages that reinforce long-term value creation.

Articulating Leverage and Balance-Sheet Strategy

The balance sheet is not merely an accounting representation; it is a central determinant of financial flexibility and market confidence; it is a statement of risk appetite and resilience. Investors and creditors assess leverage, liquidity, and funding structures as indicators of how a company will perform under stress, not just in favorable conditions.

Investor Relations supports corporate finance by framing balance-sheet choices within a coherent strategic and risk framework. Proactive communication around leverage tolerance, financial flexibility, M&A criteria (such as payback periods and expected synergy benefits), and funding priorities

Table 3.1 The capital allocation narrative framework

1. Start with the strategic intent (The "Why")
• What strategic problem does this capital decision solve?
• How does it advance the company's long-term priorities?
• How does it increase resilience, competitiveness, or growth?
2. Explain the financial logic (The "How")
• Expected returns vs. cost of capital
• Timing of cash flows
• Impact on profitability, margin profile, and capital efficiency
• Alternatives considered (and why rejected)
3. Clarify the constraints and choices
• Dividend vs. reinvestment
• Growth capex vs. deleveraging
• Share buybacks vs. strategic M&A
• Maintaining flexibility vs. maximizing returns
4. Create a map from every capital allocation decision to a set of KPIs used by investors
• ROIC/ROCE
• Free cash flow conversion
• Organic growth
• Leverage trajectory
• Cost of capital
5. Use track-record narrative to build confidence in future decisions
• Past targets met
• Discipline in capital deployment
• Measurable improvement over time
6. Provide a clear roadmap with a timeline
Investors need visibility into:
• Milestones
• Timeline to value capture
• Guidance implications
• Critical risks and mitigating factors
7. End with the Investor benefit
What does this decision mean for an investor *owning the stock*?
• Higher returns
• Lower risk
• Improved resilience
• Greater optionality
• More attractive long-term profile

enables markets to interpret changes rationally. Reactive communication, by contrast, allows uncertainty to fill the information gap—often at a high cost in valuation and financing terms.

In this domain, credibility is built through continuity. When markets understand how management thinks about risk across cycles, they grant greater flexibility during periods of disruption. Investor Relations helps establish this understanding by reinforcing consistency between stated financial principles and observed balance-sheet behavior.

Major Transactions

Major corporate-finance transactions—acquisitions, divestitures, restructurings, or refinancing events—are moments of maximum scrutiny. They test not only the economic rationale of decisions, but also the credibility of management's judgment, governance, and discipline.

In M&A communication, investors want:

- Clarity of purpose
- Realistic synergy assumptions
- Integration competence
- Proof that management understands the risks
- A path back to financial discipline.

Take the example of a multi-billion specialty minerals company that had a long-standing narrative on its value-creation criteria, supported (which is not frequent) by a clear measurement framework: to be executed, an acquisition should be able to generate a Return on Capital Employed before tax (measured by current operating income divided by capital employed) to be at least 3 percentage points above the company's weighted average cost of capital within three years of the integration.

One day, it decided to launch a friendly takeover bid for a listed company that would double its exposure to the United States, the world's largest end-market for its products. This offer was countered by a "white knight" who raised the bid twice, until the first bidder decided to walk away from the transaction. The rationale was that, while the specialty minerals company had the financial strength to make this deal, at the revised price point, it would have taken slightly more than three years to achieve its stated value-creation targets.

One might have expected the share price of the initial bidder to react negatively to the failed transaction, which, at least on paper, appeared transformational. Instead, the share price remained stable. The market recognized that the company had acted consistently with clearly articulated value-creation principles that were well understood by its shareholder base and had been endorsed over time.

Investor Relations contributes by ensuring that the strategic logic of transactions is communicated clearly and consistently, and that expectations, in particular in profit enhancement are set realistically with metrics that will be trackable over time. Markets will debate assumptions and execution risks, but they react far more negatively to gaps, inconsistencies, or perceived surprises than to disagreement over strategy.

When Investor Relations and corporate-finance operate in tandem, transactions are positioned as deliberate steps within a long-term value-creation journey rather than as isolated or opportunistic moves. This continuity materially influences how markets absorb change and reassess risk (Table 3.2).

Enhanced IR output will be required for certain high-risk situations such as:

- Highly leveraged transactions
- Cross-border M&A
- Turnaround acquisitions
- Forced or accelerated divestments
- Major shifts in business model

Table 3.2 The 10-point deal communication checklist

1. Strategic rationale
What strategic gap does this deal close?
2. Financial rationale
ROIC, synergy value, accretion/dilution, and deleveraging path
3. Integration plan
Timeline, milestones, integration team, and governance
4. Clear synergy framework
Categories (revenue, cost, capex efficiencies) and timing
5. Risks and mitigations
Operational, cultural, financial, regulatory
6. Balance-sheet impact
Leverage, rating agency dialogue, liquidity strategy
7. Guidance and medium-term targets
How does the deal change the company's growth trajectory?
8. Scenario analysis
Base, upside, and downside cases, including external factors
9. Pre-developed messaging toolkit
Key messages, Q&A bible, visuals, one-page rationale for internal and external audiences
10. Post-Announcement Reinforcement
Follow-up with investors, analysts, rating agencies, credit investors, media

For each, IR must test alternative narratives through perception intelligence well before public announcement.

Shareholder Returns

Decisions on dividends and share buybacks are interpreted by markets as signals of confidence, maturity, and capital discipline. They communicate management's assessment of cash-flow durability, reinvestment opportunities (or the absence thereof), balance-sheet strength, and its approach to shareholder remuneration, taking into account differing investor expectations. For example, a cash-rich South African company that introduced share buyback programs two years after its IPO, largely in response to international investor feedback, subsequently experienced a marked increase in US shareholder ownership.

Investor Relations helps position shareholder returns within the company's broader capital-allocation framework. Capital markets tend to penalize inconsistency more than conservatism. Sudden shifts in payout philosophy or unclear rationales for buybacks can undermine trust, even when returns appear financially attractive. Particular attention is given to the alignment between shareholder return policies and management's compensation structures and long-term incentives.

Shareholder return choices also influence the composition of the free float: retail investors and pension funds tend to favor cash dividends, while other institutional investors may prefer share repurchase programs or a combination of both. Conversely, building a stable base of private shareholders is difficult in the absence of a cash dividend.

Over time, this clarity on shareholder returns allows investors to anticipate management behavior and reduces uncertainty around future capital decisions.

Investor Relations and Corporate Finance as a System

Across all four decision domains—capital allocation, leverage and balance-sheet strategy, major transactions, shareholder returns—the strategic role of Investor Relations is the same: to translate financial decisions into a coherent capital markets narrative that reinforces trust rather than generates volatility. Corporate finance determines what decisions are made; Investor Relations influences how those decisions are interpreted, challenged, and ultimately valued.

One of Investor Relations' most valuable contributions in this context is market intelligence. Investor feedback, valuation comparisons, and peer benchmarking provide early signals of emerging constraints, opportunities, and misalignments. Used strategically, this insight improves decision quality before commitments are made. Ignored, the same signals often reappear later as valuation discounts, higher financing costs, or activist pressure.

Investor Relations for corporate finance is therefore not an extension of disclosure, nor a technical adjunct to treasury or M&A activity. It is a strategic capability that shapes how financial decisions are received in competitive capital markets, because it is the primary provider of market intelligence and investor sentiment which are indispensable to quality strategy formulation. When Investor Relations and corporate finance operate as an integrated system, companies preserve strategic flexibility, strengthen credibility, and maintain access to capital through changing conditions.

Investor Relations, Governance, and the Alignment of Company-Shareholder Interests

For capital-market participants, governance is the decision framework through which credibility is preserved when choices are made. Investors rarely observe governance structures directly; instead, they infer governance quality from behavior—how decisions are taken, how tensions between stakeholders are resolved, and how consistently stated principles are applied over time.

Companies with strong governance are afforded latitude: investors tolerate short-term volatility, support long-term investment, and remain constructive during periods of stress. Where governance is perceived as weak or inconsistent, the opposite occurs. Market tolerance narrows, risk premia rise, and access to capital becomes more constrained, and activist investors are quick to exploit such conditions.

Investor Relations plays a central role in translating governance into an investable attribute. This is not achieved by highlighting governance structures or formal processes once a year at the Annual General Meeting of Shareholders, but by making governance visible through outcomes: disciplined capital allocation, transparent handling of setbacks, coherent decision-making during transactions, and consistent engagement with shareholders and creditors for instance on the occasion of governance roadshows. In this way, governance becomes observable rather than asserted.

Governance is therefore not separate from Investor Relations strategy. It explains why some companies emerge from periods of disruption with their credibility intact while others do not, even when facing similar external conditions. Over time, it also explains why capital markets reward certain issuers with lower risk premia, greater valuation resilience, and increased strategic optionality.

Seen through a competitive lens, governance is not a defensive attribute designed merely to comply with governance codes and limit downside risk. It is an enabling one. Strong governance allows companies to act decisively without forfeiting investor trust, to pursue long-term strategy without persistent market resistance, and to rebuild credibility when inevitable setbacks occur. Investor Relations is the function through which this governance quality becomes legible, comparable, and ultimately valued by capital markets. This requires boards and governance bodies to engage regularly with Investor Relations. In practice, however, there are numerous examples where this discipline is absent, including the appointment of CEOs with no prior experience in a listed-company environment, or directors engaging directly with investors without Investor Relations involvement or appropriate training on the disclosure of material price-sensitive information.

3.8 ESG as Reshaping the Capital Story

This section is not intended as a manual on ESG communication best practices. It addresses ESG only to the extent necessary to illustrate how it reshapes the capital story and affects Investor Relations strategy.

Environmental, social, and governance considerations have become an integral, increasingly regulated component of how capital markets interpret strategy, risk, and long-term value creation. For Investor Relations, ESG is no longer a parallel narrative or a specialist disclosure topic. It often shapes the lens through which all corporate narratives are assessed.

Capital providers now routinely evaluate strategic choices—capital allocation, portfolio composition, supply-chain design, pricing power, and growth priorities—through ESG considerations. This does not replace financial analysis; it broadens, enriches, reframes it. ESG factors influence judgments about resilience, regulatory exposure, and the sustainability of returns. They therefore affect valuation, liquidity, and cost of capital across equity and debt markets alike.

From a narrative perspective, ESG complexifies the questions investors ask. Growth strategies are assessed not only for scale and profitability, but for environmental exposure and societal constraints. Efficiency initiatives are considered alongside workforce stability and operational robustness. Capital allocation decisions are interpreted in light of long-term externalities as well as near-term financial impact. In this context, ESG no longer sits alongside the capital story; it is a core component of the story and conditions how it is understood. While the value of ESG investing remains contested, and despite the fact that CEOs and CFOs complain that, except on ESG roadshows, mainstream investors never ask them any ESG-related questions, no investor presentation is complete without some form of ESG narrative and metrics. Given the significant cost of complying with ESG-related regulation, reporting standards, and stakeholder expectations, it makes economic sense to explain to shareholders how capital has been deployed in this area, which priorities have been addressed, and what broader societal or risk-mitigation benefits are expected—even where the impact on share price is indirect, long term, or non-existent.

Regardless of how the ESG mandate is allocated internally (that is, who owns the function, and whom it reports to in the organizational structure). Investor Relations plays a central role in ensuring that ESG considerations are integrated coherently into the overall investment case. Fragmented or formulaic ESG communication undermines credibility and is therefore vulnerable to accusations of "greenwashing", particularly when it appears disconnected from strategic and financial decision-making. By contrast, when ESG implications are addressed transparently and consistently within the core narrative, they reinforce confidence in management's foresight, governance discipline, and long-term orientation.

Seen through a capital markets lens, ESG is neither a moral overlay nor a reporting exercise. It is a contextual framework that increasingly shapes how risks are assessed and credibility demonstrated. Companies that integrate ESG meaningfully into their Investor Relations narrative (starting with ad hoc slides in earnings presentations) preserve strategic flexibility and access to capital; those that treat it as a separate disclosure obligation risk seeing their core story discounted or challenged.

3.9 Activism and Proxy Dynamics

Shareholder activism and proxy voting dynamics are often presented as exceptional or adversarial events. In practice, they have become a structural feature of modern capital markets and a visible mechanism through which investors express dissatisfaction—or support in the case of attacks or proxy fights. Activism typically exploits vulnerabilities, inconsistencies, or valuation gaps that capital markets already perceive, rather than creating them.

From an Investor Relations perspective, activism typically emerges where investors identify persistent gaps between stated strategy and observable outcomes, where capital allocation appears inconsistent, or where governance is seen as insufficient to discipline decision-making. Proxy advisors formalize these concerns by translating them into voting recommendations that influence broader shareholder behavior.

The likelihood and impact of activism are therefore closely linked to credibility and governance quality over time. It is worth noting that no capital structure (such as a limited free float) guarantees immunity against shareholder activism. Companies that articulate a clear strategy, apply disciplined capital allocation, and engage constructively with investors tend to retain strategic latitude even during periods of underperformance. Where credibility has eroded, similar financial outcomes provoke far more aggressive scrutiny and intervention.

Investor Relations plays a critical role in this dynamic by maintaining continuous dialogue with shareholders, monitoring evolving expectations, and translating external concerns into internal insights. Effective Investor Relations does not eliminate activism, but it reduces the risk of surprise, narrows the scope for misinterpretation, and increases the probability that engagement remains constructive rather than confrontational. One key tool is careful engagement with known activists in the investor outreach strategy.

Seen in this way, activism and proxy dynamics are not external threats to be managed episodically. They are an integral part of the competitive environment for capital. Investor Relations serves as the strategic interface that helps companies anticipate, contextualize, and respond to this feedback while preserving credibility and long-term strategic flexibility.

3.10 Confidence Formation and Market Validation

Across all capital-market situations, Investor Relations serves a single strategic objective: shaping how markets interpret, test, and respond to management behavior over time. Capital markets reward consistency, transparency, and reliability rather than perfection. What ultimately matters is whether investors understand how management behaves when conditions change—and whether that behavior proves dependable.

Market confidence develops gradually through repeated patterns of action. When strategy, capital allocation, disclosure, and delivery reinforce one another over time, investors learn how to read management decisions and calibrate their expectations accordingly. In this sense, predictability of behavior often matters more than predictability of outcomes.

That confidence is regularly tested. Periods of market stress, profit warnings, unexpected strategic shifts, or transformational transactions prompt investors to reassess whether stated principles hold under pressure. In such moments, Investor Relations plays a critical role in maintaining continuity between past commitments and present decisions, providing context, and framing events within a coherent strategic narrative. Markets tend to tolerate adverse developments when they are explained candidly and handled in a manner consistent with prior communication. Investors may still decide to sell their shares, which is inherent to their mandate; the objective is to ensure that such decisions are driven by portfolio considerations rather than negative sentiment or loss of confidence.

Confidence erodes when behavior diverges from previously articulated principles—when surprises emerge, explanations evolve opportunistically, or accountability is deflected. Once impaired, confidence can only be restored through action. This requires honest acknowledgment of what went wrong, clear corrective measures, and sustained evidence of change across subsequent reporting cycles.

Investor Relations supports this process by re-establishing a coherent narrative grounded in verifiable progress.

Seen in this way, market confidence functions as a dynamic asset. It accumulates through disciplined conduct, is tested during periods of uncertainty, and can be rebuilt through transparency and consistency over time. Investor Relations is responsible for managing this cycle purposefully across all capital-market interactions.

Companies that recognize this dynamic design their Investor Relations accordingly; those that treat market confidence as an incidental outcome of communication typically discover its importance only after it has weakened.

Investor Relations strategy is ultimately about choice and discipline: choosing which capital providers to prioritize, which messages to emphasize, which trade-offs to accept, and which behaviors to institutionalize over time. When these choices are made deliberately and anchored in corporate strategy, Investor Relations becomes a stabilizing force—one that strengthens access to capital, enhances resilience through market cycles, and supports informed decision-making at board and management level. Conversely, when IR activity is reactive, fragmented, or misaligned with strategy, it amplifies volatility and erodes trust precisely when it is most needed.

By defining a clear Investor Relations strategy, companies move from episodic communication to sustained engagement, from message delivery to relationship management, and from short-term market appeasement to long-term investability. This strategic foundation enables consistent execution, disciplined disclosure, and meaningful dialogue with investors and lenders alike. Yet strategic intent alone is not sufficient. Its impact ultimately depends on the organizational, governance, and informational foundations that support it. The next chapter therefore turns from strategy to structure, examining the capabilities and frameworks that determine whether Investor Relations operates as a reactive communications function or as a strategic capability able to sustain credibility and engagement to capital over time.

Practical Implications

- Address IR performance upstream by fixing mandate, positioning, and governance before refining execution.
- Ensure the IR mandate is explicit, aligned with management expectations, and supported by decision authority.
- Position the IRO as a strategic adviser, not merely a reporting coordinator.
- Design IR architecture to prevent predictable failure patterns.
- Treat investor sentiment as a strategic input.

The contexts examined in this chapter demonstrate that Investor Relations strategy depends on structural foundations rather than isolated responses. Credibility, access to capital, and valuation resilience are built through appropriate organizational design, sound governance, and consistent execution.

Chapter 4 examines the foundations of Investor Relations strategy, addressing how IR must be structured, resourced, governed, and embedded within the organization to operate as a strategic capability and to deliver competitive advantage consistently over time.

4

The Foundations of Investor Relations Strategy

Once the context in which Investor Relations operates is understood, the next question is how the function should be positioned inside the organization, with the appropriate mandate, reporting lines, resources, and governance to support its strategic role.

This chapter examines the structural foundations that determine whether Investor Relations can operate as a strategic capability. It focuses on organizational structure, leadership commitment, diagnostic discipline, and alignment.

Chapters 1 to 3 established that listed companies operate in a global and highly competitive market for capital, where differentiation is driven not only by financial performance, but by the consistency and strategic coherence of their engagement with investors. They also demonstrated that Investor Relations should be understood not as a communications derivative, but as a strategic discipline in its own right. The logical implication is that performance in Investor Relations is largely determined upstream, by structure rather than execution alone.

This chapter therefore addresses a single, foundational question: is Investor Relations structurally enabled to function as a strategic capability?

The chapter examines two dimensions. Internally, it explains why IR outcomes are structural: what IR is mandated to do, where it sits within the organization, who the Investor Relations Officer is as a role rather than a personality, how IR interacts with management decision-making, and how IR governance operates in practice. Externally, it addresses the reality that Investor Relations operates within pre-existing market expectations, and the

A. Guimard, *Investor Relations Strategy*, https://doi.org/10.1007/978-3-032-21679-3_4

importance of understanding investor sentiment as an input to strategy formulation.

The operational execution of legal compliance, engagement programs, tools, and measurement is addressed in Chapters 5, 6, and 7 that follow.

4.1 Why IR Architecture Determines IR Outcomes

IR architecture sets the conditions under which execution can succeed by preventing structural constraints from dominating desired outcomes.

Investor Relations performance is often judged by what the market can see: share-price reactions, earnings calls, investor presentations, roadshows, media articles, and analyst reports. Yet these visible activities are rarely the true drivers of success or failure. In practice, IR outcomes are largely determined much earlier—by the structural choices companies make about how Investor Relations is organized, governed, resourced, and embedded in corporate decision-making.

IR architecture refers to this underlying design. It encompasses the mandate of the function, its positioning within the organization, access to senior management and the board, governance interfaces, resourcing and budgeting choices, and operating discipline. These elements are largely invisible to external audiences, but they shape everything investors ultimately experience: the coherence of the equity story, the consistency of messaging over time, the credibility of management communication, the perceived expertise and authority of the market-facing executive (including the Investor Relations Officer), and the company's ability to anticipate and manage market expectations.

Well-executed IR activities cannot compensate for weak architecture. Conversely, strong architecture often allows even relatively small IR teams to deliver disproportionate strategic impact. For this reason, IR performance should not be understood primarily as a communications issue, but as a consequence of organizational design.

IR Architecture Versus Activity

A useful starting point is to distinguish clearly between IR activities and IR architecture. IR activities are what the market has access to: disclosures, meetings, calls, presentations, and responses to investor inquiries. Architecture is what enables those activities to be timely, coherent, credible, strategically aligned, and compliant. As such, it determines:

- when IR is informed of strategic and financial decisions;
- whether IR drives the development of supporting messaging;
- whether IR has the authority to coordinate market-facing communication;
- how investor feedback interpreted, and escalated internally;
- whether IR operates proactively or reactively.

Companies often invest heavily in IR activities while neglecting IR architecture—much like investing in marketing without customer segmentation or the people and capabilities needed for effective after-sales support. The result is often an IR function that is busy, visible, and technically competent—but structurally constrained. In such cases, IR effectiveness depends on favorable conditions: stable financial performance, sufficient budgets, and uninterrupted access to leadership.

When those conditions deteriorate—during periods of stress, lower profits, or crisis—the limitations of weak architecture become apparent. IR engagement is scaled back, access narrows, messaging becomes defensive, and the function shifts from shaping expectations to reacting to market pressure. What appeared robust in normal times proves fragile when resilience is most needed.

From a capital markets perspective, this distinction matters. Investors do not evaluate IR on effort or volume, but on predictability, consistency, and credibility over time. These qualities are architectural outcomes.

From Reactive to Proactive Investor Relations

Many organizations believe they have proactive Investor Relations simply because communication is polished or investor engagement is frequent.

In practice, Investor Relations is proactive when it is involved while options are still open—during planning, exploration, and evaluation phases. It is reactive when it is engaged only once decisions are fixed and disclosure becomes inevitable.

Architecture determines which of these modes is possible. Talent cannot compensate for late involvement. Conversely, strong architecture enables IR to operate upstream of announcements, even with limited resources.

Predictable IR Failure Patterns

When Investor Relations is involved late, messaging tends to become defensive rather than anticipatory. When mandates are unclear, accountability blurs, and investor trust erodes. Over time, this erosion affects how investors interpret management behavior and assess risk, even in the absence of new information. When access is personality-dependent rather than structurally embedded, IR effectiveness fluctuates with leadership changes.

In such environments, the market-facing IR role is reduced to explanation rather than interpretation—responding to questions rather than owning and articulating the company's message with authority and conviction.

These failure modes are rarely the result of poor individual performance. They are structural. They reflect architecture that is misaligned with the strategic role IR is expected to play.

Weak architecture undermines the role of Investor Relations precisely when it matters most: during capital raising, strategic pivots, or periods of stress.

IR Architecture for Risk Management and Organizational Resilience

From a management and board perspective, IR architecture should be viewed as a form of strategic risk management and organizational resilience.

Weak architecture increases the likelihood of avoidable disclosure errors, credibility gaps between strategy and execution, misinterpretation of strategic decisions, and heightened vulnerability during periods of stress, transformation, or leadership change. Strong architecture, by contrast, creates resilience. It ensures that IR insights have been integrated in the decision-making process and are available when decisions are still flexible, that market reactions can be anticipated, and that communication remains coherent under pressure and over time.

The resilience dimension becomes critical in three specific contexts:

1. *Crisis and Activist Response*

During activist campaigns, operational disruptions, or rapid financial deterioration, poorly IR architecture manifests as:

- Delayed escalation of market concerns to the board
- Inability to set up coordinated communication due to unclear governance
- Loss of institutional investor relationships because IR has been marginalized in day-to-day decision-making
- Reactive, inconsistent messaging that undermines credibility precisely when it is most valuable.

With a robust architecture in place, the company can be confident that escalation pathways remain functional even under extreme pressure, that IR has maintained sufficient investor access to understand sentiment, and that communication discipline is preserved.

2. *Strategic Transformation and M&A*

During transformational events—including M&A due diligence, integration planning, or significant business model changes—decision velocity accelerates and the need for IR input intensifies. Weak architecture typically results in:

- IR learning of material developments through external sources rather than internal channels
- Inability to coordinate messaging across multiple stakeholders during deal phases, resulting in messaging ownership being de facto ceded to investment banks and legal advisers
- Post-announcement investor backlash due to inadequate pre-announcement market intelligence gathering.

A well-defined IR architecture allows for trigger-based escalation protocols adapt to heightened decision frequency and that IR's governance linkages remain intact despite organizational disruption.

3. *Leadership Transitions*

When the CEO or CFO departs, or when board composition shifts substantially, inadequate IR architecture will lead to:

- IR effectiveness becoming personality-dependent rather than institutionalized
- New leadership lacking understanding of IR's advisory role and treating it as a subordinate communications function
- Established investor relationships becoming at risk if they have been built on individual relationships rather than institutional processes.

Strong architecture protects IR continuity through clearly documented mandate, governance processes that outlast individual leaders, and board-level understanding of IR's strategic role.

For this reason, IR architecture should not be treated as an administrative matter or delegated entirely to the IR function itself. It is a leadership choice with direct capital-market consequences. Moreover, board composition, director tenure, and board evaluation mechanisms should explicitly address whether board oversight of IR governance is adequate and sustained across director transitions.

4.2 Defining the Mandate of Investor Relations

A clearly defined mandate is the cornerstone of an effective Investor Relations function. Without it, IR lacks authority internally, credibility externally, and accountability in practice. Mandate ambiguity is one of the most common—and most damaging—architectural weaknesses in Investor Relations.

Defining the IR mandate is not about describing everything the function might touch. It is about making explicit choices regarding what IR is responsible for, what it coordinates, and what it must not own. These choices determine how IR interacts with management, how it is perceived by investors, and how effectively it can perform its advisory role. In mature organizations, this mandate is typically formalized in a disclosure policy or dedicated IR guidelines.

The Core Mandate of Investor Relations

At its core, Investor Relations exists to connect corporate strategy, performance, and capital allocation with capital-market expectations. This mandate has three essential dimensions:

- articulating the company's strategic narrative in a way that investors can understand, assess, and value;

- ensuring consistency across financial and strategic communication;
- providing management with insight into market perception and expectations.

These dimensions apply across company types and stages of development. While the complexity of execution may vary, the core mandate remains stable.

A frequent source of mandate confusion lies in the distinction between ownership and coordination.

IR owns the coherence of the equity story. It does not own the underlying business strategy.

IR may coordinate disclosure related to ESG initiatives, governance frameworks, or sustainability objectives, ensuring alignment across corporate communication. However, it does not define ESG strategy, set operational targets, or assume accountability for delivery.

This distinction is critical. Ownership implies decision rights and delivery accountability. Coordination implies alignment, interpretation, and consistency. Clear boundaries protect IR ability to function adequately—particularly when leadership expects that communication should compensate for weak or contested strategy.

Expanding the IR Mandate

While the core mandate of IR is stable, its scope often evolves as a company's capital-market exposure becomes more complex. Common triggers for mandate expansion include:

- the introduction of material debt financing or public bond issuance;
- increased reliance on credit ratings;
- rising investor focus on ESG and sustainability as valuation drivers;
- cross-border listing or an increasingly international investor base;
- transformational events, including M&A and organizational simplification or reorganization.

In these situations, IR's coordinating role typically expands—from equity-focused communication to broader capital-provider engagement. This expansion should be deliberate and explicit. It requires management to decide which additional stakeholder groups IR will address directly, which topics IR will coordinate but not own, and what additional capabilities or resources are required. This is often the case when IR's remit expands to include responsibilities for corporate communications, M&A communications, business intelligence, or the company secretariat or ESG.

Importantly, market expectations for IR quality do not diminish as scope expands; they typically intensify. An expanded remit is often interpreted as expanded access—creating the expectation that IR will be able to share more complete, better-integrated, and more authoritative information, not less. Investors and analysts interpret a broader IR mandate as implicit assurance that the company is confident in its own coherence and is willing to subject all dimensions of its narrative to expert scrutiny.

Unplanned or implicit mandate expansion is risky—and often financially risky. In smaller organizations, it frequently results in IR being expected to manage topics such as ESG or broader stakeholder relations without sufficient authority, expertise, or control. A deliberate decision to expand the IR mandate should therefore be accompanied by explicit resourcing and capability decisions.

Mandate Misalignments

Mandate conflicts most often arise from leadership expectations that are insufficiently examined.

Consider a scenario in which a CEO expects Investor Relations to manage all stakeholder engagement: equity investors, debt investors, ESG communication, media interactions, and stock market authorities.

A board assessing this expectation should ask: If IR is accountable for all stakeholder engagement, to whom is it accountable for regulatory outcomes or ESG strategy delivery? If the answer is ambiguous, the mandate is not yet sufficiently defined.

IR should accept responsibility for coordinating capital-market communication across these areas. It should not assume ownership of strategies that require distinct expertise, decision rights, and accountability—particularly where IR is neither properly resourced nor remunerated for such responsibility.

Mandate misalignment has immediate implications for accountability, trust, and risk.

When the IR mandate is unclear or misaligned, the consequences are predictable: overlapping responsibilities, inconsistent messaging, accountability gaps, cost inefficiencies, and erosion of credibility.

Conversely, a clearly articulated mandate strengthens IR's authority, protects the function from overreach, and enables constructive challenge within senior decision-making. Over time, this clarity also supports the professional standing and career progression of the Investor Relations Officer, by anchoring the role in recognized authority, judgment, and accountability rather than ad hoc execution.

4.3 Positioning IR in the Organization

Once the mandate of Investor Relations is clearly defined, the next architectural decision concerns where IR sits within the organization. This discussion is often reduced to reporting lines. In practice, IR positioning is not determined by an organizational chart alone. It is defined by access: when IR is informed, how early it is involved, and whether it can speak with authority.

Architecture only functions when senior leaders treat Investor Relations as a standing input into decision-making, not as a downstream communication step. Without sustained CEO and CFO engagement, access becomes episodic and governance collapses into formality.

Reporting Lines

Reporting lines are frequently treated as shorthand for influence. This is misleading.

An IRO reporting to the CFO may be deeply embedded in strategic decision-making—or entirely peripheral. But many of an IRO reporting to the CEO only enjoys symbolic status and limited practical involvement.

The decisive questions are not who IR reports to, but when IR gains visibility on strategic and financial decisions, whether IR is informed during exploratory phases or only once outcomes are fixed, and whether IR can escalate concerns without political friction. Consistent access to granular operational information and appropriate board-level exposure are equally important and shape market perceptions of IR authority.

Reporting lines can enable or hinder access, but they do not guarantee it.

Different reporting models can support effective Investor Relations—provided their implications are understood and managed deliberately.

IR Reporting to the CFO

This is the most common model globally. It can work well when:

- finance is closely involved in strategy formation;

- the CFO actively facilitates IR's access to broader leadership discussions;
- investor feedback is treated as strategic input;
- the CFO protects IR from pressure to soften disclosure or overcommit on performance.

In such settings, IR is informed early about strategic options, and access to the CEO and board is not politically constrained.

CFO reporting fails when:

- IR involvement is limited to disclosure preparation, sometimes even without ongoing access to internal reporting;
- strategy discussions bypass finance;
- board-level visibility into IR insights is restricted;
- the CFO treats IR primarily as a support function rather than a strategic advisor.

IR Reporting to the CEO

This model can enhance strategic alignment and signal institutional importance. It is most effective when:

- supported by disciplined governance routines;
- combined with close coordination with finance (often through formal access protocols);
- the CEO actively uses IR insight to anticipate market reactions;
- the reporting line is operational rather than merely symbolic.

It fails when:

- the reporting line is symbolic rather than operational—providing proximity without access or authority;
- governance discipline is weak, making IR involvement episodic rather than systematic;
- the CEO treats IR as a personal communications tool rather than a strategic advisory function;
- finance is excluded from IR governance, creating misalignment between financial strategy and capital-market communication.

Hybrid Models

Formal reporting to the CFO combined with structured access to the CEO and, in defined circumstances, the board often strike the most effective balance. They preserve financial discipline while ensuring that IR insight is available when strategic choices are still flexible.

Models to Avoid

Arrangements in which Investor Relations reports to the CEO's or CFO's chief of staff are typically ineffective, as they create distance from both strategic decision-making and financial authority. These configurations are rarely invisible to the market and tend to undermine perceptions of IR's mandate, authority, and access. Other suboptimal models include IR reporting to corporate communications, financial controlling, treasury, or the corporate secretariat, where the function is structurally positioned away from capital allocation and investor accountability. In such configurations, IR is more likely to be perceived as a support or messaging function rather than as a strategic interface with the market.

Formal Versus Informal Access to Leadership and Board

Access is often described as either formal or informal, and both are essential.

- *Formal access*

  Formal access includes scheduled participation in executive or board sessions and documented review processes. It provides legitimacy and visibility but is rarely sufficient on its own. When access is purely formal, it often occurs late in decision processes—after options have been narrowed and commitments made.
- *Informal access*

  Informal access refers to early visibility on emerging ideas, pre-alignment discussions, and ad hoc conversations during exploratory phases—well ahead of formal reporting cycles or major corporate events. This is where IR can add the greatest strategic value, but only when such access is structurally supported rather than dependent on individual relationships.

  The risk of relying exclusively on informal access is that it becomes personality-dependent. When the CFO or CEO who facilitated early engagement departs, informal access is often lost, leaving the incoming leadership unfamiliar with the benefit of early IR involvement.

- *Integrated Access Framework*

  Effective IR architecture requires both dimensions operating in concert:

  - Informal access is protected through cultural norms, not just personal relationships—for instance, regular "standing agendas" with the CFO that assume IR participation, or inclusion of the IRO in strategic planning sessions as standard practice
  - Formal access is meaningful because it addresses substantive issues identified through informal engagement, not procedural sign-offs
  - Escalation protocols clarify when informal discussion should trigger formal review, preventing important issues from being lost in ad hoc conversation.

Regardless of reporting line, effective IR architecture requires a minimum set of access conditions:

- early visibility on budgets, financial reporting, strategic and capital allocation discussions;
- routine alignment with the CFO ahead of financial disclosures;
- defined circumstances under which IR engages directly with the CEO or the Board;
- clear escalation paths when market implications are material.

Key IRO Capabilities

This advisory role rests on three key capabilities:

1. Understanding how investors interpret information: This requires an agile mind combined with fluency in financial analysis, valuation frameworks, and the decision-making patterns that drive investor behavior. The IRO must be able to anticipate where investor logic will diverge from management assumptions.
2. Translating strategic and financial complexity into clear, coherent narratives: This goes beyond clear communication skills; it requires the ability to identify the essential economic drivers of the business, explain their evolution over time, and position strategic decisions within a coherent long-term value creation framework.

3. Identifying gaps between management intent and market perception: This is perhaps the most critical capability. Market perception emerges not from management intention but from the cumulative interpretation of actions, communication, and outcomes over time. The IRO must be able to diagnose when perception gaps exist, determine whether they reflect misunderstanding or disagreement, and recommend how to address them.

Acting as a strategic advisor requires the IRO to think simultaneously like an analyst, an investor, and an internal leader. The role involves anticipating how decisions will be interpreted, where skepticism may arise, and which aspects of the equity story require reinforcement or clarification over time.

Importantly, advisory influence depends on timing. The IRO adds the greatest value when engaged during exploratory and evaluative phases, not after decisions are fixed. Late involvement is likely to be penalized by the market—and constrains the IRO's ability to add insight before irreversible commitments are made.

The IRO's authority derives from insight and judgment, not from formal decision rights. This distinction is essential.

IR must have sufficient authority to challenge assumptions, raise concerns, and escalate issues when market implications are material. At the same time, the IRO must not be positioned as a decision-maker. Confusing advisory authority with decision authority exposes IR to inappropriate blame when outcomes disappoint and muddies governance accountability.

Effective architecture protects this balance. It ensures that IR input is heard early and taken seriously, while preserving clear ownership of strategic and financial decisions within management and the board.

Just as trust is the ultimate bond between a company and the capital markets, trust between Investor Relations and senior leadership is a necessary precondition for effective IR architecture.

Access, escalation rights, and advisory influence cannot be sustained by formal reporting lines alone. They depend on management's confidence that IR judgment is sound, confidential, and aligned with the company's long-term interests. Without this trust, IR involvement becomes selective, late, or symbolic—regardless of governance design.

Internal trust, like external trust, is built over time through consistency of judgment, disciplined use of access, and respect for decision ownership. It is strengthened by:

- Consistency of judgment: The IRO provides counsel that is balanced, informed by market intelligence rather than political positioning, and grounded in valuation logic
- Confidentiality discipline: The IRO manages sensitive information appropriately, respects boardroom confidence, and does not use access to advance personal interests
- Respect for decision ownership: The IRO offers input and analysis but ultimately defers to management and board decision-making authority
- Long-term orientation: The IRO's counsel prioritizes long-term credibility and capital-market resilience over short-term messaging convenience
- Operational delivery: The IRO executes IR programs effectively, maintaining investor relationships and implementing communication plans with discipline.

In organizations where IR has been perceived as either excessively deferential to management or, conversely, as creating excessive constraints on communication, trust can be broken and needs to be repaired:

- If IR has been perceived as a "rubber stamp," establishing trust requires demonstrating willingness to challenge assumptions and escalate concerns, even when inconvenient to management
- If IR has been perceived as blocking communication, rebuilding trust requires clear articulation of the IRO's advisory role (not decision-making role), transparent escalation protocols, and demonstration that IR input improves rather than inhibits market communication

In either case, rebuilding trust typically requires explicit board-level discussion of IR's role, clear governance protocols that are visibly followed, and time—trust cannot be rapidly reconstructed after significant erosion.

This is enabled by candid dialogue during exploratory phases, when options are still open and market implications can still be shaped. This is particularly critical when management decides which financial objectives or guidance it wants to communicate to the market.

Accountability and Judgment

The IRO is accountable for the quality of interpretation, coordination, and escalation—not for market outcomes, and certainly not for managing the share price.

Investor sentiment, valuation, and share-price performance are influenced by many factors beyond IR's control: macroeconomic conditions, sector dynamics, competitive developments, execution against guidance, changes in cost of capital, and shifts in investor risk appetite. Holding IR accountable for outcomes rather than for judgment quality creates perverse incentives and encourages overly conservative communication, defensive positioning, and messaging discipline that erodes rather than enhances credibility.

By contrast, clear accountability standards that focus on judgment quality support several positive outcomes:

- IR credibility internally: Leadership understands that IR is being evaluated on the quality of its analysis and counsel, not on whether the market happens to agree with management's strategic choices
- IR credibility externally: Investors sense that communication reflects genuine management conviction informed by market intelligence, not communication filtered through fear of accountability for market reactions
- Constructive challenge: When IROs are confident they will not be held responsible for market outcomes they cannot control, they are more willing to raise difficult issues and offer candid counsel
- Long-term orientation: Judgment-based accountability encourages IROs to prioritize long-term credibility over short-term messaging convenience

Clear accountability standards protect IR credibility internally and externally. They also reinforce the advisory nature of the role and support constructive challenge.

4.4 The Investor Relations Officer (IRO) as Strategic Advisor

The Investor Relations Officer occupies a distinctive position within the organization. The role is neither purely a communications function nor a decision-making one. Its value lies in interpretation, calibration, and judgment applied at the interface between corporate strategy and capital-market expectations.

The IRO does not make strategy, capital allocation, or disclosure decisions. Rather, the role exists to ensure that those decisions are understood in their capital-market context before they are finalized, communicated, and absorbed by investors. This advisory positioning is central to the credibility and effectiveness of Investor Relations.

4.5 Investor Relations as a Leadership Function

The breadth of issues handled by IR—strategy, valuation, governance, risk, and market perception—makes it a natural training ground for broader executive and board responsibilities. While IR does not follow a single career path, effective practitioners typically combine financial expertise with judgment, organizational credibility, and the ability to operate under sustained market scrutiny. There are many examples of former Investor Relations Officers who have become CEOs, CFOs, Chairs, and business owners.

4.6 When There Is No Dedicated IRO

Few private companies and some smaller listed companies maintain a formally designated Investor Relations Officer. In such cases, IR responsibilities are typically distributed across finance, corporate communications, strategy, or executive leadership.

Each substitution model carries distinct implications and requires deliberate architectural choices:

- *Model 1: IR absorbed into finance*

  When Investor Relations is embedded within the finance function, its main advantage is capital-market rigor. The approach is typically grounded in financial analysis, valuation discipline, and a deep understanding of funding structures. Access to strategic financial information is immediate, and the CFO or treasurer often brings established standing with debt investors and credit rating agencies.

  Challenges emerge when financial expertise is not complemented by communication discipline. Narrative quality and coherence can weaken, investor relationships may become transactional rather than developmental, and the broader strategic narrative risks being overshadowed by earnings-centric discussions. Over time, non-financial dimensions of the company's story—such as governance, operational excellence, and organizational agility—may receive insufficient attention.

  Sustaining effectiveness under this configuration requires deliberate architectural choices. Accountability for Investor Relations must be clearly assigned to a senior finance executive, typically the treasurer or controller. Documented IR guidelines should define the executive's mandate in relation to equity investor engagement, narrative development, and escalation protocols. Ongoing coordination with corporate communications or strategy is needed to maintain narrative coherence, and the board should have visibility into how investor sentiment is monitored, interpreted, and integrated into decision-making.

- *Model 2: IR absorbed into corporate communications*

Where Investor Relations sits within corporate communications, the principal benefit lies in the quality and consistency of messaging across stakeholder groups, supported by professional communications discipline throughout the organization. This configuration also reflects a broader governance reality: heads of corporate communications have historically secured representation on executive management committees more frequently than heads of Investor Relations.

The trade-off is a heightened risk that investor communication lacks sufficient grounding in financial and valuation logic. Analyst engagement may be less analytically rigorous, and investor feedback is not always translated into actionable capital markets insight for management and board deliberations. Over time, gaps may appear in areas such as equity valuation, consensus tracking, and expectations management, limiting the function's contribution to strategic dialogue with the market.

To counterbalance these risks, structural reinforcement is required. Accountability for Investor Relations should rest clearly with a senior communications executive, supported by formal and regular liaison with the CFO to ensure financial accuracy and regulatory compliance. Governance frameworks must specify how investor feedback is escalated to financial leadership, while robust processes for consensus tracking and valuation benchmarking are essential to ensure IR insight informs financial and strategic discussions.

- *Model 3: IR led directly by senior executives (CEO/CFO)*

When Investor Relations is led directly by the CEO or CFO, typically in micro and small cap companies, the primary strength is immediacy. Investors engage directly with decision-makers, which often reinforces trust and strategic consistency. Narrative ownership is typically clear, and decision-making can be accelerated in the absence of an intermediary function.

This configuration, however, introduces structural fragility. Consistency and discipline depend heavily on executive availability and competing priorities, leading to uneven IR performance over time. Executive transitions can have a pronounced impact, as investor relationships are often personality-driven rather than institutionalized. Routine investor communication and relationship management may be deprioritized, while systematic sentiment monitoring and expectations management tend to remain underdeveloped.

Durability in this arrangement depends on formalization and the company's life cycle. Responsibilities for core IR activities—earnings calls, investor meetings, roadshows, and media engagement—should be clearly documented. Governance protocols need to define when investor feedback warrants escalation to board-level consideration. Structured processes for investor calendar management and relationship tracking are essential to ensure continuity despite executive constraints. Where scale allows, a senior staff member should be tasked with coordinating and documenting IR activity, even without a formal IRO title. Succession planning must also explicitly address Investor Relations, recognizing that executive turnover poses a material risk to investor relationships and market continuity. A reputable IR firm may bring in the professional support needed.

Regardless of structure, the absence of a dedicated IRO does not remove the need for IR architecture; it increases the importance of clarity around:

- Who performs which aspects of the IR role: Investor meetings, earnings calls, roadshows, media relations, guidance management, board reporting, sentiment monitoring
- How investor feedback is captured and escalated: Formal notes from investor meetings, periodic sentiment summaries, escalation criteria for board-level issues
- What governance discipline is applied: When is IR involved in capital allocation decisions, guidance changes, strategic announcements and even if and when does IR attend board meetings
- How consistency is maintained across transitions: Documentation, board visibility, and formal protocols that do not depend on individual relationships

For smaller public companies with limited resources, a practical approach might include:

- A senior finance executive (treasurer, controller, or CFO) designated as primary IR contact
- A documented IR charter that clarifies this executive's mandate

- A junior finance or communications staff member assigned responsibility for investor meeting coordination, calendar management, and perception tracking
- Quarterly reporting to the board on investor sentiment and any material escalation issues
- Annual review of whether the current structure remains adequate as the company grows.

4.7 Resourcing the Investor Relations Function

IR architecture, and consequently, strategy effectiveness, is only effective if it is adequately resourced. Mandate clarity, access, and governance discipline cannot compensate for insufficient capacity, misaligned skill sets, or inadequate budgeting.

At a minimum, effective Investor Relations requires:

- clear ownership of investor dialogue and market interpretation;
- analytical capacity to interpret financial performance, valuation drivers, and consensus dynamics;
- judgment and communication capability to translate complexity into coherent market narratives;
- adequate quality staffing and budgeting against mandate and objectives;
- technology infrastructure that supports research, targeting, share-ownership identification, analysis, meeting coordination, and relationship management (Table 4.1).

Team Composition Considerations

- *For Debt Investor or Credit Rating Engagement*

  Add capability in credit analysis and bond market dynamics, or establish formal liaison with CFO/Treasury. If the company has material debt outstanding or maintains active relationships with credit rating agencies, IR should include expertise in:

  - Credit spreads and bond market dynamics
  - Leverage ratios and covenant compliance
  - Cash flow forecasting and debt refinancing schedules

Table 4.1 Resourcing framework by company stage and capital-market exposure

Company stage/capital-market exposure	Minimum IR resourcing	Primary skill emphasis	Indicative budget focus
Market cap < $500M or limited investor base/early stage public companies	• One full-time IRO with strong financial literacy and investor communication experience • Selective outsourcing (roadshow logistics, meeting scheduling, basic targeting support)	• Financial analysis and core accounting literacy • Basic valuation frameworks • Clear, disciplined oral and written communication	• Essential IR infrastructure (CRM, IR website) • Targeted engagement (conferences, investor meetings) • Shareholder identification • Perception studies only if strategically material
Market capitalization: $500M to $5 bn ("mid-cap companies")	• One IRO • One analyst/coordinator • Periodic CEO and/or CFO participation in selected engagements	• IRO: strategic interpretation, market intelligence, message discipline • Analyst: financial modeling, consensus tracking, peer benchmarking, presentation development	• Analyst compensation • External advisors for complex transactions, capital structure changes, or structured perception studies • Capital Markets Day
Market capitalization: > $5 B; broad and diversified investor base ("large-cap companies")	• IRO supported by multiple analysts • Potential IR director level • Dedicated investor-event management • Possible retail shareholder interface	• IRO: strategic advisory role, board-level interface, sentiment interpretation • Analysts: valuation, forecasting, research note analysis • Event management: logistics, scheduling, execution discipline	• Full internal team costs • Ongoing external advisory support for transactions • Regular perception studies • Systematic conference participation and investor research tracking

  - Interaction between equity and credit narratives (e.g., how strategic decisions affect credit ratings).

  Alternatively, establish a formal protocol in which the treasurer or CFO owns credit Investor Relations, but IR coordinates messaging consistency between equity and credit narratives.
- *For International Investor Bases*

  Consider geographic coverage capacity or translation/localization support. If the company has material non-domestic investor base, IR infrastructure should include:

  - Capability to engage with investors in key geographic markets (EMEA, Asia–Pacific, etc.), including local presence
  - Translation support for key materials (annual report, investor presentation, guidance updates) as appropriate
  - Understanding of local governance expectations, disclosure requirements, and investor preferences, regardless of whether the company y is dual-listed or not
  - In very large organizations, potentially regional IR resources or relationships with local IR firms.
- *For ESG-Focused Investor Engagement*

  Develop capability to translate ESG metrics into valuation and risk terms, or establish clear interface with Sustainability function. ESG is increasingly material to investor valuation, but IR's role is not to own ESG strategy delivery. Instead, the IRO will focus on:

  - Translating ESG metrics and objectives into terms that matter to valuations (e.g., regulatory risk, competitive advantage, operational resilience)
  - Coordinating messaging between ESG disclosures and investor communication
  - Escalating ESG-related investor concerns that may have capital-market implications
  - Educating investors on how the company's ESG strategy supports long-term value creation (Table 4.2).

Table 4.2 Basic IR function staffing architecture

Company profile	Minimum viable	Fully resources	Critical in-house
Growth-stage, < $2B	Solo IRO	IRO + Analyst	Market intelligence, strategy
Mid-cap, Institutional heavy	IRO + Analyst	IRO + 2–3 Analysts + Communications	All core functions
Large-cap, Complex cap structure	IRO + Sr. Analyst	Full team + specialized roles	Executive access, governance

Outsourcing Investor Relations

Outsourcing Investor Relations is primarily an architectural question rather than an operational—or budget—one. The guiding principle is straightforward: companies should retain internal ownership of investor relationships, strategic interpretation, and governance, while selectively outsourcing execution-heavy or highly specialized activities. Where Investor Relations is outsourced in its entirety—most often in smaller organizations—the risk is not outsourcing per se, but the loss of internal judgment, continuity, and accountability.

Investor engagement, narrative ownership, board interface, and the interpretation of investor sentiment must remain internal, as these activities define how the market understands management intent and behavior. By contrast, operational elements such as event logistics, presentation production, technology support, translation, and certain forms of external research can be outsourced efficiently, provided they remain clearly directed and supervised by the company. Specialist advisory support may also be appropriate during transformational events such as mergers, capital raises, or restructurings.

Effective outsourcing requires discipline. External providers must operate under strict confidentiality, and control over investor targeting, meeting agendas, and key messages should never be delegated. Outsourced activities need regular review to ensure they continue to serve strategic objectives rather than becoming disconnected execution layers. Where external research is used, internal analytical capability remains essential; interpretation and decision-making cannot be outsourced without weakening the function.

Resourcing decisions more broadly should be revisited regularly as mandates evolve. Changes in investor-base composition, expansion into debt or ESG communication, rising activism risk, geographic complexity, leadership transitions, or shifts in technology all affect the adequacy of IR resources.

These considerations warrant periodic review by management and explicit discussion at board level, particularly where resource gaps create material exposure.

Resourcing is therefore not an execution detail. It is a structural decision that directly determines whether Investor Relations can operate with authority, continuity, and trust over time. Strong architecture without adequate resources is ultimately unsustainable—especially in smaller organizations, where the IRO often carries broad responsibility with limited support.

4.8 Investor Relations Processes and Governance

Investor Relations governance defines when IR is involved. This is different from what IR decides.

Governance discipline determines whether IR insight informs decision-making while options are still open, or whether it is applied retrospectively once decisions are fixed. Clear sequencing and escalation logic are therefore central to effective IR architecture.

Weak governance leads to late involvement, inconsistent messaging, and avoidable trust-damaging risks. Strong governance ensures that IR input is available when it can still influence framing, timing, and expectations.

Governance discipline is particularly critical during periods of transformation, capital raising, guidance updates, or strategic change, when market interpretation materially affects valuation and access to capital.

IR Sequencing and Documenting

Most strategic and financial decisions evolve through identifiable stages:

1. Exploration: Preliminary assessment of options (e.g., preliminary acquisition targets, new product opportunity, response to market disruption)
2. Evaluation: Detailed analysis including impact on analyst estimates, investment recommendations, and valuation multiples
3. Commitment: Preliminary decisions made, internal resource allocation approved (e.g., first draft announcements, board briefings)
4. Execution: Public announcement, regulatory filing, investor communication (press release, conference calls, roadshows).

IR value is highest during the early stages, when alternatives are still under consideration and when management thinking is still open to market-informed input.

Common failure patterns arise when IR is engaged only at the commitment stage. By then, options are constrained or insufficiently assessed, and market reactions must be managed rather than anticipated. This is the reactive posture that undermines long-term credibility.

Effective governance explicitly defines which categories of decisions require IR involvement and at which stage. The determination should be made at the governance level, not left to case-by-case judgment.

A recurring governance challenge is determining when an idea moves from early exploration to serious consideration—and therefore requires automatic involvement from Investor Relations. In practice, this threshold is reached once management time and analytical resources are formally committed, external advisers are hired, scenarios begin to converge, capital-market implications become material, disclosure obligations are triggered, or board committees are asked to provide input or approval. At that point, IR involvement should be automatic rather than discretionary.

IR governance defines in advance when IR must be engaged across a range of situations, including capital allocation decisions, guidance changes, strategic pivots, financing transactions, leadership or governance changes, activist situations, proxy contests, and merger activity from exploration through integration. Regardless, IR should be involved early enough to assess market implications, contribute to messaging and sequencing, and monitor investor response.

Formal access to senior management, however, does not substitute for continuous interaction. To be effective, IR-leadership engagement has to be sustained and iterative. Informal exchanges—brief check-ins, judgment calls on emerging investor concerns, and ongoing interpretation of market signals—often matter more than formal reports or scheduled meetings. While structured routines provide predictability, it is frequent interaction that ensures IR insight arrives early enough to influence decision-making.

In larger organizations, this interaction is typically supported by defined cadences, such as brief daily check-ins during market hours, weekly reviews of consensus and sentiment, share-price evolution, peer benchmarking, and intensified alignment in the days preceding major announcements. Smaller organizations may of course rely on less formal structures, but the discipline remains the same: regular visibility between IR and leadership, deliberate preparation ahead of market-sensitive events, and prompt debriefing once investor feedback emerges.

Documenting IR involvement and escalation decisions reinforces this discipline. This is what makes IR guidelines and policies such a useful document. Internally, it provides clarity on when IR was consulted, how its input informed decisions, and how accountability is maintained over time, including through personnel transitions. Externally, it supports compliance and defensibility should disclosure decisions later be questioned by regulators or market authorities. Documentation need not be burdensome. A brief record capturing when IR was engaged, the market implications considered, and how this input shaped communication and timing is typically sufficient. The objective is clarity, continuity, and a defensible governance trail.

4.9 The Board's Role in IR Architecture

While executive governance determines day-to-day IR effectiveness, the board plays a critical role in affirming IR architecture and ensuring accountability.

From a board perspective, IR architecture should be viewed as a governance and risk-management matter. Best practice shareholder engagement strategies suggest that the board should be responsible for ensuring that IR is structurally enabled to support strategic objectives and capital market credibility.

When the IR architecture is weak, the board's ability to assess IR effectiveness is compromised. When IR lacks access to senior information, market-relevant signals are lost and disclosure risk increases. Moreover, when leadership transitions occur (new CEO, CFO, or board chair), weak architecture creates vulnerability because IR effectiveness becomes personality-dependent.

Board Oversight of IR

When it is formalized, Board oversight of Investor Relations typically sits with the audit committee, strategy committee, or a dedicated capital markets committee, depending on company structure. The specific forum matters less than clarity of responsibility. At a minimum, the board should have visibility into how IR is positioned and resourced, its access to decision-making, how investor sentiment is monitored and interpreted, and how escalation decisions are handled. Oversight should also test whether IR architecture remains aligned with the company's risk profile and capital-market exposure.

At regular intervals—annually or biennially, and more frequently following material change—the board should review whether the foundations of Investor Relations remain fit for purpose. This includes confirming that the

IR mandate is clearly defined, that reporting lines and access support early involvement in strategic decisions, and that escalation protocols function as intended. The review should also assess whether IR has sufficient authority to raise concerns candidly and whether governance processes are respected in practice.

Periodic board updates should address market sentiment and perception, focusing on investor confidence trends, recurring themes in feedback, relative valuation positioning, and changes in shareholder composition. The objective is not exhaustive reporting, but early detection of gaps between management intent and market interpretation.

Not all investor feedback warrants board attention. Escalation should be reserved for situations where market signals indicate heightened risk or structural misalignment. These include persistent trust gaps between management and investors, valuation risks arising from strategic decisions that the market interprets differently than intended, disclosure breakdowns, significant shifts in investor confidence or shareholder composition, leadership transitions with capital-market implications, and proxy advisory opposition that signals governance concern.

Clear escalation criteria serve a dual purpose: they prevent material issues from remaining unaddressed, while avoiding the elevation of routine market noise to board level. When escalation occurs, the board's role is to determine whether communication requires refinement, strategic assumptions merit reassessment, or governance oversight should be strengthened. In rare cases, sustained market skepticism may point to deeper execution or leadership issues that warrant direct board intervention.

Board-Level IR Reporting

Board-level IR reporting is a core governance responsibility of the Investor Relations function. Its purpose is not only to account for IR activity, but rather to equip the board with insight into how the company is understood, valued, and assessed by the capital markets.

In practice, board-level reporting on Investor Relations should prioritize insight over activity. It should be presented by the IRO in person during a Board meeting, at least once a year. While metrics such as investor meetings, free-float coverage, or engagement intensity have contextual value, they are secondary to understanding how the market is interpreting the company's strategy and risk profile. Effective reporting focuses on market expectations, emerging concerns, and the degree of alignment—or misalignment—between management intent and investor perception.

At its core, board-level IR reporting should provide a clear snapshot of market sentiment. This includes trends in institutional investor confidence, recurring themes in investor feedback, valuation positioning relative to peers and historical ranges, and any material shifts in shareholder composition. Boards should also be informed about the quality and direction of analyst coverage, including changes in ratings, consensus revisions, divergent assumptions, and the implications these may have for market expectations.

Beyond sentiment and consensus, reporting should surface emerging investor themes that may signal perception gaps or future risk. These often include questions around strategy execution, ESG priorities, regulatory or competitive developments, and relative positioning versus peers. Where strategic decisions have been announced, IR reporting should assess how the market is interpreting those decisions, whether valuation outcomes align with management intent, and what early signals suggest about investor acceptance or skepticism.

Changes in shareholder composition warrant particular attention, especially where they may affect engagement priorities, voting dynamics, or exposure to activism. Trend analysis over time is equally important, enabling the board to distinguish between temporary market noise and sustained shifts in confidence, and to understand what factors are driving improvement or deterioration.

Share-price performance and valuation metrics provide necessary context but should be interpreted analytically rather than descriptively. The focus should be on how valuation evolves relative to peers, indices, and cost of capital, and how these movements relate to financial performance, guidance, or strategic announcements—rather than on short-term price movements in isolation.

The cadence of IR board reporting should align with strategic planning cycles and major decision points. Quarterly updates are typical for larger companies, while smaller organizations may opt for semi-annual or annual reviews, supplemented as needed during periods of heightened change, transaction activity, or market stress (Table 4.3).

4.10 Identifying Investor Sentiment and Market Expectations

Understanding investor sentiment and market expectations is central to effective Investor Relations. Sentiment provides the external reference against which IR priorities, messaging, and judgment are tested. Without it, even

Table 4.3 Board-level Investor Relations reporting overview

Reporting area	Purpose	Key elements reviewed
Market sentiment snapshot	Assess overall investor confidence and perception	Institutional investor confidence trends; recurring concerns or themes; valuation positioning versus peers and historical range; material shifts in investor-base composition
Analyst coverage and consensus	Understand expectations-setting and external interpretation	Number and quality of analyst coverage; rating distribution and recent changes; consensus earnings revisions and implications; divergent or outlier analyst assumptions
Emerging investor themes	Identify perception gaps and forward-looking risks	Recurring investor questions; ESG-related focus and engagement impact; regulatory or competitive concerns; peer comparison insights
Capital-market implications of strategic decisions	Test alignment between management intent and market response	Market interpretation of recent announcements; alignment between valuation impact and intended outcomes; early signals on major initiatives (transformation, M&A, exits)
Shareholder composition changes	Anticipate engagement and voting dynamics	Shifts in investor base; concentration of activist or ESG-focused investors; geographic or investment-style changes

Reporting area	Purpose	Key elements reviewed
Sentiment trend analysis	Distinguish noise from structural change	Comparison with prior periods; drivers of sentiment improvement or deterioration; forward-looking assessment of likely sentiment trajectory
Share-price performance and valuation context	Provide valuation context without over-emphasis	Absolute share-price performance; valuation multiples versus indices and peers; changes in cost of capital or equity risk premium; correlation with performance, guidance, or strategic events

well-structured IR functions risk operating on internal assumptions rather than market realities.

This section shifts the focus from internal enablement to external interpretation—how investors perceive the company, how expectations form, and how confidence or doubt accumulates over time.

4.11 Market Insight and Expectations Management

At its core, IR seeks to understand how a company's strategy, execution, and governance are perceived over time, identifying where confidence or doubt resides.

Market expectations do not emerge solely from disclosures, nor from media coverage or research reports taken in isolation. They are formed through the cumulative interpretation of a company's actions, leadership credibility, quality of execution, and track record over time. IR influences these expectations through deliberate communication and engagement. A structured assessment of market perception and expectations provides the context in which IR strategy is developed and all subsequent activities are calibrated.

Understanding how the market perceives the company, both at a given point in time and over time, does not imply that corporate strategy should be adapted to prevailing investor preferences. The purpose of sentiment analysis is to inform strategic decision-making. The responsibility for setting strategy lies with the board and executive management. IR ensures that decisions are made with a clear understanding of their capital-market implications.

When used properly, sentiment analysis enables management and boards to:

- Anticipate reactions to strategic decisions before they are announced
- Distinguish between misunderstanding (addressable through communication) and disagreement (requiring either strategic adjustment or acceptance of market skepticism)
- Identify where communication can strengthen credibility without compromising long-term objectives
- Clarify whether market resistance to a given decision reflects a lack of information, a trust deficit, or a structural constraint that transparent communication alone cannot resolve.

The risk arises when sentiment feedback is treated as instruction rather than intelligence. Mature IR functions anchor sentiment analysis in long-term strategy, distinguishing carefully between:

- Short-term sector rotation or sentiment shifts that are driven by macro factors because they differ fundamentally from persistent investor concerns about the company's strategy or execution.
- Perception gaps that can be addressed and structural constraints that cannot: Some investor skepticism reflects incomplete information and can be resolved through better communication; other skepticism reflects legitimate business risks that communication alone cannot eliminate.
- Investor preferences and fiduciary responsibilities: management and the board retain ultimate responsibility for deciding strategy based on long-term value creation logic, not short-term investor preference.

Sentiment analysis allows leadership to act with foresight and avoid being defensive when engaging with investors.

4.12 Investor Perception and Sentiment Assessment

Understanding investor sentiment requires systematic tracking. Effective companies establish ongoing mechanisms to capture, analyze, and act on how investors and analysts perceive the company, from informal surveys to structured perception studies.

Below is a three-tier approach to sentiment monitoring:

- *Tier 1: Formal Perception Studies*

  Conducted typically every 18–24 months or when significant corporate events require reassessment. These studies involve confidential interviews with major institutional investors, sell-side analysts, and proxy advisors. External advisors typically conduct these 30–45 minute interviews to ensure candor and independence. Some boards mandate these studies at least annually if the company faces elevated capital-market risk (activism risk, strategic transformation, competitive uncertainty).

  Key topics in formal perception studies typically include:

  - Key areas of investor interest and concern
  - Confidence in management credibility and strategic execution capability

- Clarity of the equity story, financial and operational reporting, and competitive positioning
- Perception of governance practices and board quality
- Credibility gaps between management claims and market perception
- Relative valuation assessment versus peers
- Effectiveness of Investor Relations practices and accessibility of management

The resulting analysis identifies common themes, outlier perspectives, and actionable insights to inform corporate and IR strategy refinement and board-level discussions of market positioning. While such studies can require a substantial financial commitment, their value lies entirely in how the findings are acted upon., demonstrating to investors that their feedback is taken seriously. In some companies, board charters call for an independent perception study to be conducted annually.

- *Tier 2: Monthly Consensus Tracking*

For companies with decent analyst coverage—typically at least three analysts—analyst consensus, recommendation distributions, changes in earnings estimates and target prices, and research narratives together offer continuous insight into evolving market sentiment. This monitoring benchmarks the company's metrics against peers and tracks changes in analyst assumptions about:

- Business drivers and competitive positioning
- Margin trajectory and profitability drivers
- Growth rates and market share
- Capital allocation and shareholder return expectations.

Monthly tracking data might include:

- Analyst consensus earnings estimates (current year and next year at least), presented as low, high, median, and average values.
- Distribution of investment recommendations and changes in period (upgrades, downgrades, initiations)
- Target price distribution and median
- Key themes in recent research
- Peer comparison (valuation multiples, growth expectations, rating distribution).

- *Tier 3: Monthly Executive Reporting*

A concise report to the CEO, CFO, and Board summarizes key sentiment indicators, analyst activity, and emerging perception themes. These insights should be presented before board meetings, earnings announcements, ensuring capital-market intelligence remains visible to decision-makers.

Example monthly report structure:

- Sentiment summary: key changes in analyst consensus, notable research, investor concerns
- Valuation context: P/E, EV/EBITDA, and other multiples relative to history and peers
- Analyst activity: recent research notes, rating changes, initiation/termination of coverage
- Themes: recurring investor questions, concerns arising in recent meetings
- IR activities: number of investor meetings, split between current shareholders and prospective investors, sell-side analyst interactions.
- Peer benchmarking and market intelligence.

These findings, along with recommendations from perception studies, should be documented and retained, with board-level summaries prepared for disclosure in governance records. This creates accountability for how sentiment insights influenced IR strategy and ensures that sentiment monitoring supports—not undermines—legitimate strategic decisions.

4.13 Sentiment and Expectations Management

Sentiment analysis aids expectations management and guidance policy. When perception studies reveal material misalignment between investor assumptions and management's view of business drivers, growth rates, margin profiles, or value-creation mechanics, the guidance framework and disclosure policies can be refined to improve investor understanding.

This approach differs from changing stated objectives or "guidance" based on operational performance. Instead, it focuses on refining the clarity and accuracy of the guidance framework.

Sentiment insights can be used to the following effect:

- If sentiment research shows investors underestimate the company's pricing power or market share resilience, disclosures can be enhanced to address these blind spots—for example, by providing more granular pricing data, discussing competitive positioning, or explaining how pricing is protected by customer contracts or switching costs.

- If analysts' consensus estimates are based on assumptions that differ from management's actual model, the guidance framework can clarify the company's true economic drivers. For instance, if analysts assume margin pressure from wage inflation but management has structural cost offsets, clarity on these offsets improves understanding.
- If investors overestimate competitive threats or regulatory risks, supplemental disclosures can adjust these perceptions—for example, by providing data on competitive wins, customer retention, or likelihood of regulatory outcomes.
- In cases where market expectations for growth, profitability, or cash generation are overly optimistic, guidance revisions (rather than operational changes) can help set realistic expectations. This preserves credibility by preventing repeated disappointments. The key is to adjust expectations before they disappoint, not after. Quite importantly, the market will forgive a guidance revision, but not two consecutive guidance revisions.

The relationship between sentiment and guidance is iterative. Sentiment insights inform guidance frameworks, shaping market expectations, which are then tracked and validated through subsequent rounds of sentiment analysis and consensus monitoring.

When mandate, governance, access, sentiment tracking, and resourcing are aligned, Investor Relations functions as a strategic capability rather than a reactive support activity. These architectural choices determine whether IR can exercise informed judgment, build investor trust, and support sustained access to capital.

Practical Implications

- Ensure the IR mandate is explicitly defined, aligned with management expectations, and supported by decision authority before executing.
- Position the IRO as a strategic adviser.
- Design IR architecture to prevent predictable failure patterns.
- Treat investor sentiment as a strategic input.

This chapter established that Investor Relations outcomes are determined by structural foundations: mandate, positioning, resources, governance, and diagnostic discipline. It showed that IR must be architecturally enabled before it can function as a strategic capability. Structure alone, however, does not create competitive advantage. The next chapter examines the core Investor Relations strategies through which this capability is translated into deliberate choices about communication, positioning, and engagement in the competition for capital.

5

Core Investor Relations Strategies

With the organizational foundations of Investor Relations established, the focus turns to the strategic choices that determine how the function creates value, shapes market perception, and supports the company's long-term access to capital. This chapter examines the core Investor Relations strategies and how they function together to create competitive advantage.

Effective Investor Relations requires more than sound organizational structure and clear authority. It requires disciplined execution—a coherent strategy that aligns narrative, disclosure, stakeholder engagement, and governance across any market conditions.

This chapter brings together the individual building blocks of effective Investor Relations and examines how they function as an integrated system. It shows how narrative, disclosure, stakeholder engagement, and governance interfaces interact over time to shape reputation, valuation, and access to capital. Rather than treating Investor Relations as a collection of activities, the chapter explains how IR works in practice: as a coordinated framework that aligns communication discipline, market engagement, and institutional trust around long-term value creation.

This chapter explores how companies deliberately shape market outcomes by:

- Establishing perception and reputation through a disciplined investment narrative that connects strategy to performance
- Managing expectations and valuation through transparent disclosure and financial reporting that reduces uncertainty

A. Guimard, *Investor Relations Strategy*, https://doi.org/10.1007/978-3-032-21679-3_5

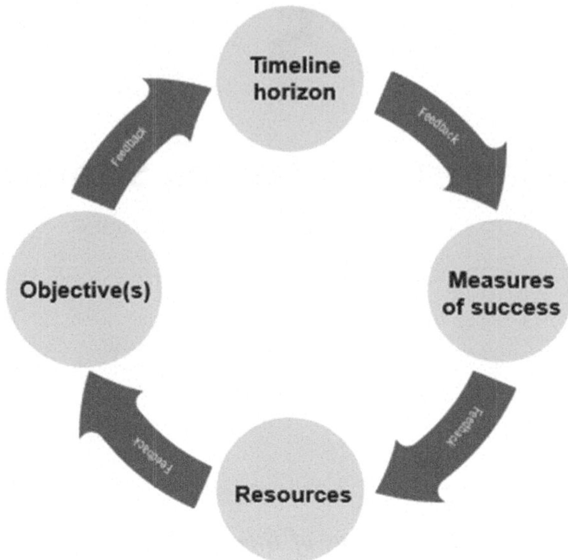

Fig. 5.1 Nurturing your IR strategy: The feedback loop

- Building shareholder base resilience across market cycles by diversifying ownership and deepening investor conviction
- Navigating investor scrutiny through structured governance engagement and Board-investor dialogue
- Ensuring message coherence across financial, corporate, and governance communications as stakeholder boundaries blur (Fig. 5.1).

5.1 The Art and Science of Crafting the Narrative

Crafting the Investor Relations narrative is both a strategic discipline and a practical craft. It sits at the intersection of corporate strategy, financial reality, and market psychology. At its core, the narrative is neither a promotional exercise nor a stylistic spin on disclosure. It operates within strict legal and regulatory boundaries and derives its credibility from analytical rigor, factual integrity, and consistency over time.

The IR narrative is the structured articulation of how a company creates value, why that value is sustainable, and how management intends to steward capital across cycles. In this sense, crafting the IR narrative is not a cosmetic exercise. It is the disciplined marketing of the company's value proposition to the capital markets—grounded in evidence, constrained by regulation, and tested continuously through investor dialogue and market feedback.

It is therefore essential to understand how to define the equity story, articulate the value-creation logic, clarify time horizons, and ensure narrative consistency—including how material ESG factors are embedded in strategy, risk management, governance, and capital allocation, rather than treated as a parallel or discretionary storyline.

Mastering the art and science of crafting the narrative requires far more than good writing. It demands strategic judgment, financial literacy, and the authority to determine not only what the company communicates, but why, when, and to whom. Narrative discipline is as much about sequencing and selectivity as it is about substance, clarity, and readability.

All in all, the equity story should always follow these guidelines: focus on transparent communication and investor relationships. Make your company intelligible, accessible to investors, and too valuable to sell.

The objective of this section is to provide a structured framework for the development of core Investor Relations messages. It sets out the thematic architecture that enables companies to articulate how they operate, compete, create value, and manage risk over time. This framework serves as a reference for consistent message development across financial and non-financial dimensions and is illustrated by the accompanying table of Investor Relations messages by theme.

Contrary to what is sometimes assumed, Investor Relations is not solely about:

- company finances, numbers, and consolidated financial statements, which quickly become historical once disclosed;
- positive developments or favorable outcomes.

It is widely accepted today that a significant proportion of a company's value—often estimated at one-third or more—is attributable to non-financial and intangible assets that are not captured in financial statements. Moreover, experience shows that companies that demonstrate humility, transparency, and accountability when performance disappoints tend to preserve trust more effectively than those that communicate only success.

As a result, the scope and required expertise of Investor Relations continue to expand. Portfolio managers increasingly incorporate additional variables into their valuation models and investment criteria, including innovation capacity, intellectual capital, research and development, use of technology, corporate brand strength, management reputation, governance quality, sustainability practices, and broader social and environmental factors.

A company's strategy cannot be analyzed solely through reported figures, which represent only the visible surface of a far more complex reality.

The boundaries between financial, technical, operational, commercial, organizational, social, and environmental factors have therefore become increasingly blurred. This makes consistency across time, formats, and communication channels more difficult—but also more critical—than ever before.

Against this backdrop, the messages developed and delivered by Investor Relations should inform the market about:

- the company's overall vision and strategic direction;
- both favorable developments and emerging challenges;
- its sources of competitive advantage;
- its business model, and how it drives performance, measured through indicators used internally as well as by the market's preferred metrics;
- its prospects and long-term ambitions.

It is essential that companies strive to maintain a comparable level of transparency and disclosure quality over time, including after the IPO phase. As a matter of principle, issuers should avoid presenting selectively favorable pictures of performance.

Finally, in its efforts to educate the financial markets about its business, a company should systematically define acronyms, financial ratios, and technical terminology, ensuring that its narrative remains accessible, intelligible, and comparable across audiences and geographies.

Below is a workable Investor Relations narrative architecture designed to ensure that all Investor Relations communication is anchored in a coherent, durable logic for value creation, rather than in episodic messaging (Table 5.1).

Writing Clearly

Writing clearly is a "must-have" skill. It can really enhance reputation, or it can deter your target audiences from reading anything that your company writes. You should entice your readers, not overwhelm them. In certain countries, the regulator is requiring that texts be written in a clear and readily understandable style, given the excesses of "legalese" contained in financial documentation. Indeed, this is quite a challenge as the same document will be

Table 5.1 The narrative architecture

The narrative architecture
• **Long-term value-creation logic** What fundamentally drives sustainable value over time
• **Strategic priorities** Where management is deliberately allocating focus and capital
• **Financial performance drivers** How strategy translates into financial outcomes
• **Risk and uncertainty framing** What could disrupt the strategy and how it is managed
• **Externalities and sustainability** How ESG factors, regulation, and geopolitics affect value creation
• **Evidence hierarchy** Which facts, metrics, and milestones matter most

targeted at varied audiences, with varying levels of understanding, education, and knowledge.

The language used should be direct and simple, reflecting your company's personality in an authentic manner.

Bridging the Language Divide

Getting your message across multiple languages can be another IR challenge. It may therefore be advisable to hire professional copywriters and native speakers.

If your company's official language is not English, it is quite likely that you will need the services of a translator for some or all of your Investor Relations tools and documents. Not only should the translated document reflect the original content accurately and faithfully, it must also convey the same image of quality and remain an easily intelligible and thoroughly pleasant read.

This is unfortunately not always the case, in part because the relationship between IR teams and translators is not always as effective as it should be. Timing constraints are a recurring issue, particularly when translating earnings releases whose content may change up until the last minute. In addition, because English is the international language of finance, many IROs in non-English-speaking countries speak and write sufficiently good English to believe they can accelerate the process by translating documents themselves.

Yet, a better understanding of each other's constraints, needs, and objectives can lead to a more effective and mutually beneficial working relationship.

Here is a list of recommendations for IROs and translators on how to best work together:

- Identify what needs to be translated. Whether your shares are listed in a foreign country or not, the decision should not be driven by cost or regulatory considerations only. Your IR strategy may include catering to a large retail shareholder base or targeting investors in a country where the national language is not English. As a courtesy to this audience, you may want to have your slideshow translated or come to meetings with handouts in this region's language. This is particularly valid when your company has operations locally and you can use their brochures, for instance. Conversely, you need to be aware of the fact that investors in your home country may resent it if you do not bother using slides in your home language and use English slides instead.
- Choosing (and retaining) the right translator. It is possible that you may not find the perfect translator from day one and may need to shop around a bit. Ask your peers whom they work with and do not hesitate to ask your local teams abroad for advice or support.
- Work together more efficiently:
  - Talk to each other. Far too often, communication between IR and translators is done via email. Every now and then, you should talk to put the messages in context, to gather feedback on how previous translations have been perceived by their end-users such as analysts, investors, journalists, and how workflows between IR and translators can be further improved;
  - Brief your translator. Because translators are not machines but human beings, they have a work process and speed of their own. Discuss your project timeline with your translator and see how it is going to work out for both of you;
  - Provide him or her with as much supportive material or background Information as you can, such as analysts' reports, including a contact person in your IR organization;
  - Keep your translator regularly informed of what is going on at your company, by adding her or his name to your corporate mailing lists;
  - Help the translator develop and maintain a translation glossary that is specific to your company and industry.
- Protect yourselves legally:

  - If price-sensitive information is being translated, make sure the translator has signed a non-disclosure agreement and has the proper measures in place to store your information and exchange it with you safely;
  - You may want to mention that your earnings release or annual report is a translation from another language which is provided for information purposes only, and add that in the event of discrepancies between this and the original version, the latter will prevail.

- Write clearly. If the message in your home language is not easily understandable, you should not be surprised if it does not come out clearly in the translation either.
- "If you pay monkeys, you get peanuts." IROs should be careful with translation costs that are priced at a very low per-word rate. Yes, there exists software that provides automated translation very cheaply. (If you have never done so, try to translate any web page from your home language into another one and see the results. You don't want your earnings release to be that confusing). At present, this software is unable to actually rewrite your text. And this is precisely what is going to make or break the quality of your IR message in a foreign language. You need a professional translator for this and it has a price.
- Translation is not only about words and meanings. It is also about respecting typographical conventions. These can be industry, but also language or country specific (for instance, the use of comma decimal marks or of period decimal marks is not the same the world over). Make sure everyone involved is aware of and respects these.

Table 5.2 illustrates how Investor Relations messages can be structured across core themes to support a coherent and credible equity story.

Financial and Strategic Messages

The Business Environment

Listed companies must describe the business environment, the sector, and the cycles in which they operate, specifying the following:

- Regulations that affect their activity in terms of obligations, business opportunities, and future performance;
- The economic environment as reflected in growth rates in the countries in which they are established, interest rates, exchange rates, raw

Table 5.2 Core narrative framework for the equity story

Core narrative theme	Role in the equity story	Key message focus
Market / operating environment	Establishes the context in which the company competes and creates value.	Market dynamics, macroeconomic trends, regulation, competition, sector structure, cyclicality and demand drivers.
Business model	Explains how the company generates revenue, margins, cash flow and returns	Clients, revenue streams, growth drivers, pricing, cost structure, margin drivers, scalability and resilience of the model, business-model risk factors, competitive advantages and barriers to entry.
Strategy	Shows how management intends to create value over time.	Strategic priorities, operational objectives, financial objectives, investment plans, growth initiatives, capital allocation framework.
Organization	Demonstrates the capabilities, operating infrastructure, systems and culture that support execution	Brand awareness, reputation, product quality, intellectual capital, human resources, culture, adaptability, processes, risk management and communication discipline.
Teams / management quality	Builds confidence in leadership judgment and execution capacity.	CEO reputation, management experience, credibility, incentive alignment, succession depth, ability to attract and retain key talent, partnerships and networks.

Core narrative theme	Role in the equity story	Key message focus
Performance / financial strengths	Provides evidence that the equity story is being delivered.	Reported performance, segment analysis, cash generation, returns on capital, M&A integration and value creation track record, sensitivity to key external factors such as exchange rates, interest rates and raw material prices.
Sustainability / corporate governance	Reinforces long-term credibility, responsibility and resilience	Governance quality, transparency, material sustainability priorities, stakeholder relationships, regulatory alignment, risk oversight and disclosure discipline

materials prices, climate trends, consumer spending patterns, and so on. This description should include an analysis of a company's sensitivity—or absence thereof—to the key exogenous factors to which it is exposed and any seasonal aspects of their business;
- The competitive environment and their positioning relative to their main competitors.

In addition to own company data or estimates, it is advisable to educate the investor or the analyst about your macroeconomic environment. Provide external information sources and list them.

Presenting the competitive environment requires objectivity and caution. Using disparaging language about competitors will inevitably backfire on corporate reputation. Remember that investors and analysts can provide a wealth of information on the competitive environment, which makes the dialogue IROs have with them all the more interesting.

Among various skills, an IRO who is as knowledgeable as can be about the company's sector and cycle, will be able to do the following:

- Identify and help develop sector-specific indicators;
- Anticipate upturns and downturns and develop effective messages. These will notably highlight the company's strategy and actions to adjust to a changing environment. For instance, if your company has an international footprint, explain how regional differences may positively affect your business and product cycles.

In this respect, you should also be able to notice when investors are wary of lengthy explanations by management of the economic environment in which its company operates. The reason is simple: They are already well aware of it and overflowed with macroeconomic information.

The Organization

Messages will focus on the legal structure of the company and the governance rules in place. Information about corporate governance is tightly regulated and is required by most of the world's major stock exchanges.

Analysts, investors, and journalists will partly evaluate the company's reputation on the basis of awards and positions in various rankings for product or service quality.

This is also an opportunity for a company to describe the quality of their human resources, labor policies, employment attractiveness, and sustainable development policy.

Corporate business vision and mission statements may also be published to create a framework of values adopted within and around the company, associating all the company's stakeholders, including the financial markets.

Human Capital

Companies will focus on the experience, depth, and diversity (gender, geographical origin, education) of senior management skills, providing all the information needed to allow markets to evaluate their renown and reputation.

This is one highly visible area in which dynamic interaction is required between financial, corporate, and internal communications.

Companies highlight their track record in terms of financial results as well as achievements in other fields: industrial, commercial, and technological achievements, for instance. Wherever and whenever possible, they provide the following:

- Presentation of their different businesses and respective market positions. In this respect, communicating on market shares and leadership is tricky, particularly when it comes to financial or transaction-related documentation: Market authorities may require that these messages be supported by third-party evidence.
- Historic trends and performance comparisons. For instance, comparing results over a period of several years (such as in "Sales growth exceeded 5 percent for the third year in a row"), and not simply with the previous one ("Sales were up 5 percent compared to the previous year"), gives a sense of strength and credibility of management's ability to implement strategic directions.
- The breakdown of performance is given for each division and geographic area, in accordance with applicable accounting standards, and in a manner that is consistent with their overall organization.
- The business or sector-specific indicator is mentioned in the previous section.

These "extra efforts" will give corporate messages even more impact.

Reported performances should also be explained by the internal and external factors that helped make them possible: Successful price increases for the company's products compensating for inflation in raw materials, restructuring measures positively impacting the cost base, lower interest rates, and decrease in indebtedness reducing financial charges, and so on. Here again, there is an educational role for Investor Relations to play.

Past performances should wherever possible be correlated with the objectives the company has communicated to the markets. This is an opportunity to discuss milestones in achieving its strategy and explain whether if it is ahead or behind schedule.

What company management in general and Investor Relations in particular should refrain from doing is publicly criticizing how the company is perceived by the financial markets. It is not for the CEO to voice an opinion on how cheap or undervalued he feels the company is.

Business Model

The presentation of a company's business model is focused on the financial criteria and on the key performance indicators that are applied in strategic planning and in the setting up of realistic targets and credible objectives. Examples include the following which can be presented as absolute figures, percentages or ranges:

- Compound annual growth rates;
- Revenue breakdowns by division (or product lines) and geographic area;
- Market shares;
- Annual research and development expenditure;
- Operating income as a percentage of sales;
- Dividend payout ratio;
- Cash flow as a percentage of sales, before and after capital expenditure ("free cash flow");
- The capital intensity of the business as expressed through capital expenditure as a percentage of sales;
- Net debt-to-equity ratios;
- Cash and cash equivalents.

The internal financial reporting systems must be structured to provide data that are relevant to the understanding of the company's business model. In this respect, international accounting standards require that financial reporting and internal organization match. For instance, if your business is organized by product lines as opposed to geographical regions, you will see to it that this is part of the presentation of your business model.

Also, it is worth mentioning that a company-specific, "adjusted" ratio is a message, not only the result of mathematics, and therefore requires careful and sustainable articulation.

In certain cases, some corporate governance and socially responsible investment metrics are factored into the business model as well. All can serve as a basis for management compensation and for the attribution of performance-related pay, either in cash or in shares, when such remuneration policies are in place.

Companies must be vigilant not to give in to passing trends that favor one ratio over another. If they are in the process of launching a financial operation, they may also have to withstand pressure from investment banks that want to structure the business model to make it attractive to their own clients, possibly to the detriment of the ideal shareholder base targeted by the company, and away from the way management is actually running the company. Note that portfolio managers pay close attention to how robust and proven the business model is in making their investment decisions.

The business model presented to the market should be stable over time except where significant events such as acquisitions cause it to change.

Companies that present their business models clearly show that visibility on their activity is good, even if they do not give targets. The simpler and clearer the business model, the easier it will be for analysts to build their models and determine the value of the company. Companies that are reluctant to provide quantified targets will find that a well-articulated business model can serve as an effective substitute.

Lastly, do not exasperate analysts by reclassifying your segmentation and financials too often. It means that they have to rewrite their entire valuation model. Try to keep your core presentation uniform year after year. If, for instance, you have changed the fundamentals of your business through a major acquisition, provide a detailed reconciliation and variance analysis. If this applies to your company, make sure you properly explain measures that contrast with your country's Generally Accepted Accounting Principles (GAAP) and reconcile to the reported numbers.

Presentation of Company Strategy

Companies should develop specific presentations for the senior management to talk about their longer-term strategy and not simply make it a part of their results announcements. The goal is to attract maximum attention and not be distracted by short-term achievements which investors will already be aware of anyway.

When discussing their strategy, companies should also provide performance indicators:

- that enable the market to evaluate how successfully a strategy is being implemented;

- for which management is accountable.

Consistent with the philosophy that' what is not measured cannot be managed', the following principles should apply:

- Align internal and external key performance indicators ("KPIs");
- 1 strategic objective → 1 key performance indicator;
- No key performance indicator available? No message.

In other words, management should exert extreme caution before it communicates a strategic objective for which no metric exists to track progress or hold management accountable. It is wise to stay away from mainstream, generic messages that can apply to virtually every company ("profitable growth," "value creation" are good proxies of this) and become meaningless if not properly substantiated.

Strategic messages are particularly important when the goal is to prepare the market for changes resulting, for instance, from an acquisition or a move into a new geographic area or the appointment of a new CEO. Such news will be readily understood, and maybe even endorsed by the market as soon as it is announced if it is consistent with the strategy the company has presented over time. Investors do not like surprises. This is another reason why communications too must be long-term oriented. The share may trend higher or lower in the two days that follow a strategic announcement, but the important thing is where it stands two years later.

A clear explanation of the strategy goes hand in hand with a clear explanation of the risks attached to it.

Strategy messages should be developed together with those supporting the business model. This can be done using the capital allocation approach: what can be invested? What can be returned to shareholders?

Shareholder Value Creation Messaging

The concept of shareholder value creation has become one of the most widely endorsed messages in financial communications and Investor Relations. It is virtually every listed company's official goal to create value for its shareholders. Unfortunately, it has become far too generic to be as compelling as it may have been in its early days. The reason lies in the absence of substance attached to it.

Shareholder value creation as a strategic direction and as a message becomes relevant if and when it describes the levers used by management to achieve this much-desired ambition. Financial communications will then focus on communicating their respective characteristics, roles, and targets. Aiming at presenting the company's strategy as geared to creating shareholder value, these messages can be articulated around the following levers:

- Financial levers:
  - Increase earnings per share;
  - Improve total shareholder return;
  - Generate investor trust;
  - Raise return on equity (ROE), return on capital employed (ROCE);
  - Lower the cost of capital;
  - Offer attractive shareholder remuneration policy, via regular dividend payments, share buyback programs, rights issue, and other non-dilutive instruments.
- Operating and strategic levers:
  - Create value for customers;
  - Grow with mergers and acquisitions (M&A);
  - Steady organic revenue growth;
  - Tight cost control;
  - Best practice-driven corporate governance;
  - Human resources and compensation policies.

  In addition,

- The company will want to stress that it has developed proactive Investor Relations program and made shareholder value creation an intrinsic part of its corporate culture; and
- Communicating on shareholder value creation truly becomes powerful when quantified targets are associated: "We are increasing our return on equity (ROE) target, in the range of 33–36 percent."

In order to curb excessive communications in this area, certain legislators have decided to formally require that it be

- based on a consistently applied and clearly explained methodology;
- reviewed by the statutory auditors if the information is to be part of the issuer's legal documentation (in a prospectus, for instance).

Lastly, investors need to be able to reconcile indicators used to track shareholder value creation with the company's consolidated financial statements.

Because just about any company can claim it wants to create value, credibility lies in the respect of the following recommendations:

- Explain why you chose those value-creation indicators in particular;
- Consider having them audited, if not already required by law;
- Post the definition of these metrics on your website;
- Be consistent through good times … and bad.

Environmental, Social, and Governance (ESG)

Closely linked to corporate governance, sustainable development has evolved from a broad political, social, and economic concept—defined by the United Nations as development that "meets the needs of the present without compromising the ability of future generations to meet their own needs"—into a core component of corporate strategy, risk management, and capital allocation. What was once described primarily as corporate social responsibility (CSR) has expanded into a far more structured and decision-relevant framework encompassing environmental, social, and governance considerations.

These issues now span wide areas of corporate activity, including:

- environmental performance, climate risk, health and safety, and resource management;
- social factors such as workforce practices, human capital development, and community impact;
- governance structures, controls, and accountability.

As a result, sustainability considerations are no longer treated as peripheral or purely reputational. The growth of responsible and sustainable investment has been accompanied by the mainstream integration of ESG factors into investment analysis and portfolio construction, as well as by the emergence of specialist ESG advisory and rating ecosystem. What began as a niche segment of socially responsible investing has become embedded in the fiduciary responsibilities of asset managers, with ESG considerations increasingly influencing risk assessment, cost of capital, and long-term valuation.

This evolution has materially changed the role of Investor Relations. ESG sits now firmly at the intersection of financial and non-financial disclosure, with direct implications for valuation, access to capital, and investor confidence. Regulators in many jurisdictions now require standardized sustainability disclosures, while investors and data providers expect consistency, comparability, and auditability of ESG data. Dedicated ESG presentations, integrated reporting, and targeted investor engagement have therefore become part of the IR toolkit, whether managed directly by IR teams or in close coordination with sustainability, finance, and legal functions.

In this context, sustainability communication is no longer primarily a branding exercise. While it can enhance reputation, it also comes with real operational demands. ESG data must be produced using robust reporting systems, aligned with regulatory frameworks and external benchmarks, and capable of standing up to investor scrutiny. These requirements add complexity and cost, reinforcing the importance of using the same information internally for management decision-making, risk oversight, and strategic planning.

Reporting frameworks have also matured. The Global Reporting Initiative has long played a foundational role in shaping sustainability disclosure, but it now operates within a broader ecosystem of standards, regulations, and assurance expectations. ESG reporting has shifted decisively from voluntary narrative to structured, regulated disclosure, particularly in markets where sustainability and governance requirements are tightly linked to capital markets supervision.

Some IROs may still observe that ESG questions do not dominate every investor meeting, particularly outside dedicated sustainability-focused funds. However, this perception increasingly understates how ESG information is used. Today, ESG factors are often embedded upstream in screening models, risk frameworks, voting policies, and engagement priorities, rather than raised explicitly in every interaction. Weak or inconsistent ESG disclosure can therefore limit investor interest long before a meeting is requested.

From an Investor Relations perspective, proactive ESG communication is no longer optional. It shapes how issuers are assessed, compared, and filtered in the competition for capital. ESG performance and disclosure act as proxies for management quality, governance discipline, and long-term resilience. Companies that fail to articulate a credible sustainability strategy risk being excluded not only on ethical grounds, but on perceived financial and governance risk.

What once appeared peripheral has become structural. For IR teams, the challenge is no longer whether ESG matters, but how effectively ESG considerations are integrated into the core equity story, financial narrative, and ongoing investor dialogue.

Here are some tips on how IR can successfully address ESG:

- Proactively address ESG issues on quarterly analyst calls, investor days, etc. It may simply be about presenting a couple of meaningful sustainability metrics every time on every occasion (safety improvement ratios, waste recycling ratios, number of independent directors, commitment to net zero emissions, etc.). This will help support your growth strategy by talking about the processes in place to improve operating efficiency, reduce costs, and minimize risks.
- Be involved in the creation of new, ESG metrics that can be specific to your company, your industry.
- Build the business case for sustainability with success stories and Returns On Investment on revenue and costs (such as resource efficiency and cost savings, employee productivity, innovation and growth, diversity).
- Highlight what makes your performance viable, sustainable, over the long term: discuss R&D expenses, customer retention, customer satisfaction, revenues from new products, etc.
- Engage with a broader set of stakeholders, including ESG fund managers and analysts. Ask them which ESG indices matter to them, share this information with other entities in your organization which deal with different stakeholders. Balance the pros and cons of seeking ESG rating.

Should you need one last reason, remember that investors are risk-adverse and love sustainability. They are prepared to pay a premium for that predictability.

Investor Relations for Employee Shareholders

Investor Relations also targets employee shareholders, even if in most cases these are being taken care of by a dedicated department, quite often within the human resources department. Regulatory and fiscal frameworks often promote employee savings plans with employees being offered company shares at particularly attractive prices. In this instance, Investor Relations should complement labor policy and focus on the following:

- Assuring consistency—including in terms of regularity—between the external image (that presented to the press, for instance) and the internal one;
- Developing a specific communications strategy for these shareholders.

The tools applied specifically to this aspect of Investor Relations include the following:

- Townhall meetings, internal roadshows;
- Intranet (possibly managed by the bank where the shares are deposited);
- Up-to-date share prices, models for personal portfolio management and valuation, and calculation of capital gains and losses;
- Regulatory information about material non-public information, insider trading, the conditions under which shares can be traded, and the issue of stock options.

The person in charge of employee shareholding schemes will work with the IRO to develop employee-specific educational messages about the following:

- Personal wealth management. The long-term yields of stocks (usually higher than any other form of investment), different tax benefits, and changes in legal measures as well as tax incentives governing employee share ownership.
- Strategy. The risk-reward ratio of equity investments based on salary, convergence between the employee shareholders' interests and those of the company and its other shareholders, personal contributions to overall company performance and increase in the stock price.
- Pedagogy. Participation in promoting the company's image, brand, and values.

5.2 Managing Investor Expectations

Managing investor expectations is not limited to providing earnings guidance. It is about shaping how the market interprets uncertainty, time horizons, sensitivity to external factors and the conditions under which strategic and financial objectives can be achieved.

Regulations do not usually require companies to provide quantified outlook and objectives—also known as "guidance"—as opposed to qualitative statements. But markets do: it is a key factor in determining valuations. In certain cases, the provision of forecasts in the company's issue prospectus may be subject to statutory audit.

If the company decides to provide some form of indication of its future performance in a forward-looking statement, it is better to do it as efficiently as possible. This is an extremely strategic decision in which the IRO must necessarily be closely involved.

It is not within the scope of this book to recommend whether or not companies should provide more or less detailed guidance, or how often they should do so, if at all. Actually, some companies may avoid giving any kind of guidance by consistently providing quality information about their business and current performance every time they report results, along with a thorough description of their business model. The important thing to remember is that providing the "long view" is a continuous dialogue.

Forecasts, Objectives, Outlook, and Guidance

Depending on market regulations, these terms can have very different meanings and can imply legal obligations that it is better to be aware of before you go public. As previously mentioned, forecasts must be approved by statutory auditors and not simply calculated by management.

Objectives are different from forecasts and therefore a bit more flexible. They can often be used to communicate approximate targets or ranges, although the latter must not be too wide if they are to be credible.

Outlooks leave a good deal of leeway, depending on the time horizon covered by the company's strategic objectives and the type of qualitative and/or quantitative indicators used. Drafting the outlook statement requires wordsmithing skills of the highest order.

So does the translation of these terms into other languages.

Few IR decisions have a greater long-term impact on credibility than how a company frames its outlook. Whether to provide formal guidance, qualitative direction, or no forward-looking indications at all is not a technical choice but a strategic one. Guidance shapes investor behavior, management discipline, and market expectations over time—and reversing course can be costly. In volatile or uncertain environments, the challenge for Investor Relations is not precision, but consistency and honesty about visibility. Managing expectations therefore requires clarity about time horizons, risk factors, and decision-making processes, as well as the discipline to intervene early when expectations drift materially from reality.

Selecting Guidance Indicators

As discussed above, companies should allow the market to evaluate their performance based on the same indicators used internally. The idea is to stay away from long-term goals that are too generic and to provide some kind of a dashboard, combining standard financial information (sales, profitability, cash flow, etc.) and operating data that are specific to the company (geographic footprint, new clients, utilization rates for industrial facilities, etc.). It is also an opportunity to give more explanation about the business model.

The IRO is the best person to identify the indicators analysts are following and to give this information back to accounting and reporting departments. Demand for this information will be met bearing in mind constraints relating to the internal information systems and the possibly strategic (therefore confidential) nature of the information being sought. It is recommended that companies study the analysts' valuation models when deciding on the indicators to be communicated to the outside world and guided upon. This analysis will allow the IRO to anticipate what consequences the selection of specific objectives may have on the company's share price. It must however be kept in mind at all times that the market will first focus on certain unavoidable metrics such as net income, earnings per share or revenue growth. Results announcements are first read by software and increasingly interpreted by artificial intelligence systems programmed to identify and prioritize such metrics.

Whatever objectives the company ends up using, it will in all cases need to provide factual information about the working assumptions behind, whether these relate to the macroeconomic environment or factors that are specific to its businesses ("Our projected guidance assumption of 90.3 million dollars in non-operating items, excluding the foreign operations, is contingent upon the final results of our 2008/2009 loan agreement."). It may also be necessary to review the key risk factors associated with the realization of these targets. This is, by the way, an additional opportunity to show that the management team is aware of a range of possible long-term scenarios and has a clear strategy for dealing with each.

Depending on their type and degree of reliability, objectives may be any of the following:

- Qualitative ("Net income for the current year should be slightly higher than in the previous year.");
- Quantitative ("Sales are expected to exceed 850 million euros in three years' time.");
- Ranges ("Management expects cash flow from operations to be between 300 and 400 million dollars in the medium term.");
- Worst-case or best-case scenarios ("A 10 percent increase in oil prices would add some 300 million dollars to our cost structure." "Given the exposure that our large development pipeline gives us to short-term interest rate fluctuations, increases or decreases in short-term interest rates could have positive or negative impact on our financial results.").

Absolute values should be avoided and targets should always be expressed in the conditional.

The importance of the objectives delivered to the market should not be overestimated or underestimated. In the event of an inquiry by market authorities or lawsuit, listed companies may be required to justify their disclosure content and procedures. Targets should be as consistent as possible with the company's internal earnings forecasts and based on information available at the time the forward-looking statements are made.

The same discipline that applies to financial guidance increasingly applies to non-financial commitments that influence valuation and risk perception. Decarbonization pathways, capital expenditure intensity, social commitments, and governance transition timelines are now scrutinized by investors at reporting moments through the same lens as financial outlook: credibility of assumptions, clarity of time horizons, internal consistency, and execution risk. When companies choose to communicate targets or trajectories in these areas, they implicitly shape expectations that will be tested at each results announcement. As with financial guidance, articulating the underlying assumptions, constraints, and sensitivities is therefore essential to avoid misinterpretation, loss of credibility, or unintended volatility.

Choice of Time Horizon

The market expects companies to provide earnings forecasts across multiple time horizons, including the current quarter, half year, full year, and at least the following year, as well as indications regarding subsequent years where possible. The level of precision that analysts, in particular, seem to be counting on is sometimes exaggerated. Indeed, companies are supposed to help analysts do their job efficiently, but not do it for them. Every IRO will tell you that these boundaries can be a source of misunderstanding between the issuer and the markets.

Financial markets and listed companies do not trade in the same time horizon, and it is truly difficult to reconcile them. It is always in the company's interest to align the targets it makes public with its management methods. For instance, firms that have five-year strategic plans should provide an outlook covering that period, together with appropriate cautionary language.

On the contrary, if a company is going through difficult period, short-term news flow will be critical.

There are proven advantages to giving targets for the medium and long terms.

There is less risk of repeated changes to the said targets over the period, meaning that:

- earnings estimates are in a more narrow range;
- The share price is less volatile;
- The stock is more attractive to long-term investors. University research tends to show that companies that provide objectives for longer periods have a better chance of attracting long-term investors;
- The targets are more consistent with the company's business model;
- It is easier to reconcile internal objectives and external guidance.

Companies that use longer time horizons for their strategic objectives can blend qualitative and quantitative targets. For example, they might say, "Operating margin should continue to expand at the same pace as last year. Management is reiterating its target of achieving a 10 percent operating margin by the end of its five-year strategic plan."

Research has shown that there is no lasting negative impact on the valuation of companies that stop or fail to provide guidance for the following quarter and focus instead on the full year or a longer period.

Managing Change in Guidance Policy

Companies may have to revise their targets upward or downward, suspend or discontinue the practice altogether in response to reported results and/or a change in the underlying assumptions supporting the original guidance.

From a legal standpoint, such revisions constitute price-sensitive, insider information that must be made public by a press release (or a statement filed with the home exchange). This is often done when earnings are reported, but can also take place outside the reporting period when management becomes aware that the guidance will not be met. Yet particularly in the United States, the forward-looking statements included in the earnings releases or presentation frequently state that "the company undertakes no obligation to publicly update or revise any forward-looking statements, whether as a result of new information, future events, or otherwise." This type of statement does not comply with the regulations of other countries where, precisely, companies do have the obligation to update the markets in case of any material change to previously disclosed information.

Similarly, some will argue that, in between two reporting periods, a company should not respond to the question, "Are you confirming your earnings objectives?" as this might be deemed to constitute price-sensitive information.

Companies that provide targets for the medium and long terms will not necessarily have to add one year to their guidance every year, except under special circumstances (if they have acquired or divested themselves of a major portion of their activities, for instance).

As we have seen, there are many ways for companies to keep market participants informed of their prospects, their strategic goals, and their financial objectives. With time, these targets may become unachievable or irrelevant, whatever the reason may be. If there is a guidance policy in place, management, and the board of directors in most cases, can decide to revise it and even put an end to this practice.

Because the value of a share is largely based on the investor's expectations (for instance, dividend distribution, potential capital gain), it is therefore the company's duty, and quite often a strict legal requirement, to communicate this change. This is highly price-sensitive information.

Elaborating on the reason for change is a challenging Investor Relations exercise, sometimes akin to a crisis communications exercise. For sure, it will not go unnoticed, but, over time, it can also be beneficial to the company, if it is properly crafted.

Circumstances may dictate that a company changes the way it provides guidance. This evolution can be driven by external and internal causes such as:

- *Macroeconomic and geopolitical factors*. In this instance, you may want to avoid being penalized for not being able to factor into your guidance the impact of elements over which your company has no control and whose volatility may greatly affect your ability to achieve your target, for good or bad. These factors include taxes, interest rates, currency, raw material prices, government-administered prices, and other arbitrary price-setting mechanisms. Most notably, the 2008 Global Financial Crisis and the COVID-19 pandemic led many companies to suspend guidance or fundamentally reconfigure it.
- *The performance track record*. A company that has consistently missed its earnings targets (and analysts' estimates) will undoubtedly have suffered both share price damage and a loss of investor trust. It may have to do with the quality and the reliability of its information systems, the inability to accurately forecast performance, an overly optimistic new management, or the incapacity to anticipate and adjust to a volatile operating environment.

It can take several quarters or reporting periods before these issues can be remedied and a more cautious stance taken.

- *The business model*. This can be the case when part of your profits becomes more heavily dependent on any of the above macroeconomic factors, following a large acquisition, a major asset disposal, the launch of a new product, or a large investment in a new country. Another example justifying a change in the guidance policy may have to do with increasingly longer-term contracts, with actual profit generation scheduled toward the end of the period, or beyond the current guidance horizon. These elements may increase or, on the contrary, reduce the predictability of the objectives you have disclosed for a given period.
- *Management*. A new chief executive officer may not feel committed to the objectives set by its predecessor and want to discontinue the policy. Or, the company may have learnt the lesson from a history of profit warnings and want to rebuild market trust and establish a reputation for reliability.
- *Competitive environment*. A change in the way the company's direct competitors and peer group communicate their prospects may prompt the decision to revisit the guidance policy. Indeed, guidance provision can be a differentiator in investors' decision-making process, and, as a consequence affect the company's valuation.
- *Share ownership*. A change in shareholder structure may well require guidance policies to be aligned within the same group of companies, when several of them are listed. New majority shareholders may also require that the communication of a business and financial outlook be updated to suit their own objectives.

Revisiting a guidance policy implies setting goals differently. This can take various forms:

- Updating the current guidance;
- Moving from qualitative to quantified goals, or the other way around;
- Using a different set of key performance indicators and financial metrics;
- Lengthening the time horizon (rather than shortening it, usually);
- Discontinuing guidance altogether.

With the exception of this most extreme change, these forms can be combined as described earlier, in order to form the new guidance policy.

Given the risks involved—increased volatility, reduced analyst coverage, poorer financial reputation, just to name a few—switching from one guidance policy to another has to be a well-thought-out decision. It requires that management, the board of directors and the Investor Relations team be fully aligned.

In order for it to go as smoothly as possible, the change needs to be articulated in a timely and credible manner. Timing is important when you consider changing your guidance policy, as investors will wonder why you do this now.

In particular, if the new guidance results in less transparency (or if it is perceived as such), analysts and investors are likely to resent the change and be vocal about it. They will argue that, from now on, it will be more difficult for them to come up with realistic earnings estimates and make a well-informed investment recommendation or decision.

As the primary contacts for data-hungry sell-side analysts and investors, Investor Relations officers have a very important role to play in conducting the change in guidance policy. This will involve

- working closely with management in order to list the pros and cons of changing earnings guidance;
- analyzing industry practices, considering if, when and how other companies have revised their guidance policy in the past, and what market reactions have been, both upon the announcement and in the longer run;
- writing the rationale for the change, possibly including stopping earnings guidance;
- identifying metrics that are core to the valuation of the company, consistent with the execution of the strategy over a more extended horizon, and for which some kind of outlook should therefore be provided;
- submitting the calendar and the content of a new guidance policy for discussion and approval.

Because developing an effective new guidance policy is often a question of "give" and "take," the "give" part is a critical success factor. If the company decides to limit the number of metrics it sets objectives for, or to move away from guidance and only communicate longer term, qualitative directions, it will be best advised to compensate for this perceived decrease in disclosure by:

- enriching its messages with more facts and data that are relevant to understanding its business model and long-term strategy;
- providing more information on the drivers of its end-user markets;
- being more specific about the external constraints, the macroeconomic assumptions that can affect its performance.

Providing guidance is hardly ever a legal requirement. Furthermore, it has yet to demonstrate that its benefits substantially outweigh its costs.

It can actually well be the opposite, given the costs incurred in preparing the guidance and managing the company toward those goals … and missing them.

The many benefits of guidance usually include transparency, an effective way to establish realistic earnings consensus, achieve higher valuation, increased liquidity, and lower volatility. It is also a powerful internal incentivization (and compensation) tool and illustrates management's commitment to meet or even exceed the objectives. Furthermore, it is supposed to simplify the life of Investor Relations officers as it satisfies the requests from sell-side analysts. Arguably, monitoring earnings consensus without any form of guidance can be a difficult exercise that requires skill, caution, and a perfect understanding of the potential legal implications. These are extremely powerful reasons why companies that do provide guidance are not keen to move away from this practice. One could observe that these are the same companies that complain of the short-termism of the stock market.

Costs far exceed these benefits when guidance is missed, not to mention the impact on the company's reputation. In addition, there are investors who do not invest in companies that do not provide guidance.

Yet, those companies that have made the leap and stopped providing guidance have not necessarily suffered from it over the longer term. They ensured they demonstrated sustained improvement in performance and communicating progress against strategic directions. What has been proven to work is also to provide additional contextual, operational information to help the market better understand the various metrics that can influence a company's future performance. This is ultimately what investors are interested in. Where is the company heading? What are the metrics that matter? What type of performance is really sustainable? What is the time horizon that makes sense for a strategy to be fully implemented?

Lastly, there is no such thing as a perfect moment to announce a change in guidance policy. In any case, the announcement should make it clear and intelligible, with a substantiated rationale for doing so. The news should not be buried somewhere in the text, with the hope that nobody will notice. This would only make matters worse.

All in all, companies are well advised to think twice before embarking on providing guidance.

5.3 Periodic Financial Reporting

Financial reporting is one of the most underestimated—and most powerful—strategic levers in Investor Relations. While guidance shapes forward expectations, periodic financial reporting is where those expectations are tested, recalibrated, and either reinforced or questioned. Over time, it is the quality and consistency of financial reporting that determines whether management credibility compounds or erodes.

In practice, financial reporting is not merely about publishing numbers. It is about translating performance into meaning, providing decision-useful context, and anchoring valuation through disciplined disclosure. Companies that treat financial reporting as a compliance exercise consistently underperform in the competition for capital—regardless of underlying results.

Earnings Announcements

Every earnings announcement is a valuation event. It updates the market's understanding of the company's trajectory, resilience, and execution discipline. Over successive reporting cycles, these updates accumulate into a perception framework that influences analyst models, investor confidence, and ultimately the cost of capital.

High-quality financial reporting enables investors to answer three fundamental questions with confidence:

- What has changed since the last reporting period?
- Why did it change?
- What does this imply for the future trajectory of the business?

When reporting fails to address these questions clearly, the market fills the gaps—often incorrectly. Volatility, mispricing, and credibility discounts are rarely the result of "bad numbers" alone; they are more often the consequence of weak explanation.

The Earnings Press Release

The earnings press release is the backbone of the financial reporting cycle. It is the most widely read, most frequently quoted, and most immediately market-moving disclosure document. For many investors and analysts, it is the primary source of information—sometimes even more influential than the earnings presentation or conference call. For the purpose of this book, we will not address the reporting formats still used in certain emerging jurisdictions, where earnings announcements often follow a template focused primarily on compliance. The press release remains the foundational disclosure document: the first formally disseminated earnings communication, the reference point for media, investors, analysts, and data providers, and the format most consistently distributed across newswires, exchanges, company websites, and financial platforms.

Effective earnings releases share several defining attributes:

- They are driven by investor logic, not accounting form
- They surface material developments early in the text structure, rather than burying them in detail
- They articulate performance dynamics, not just outcomes
- They anticipate investor questions instead of reacting to them.

A Multi-Dimensional Financial Analysis Framework

One of the most frequent and damaging reporting weaknesses is an exclusive reliance on year-on-year comparisons. This is ignoring the market's language. While year-on-year data is legally required, it rarely reflects how investors and analysts actually assess momentum.

Professional investors think sequentially. They look for:

- Acceleration or deceleration trends
- Inflection points
- Evidence of stabilization or deterioration across consecutive periods

Sequential analysis allows companies to highlight resilience, recovery, or emerging pressure points long before they become visible in annual comparisons. It is particularly powerful in volatile or crisis environments, where year-on-year figures may obscure meaningful recent progress or deterioration.

Companies that consistently integrate sequential analysis into their earnings releases demonstrate analytical maturity and significantly reduce the risk of being misread by the market.

For instance, when a company reports full-year results, this usually marks the end of a quarterly or semiannual reporting cycle. Therefore, it should not limit itself to comparing the full-year numbers to the prior-year performance, but also to how the second half has performed versus the first half of the year, and to how the fourth quarter has performed versus the third. Analysts and investors analyze a company's performance with that lens and companies should do so too. Furthermore, it is a potent source of messaging, such as "third consecutive quarter of revenue growth" or "sales rebounded in the second half, from a low base in the first six months of the year." This is also likely to be consistent with how management analyzes performance in internal reporting.

The other dimension that this analytical framework brings into focus is the strategic dimension: how full-year results demonstrate steady, effective strategy execution over several years, in line with stated objectives and, potentially, long-term guidance.

Another structural flaw in earnings reporting is starting with text rather than analysis. Drafting an earnings release directly in a word-processing document often results in descriptive reporting that misses strategic emphasis.

An effective alternative process includes:

- Beginning with financial and operational data analysis
- Identifying trends, inflection points, and anomalies
- Visualizing those dynamics through charts or tables
- Deriving key messages from the analysis
- Building the earnings release around those messages

This approach ensures that narrative is evidence-based and that key messages are supported by data rather than retrofitted after the fact. It also facilitates consistency between the earnings release, presentation materials, and management commentary.

Timing and Process

Starting the earnings reporting process too late before the regulatory deadline is one of the most reliable predictors of poor disclosure quality. Rushed reporting increases the likelihood of:

- Weak or incomplete analysis
- Unclear messaging
- Inadequate internal alignment
- Management being unprepared for investor questions.

High-performing IR teams treat earnings reporting as a multi-week strategic process, not a last-minute drafting exercise. Adequate time allows for scenario analysis, stress-testing of messages, and rehearsal of management responses.

As a rule of thumb, earnings releases that go through too few iterations lack depth; those with too many iterations often suffer from message dilution and internal politics. Discipline lies in clarity of ownership and early agreement on key messages.

The drafting of an earnings announcement can start even before preliminary numbers are available. For instance, assuming your performance is fairly linear month after month, you can start developing key messages for the first six months based on consolidated financial reporting for the first five months. An Investor Relations Officer who is constantly kept in the loop of how the business is doing and is financially literate, will know how to start working early on the six-months announcement before the preliminary financial statement is available.

Ownership of the Earnings Release

While finance, legal, and accounting functions play essential roles in the reporting process, the strategic ownership of the earnings release must sit with Investor Relations which acts as the bridge between numbers and narrative—ensuring that financial outcomes are interpreted through a strategic lens. The decisive factor is not technical accuracy alone, but familiarity with investor expectations, modeling behavior, and perception risks.

When earnings releases are driven primarily by accounting logic, several problems tend to arise:

- Financial results are disconnected from strategy
- Execution challenges are underexplained
- Management does not receive full credit for strategic progress
- Investor confidence weakens despite solid performance.

Addressing Underperformance and Bad News

Markets are less unforgiving of bad news than they are of poorly handled bad news. Attempts to bury negative developments, soften language excessively, or delay acknowledgment almost always backfire.

Credible financial reporting addresses challenges directly, explains causality, and outlines management's response. This approach does not amplify negative reaction; it contains it. Over time, companies that demonstrate transparency in difficult periods benefit from lower volatility and stronger long-term investor trust.

The Outlook Section

Neglecting the outlook section is one of the most damaging omissions in earnings reporting. It is one of the most underutilized value drivers, especially in less sophisticated markets. Even in the absence of formal guidance, investors expect management to articulate directional assumptions, key sensitivities, and areas of uncertainty.

An effective outlook section:

- Connects reported performance to future drivers
- Clarifies what management is watching most closely
- Frames uncertainty arising from external factors
- Reinforces strategic priorities.

Silence or boilerplate language in the outlook section is often interpreted as uncertainty—or worse, lack of control.

Over time, financial reporting quality becomes a reputational asset. Consistent excellence in reporting signals Company, CEO, CFO, and IRO discipline, preparedness, and a good understanding of the needs of capital markets. It also materially reduces the burden on guidance, as well-articulated reporting narrows the range of investor assumptions.

Companies that master financial reporting do not merely inform the market—they lead it (Table 5.3).

High-quality financial reporting is what makes guidance credible. Without disciplined, consistent, and analytically robust reporting, guidance becomes aspirational rather than grounded. Each results announcement tests whether prior assumptions still hold, whether execution is unfolding as expected, and whether management has earned the right to influence forward expectations. In this sense, financial reporting is the operational backbone of guidance: it is where promises are reconciled with performance and where the market decides how much trust to place in what comes next.

5.4 Ongoing Disclosure and Special Situations

Ongoing disclosure refers to the continuous obligation of listed companies to assess and, where required, disclose information that may be price sensitive, irrespective of the periodic reporting cycle. Unlike periodic disclosure—which is set by regulatory deadlines and follows a predefined content—ongoing disclosure is event-driven, situational, and dependent on judgment exercised in real time.

Across jurisdictions, this obligation is framed through different regulatory constructs, including *price-sensitive information*, which is also known as *inside information*, *material nonpublic information (MNPI)*, or obeys to *fair*

Table 5.3 Earnings-release governance checklist

1. Strategic ownership
☐ Has clear ownership been assigned to Investor Relations for the overall narrative and investor logic?
☐ Is the earnings release driven by investor relevance or by accounting form?
☐ Has management explicitly defined the *three messages they want the market to retain* from the release?
2. Analytical readiness
☐ Has sequential analysis (quarter-on-quarter or half-on-half) been performed alongside year-on-year comparisons?
☐ Have trend inflection points, momentum shifts, or early-warning signals been explicitly identified and articulated accordingly?
☐ Are internal dashboards and external disclosures aligned in structure and interpretation?
3. Message discipline
☐ Does the opening section of the earnings release highlight the most material developments of the period under review—positive or negative?
☐ Are key financial outcomes clearly linked to strategic decisions, quality of execution, or external factors?
☐ Is negative information addressed upfront, with causality and management response clearly articulated?
4. Outlook and forward-framing
☐ Is there an outlook section or forward-looking commentary that provide directional insights either quantitatively or qualitatively?
☐ Are assumptions, sensitivities, and areas of uncertainty framed consistently with prior disclosures?
☐ Does the outlook reference capital allocation, investment priorities, and longer-term strategic objectives?
5. Process and timing discipline
☐ Has the earnings announcement timeline been respected?
☐ Was the earnings-release process initiated early enough to allow for analysis, challenge, and iteration?
☐ How many reviews has the draft announcement gone through and how does this compare with previous announcements?
☐ How thoroughly have potential investor and analyst questions been anticipated and stress-tested against the final text?

(continued)

Table 5.3 (continued)

6. **Governance and risk control**
☐ Have finance, legal, and IR jointly validated accuracy, consistency, and disclosure compliance?
☐ Does the final version integrate input from HR and corporate communications?
☐ Is the release fully consistent with prior public statements, guidance frameworks, and messaging conventions?
☐ Have cybersecurity and information-leak risks been assessed and mitigated prior to publication?
7. Management preparedness
☐ Has there been a dry-run of the earnings call with CEO and CFO to ensure they are comfortable defending results in real time?
☐ Is there a clear plan for post-release engagement, feedback capture, and internal debriefing?

disclosure requirements. While terminology varies, the underlying principle is consistent: information that is not publicly available and that a reasonable investor would consider important in making an investment decision must not be selectively disclosed or used for trading purposes. Failure to disclose such information appropriately—or to control its dissemination—can distort market integrity and expose companies and individuals to significant legal and reputational risk.

In practice, the boundary between what constitutes disclosable information and what remains internal is rarely clear-cut. Materiality is contextual, forward-looking, and often cumulative. Information that appears immaterial in isolation may become price sensitive when combined with prior disclosures, market expectations, or prevailing conditions. Moreover, the timing of disclosure requires careful assessment: premature disclosure can mislead, while delayed disclosure can undermine trust and compliance.

Ongoing disclosure therefore cannot be reduced to mechanical rules or checklists. It requires disciplined judgment, informed by an understanding of market expectations, regulatory principles, and the company's own disclosure history. Investor Relations plays a critical role in this process by acting as an interpretive interface between management, legal counsel, and the market—helping to assess when evolving information crosses the threshold from internal insight to disclosable fact.

It is within this framework of ongoing disclosure—where judgment, timing, and consistency are paramount—that special situations such as profit warnings, mergers and acquisitions, shareholder activism, leadership changes, and crisis events must be managed.

Not all special situations call for the same level of immediacy, quantification, or messaging precision. What they share, however, is the need for disciplined judgment around materiality, timing, and consistency with previously communicated assumptions or facts. In this section, special situations are addressed through the lens of disclosure governance—focusing on when and how Investor Relations should intervene to preserve credibility under stress.

Profit Warnings and Pre-announcements

There are three main situations in which companies can issue profit warnings and pre-announcements:

- When they realize that between the end of the reference period (for instance, the end of the quarter) and the scheduled earnings release date the

actual results will be significantly below or above the targets announced to the market. In most cases, the overshoot or shortfall will relate to operating income, net income, or earnings per share;
- When, in the course of the reference period, an event occurs that makes the targets announced obsolete;
- When companies realize that their actual earnings will fall short of the analyst consensus as published by specialized vendors or the company itself.

With the exceptions of certain jurisdictions that stipulate a quantified threshold that triggers the pre-announcement (for instance when it appears that net income will be 20% above or below last year's), it is up to the company to decide whether the discrepancy between the actual figures and its own targets or analyst expectations justifies a profit warning. While such a warning will have an immediate impact on the stock price, failure to issue one will undermine the company's credibility, and investors may be even more disappointed when results are actually published.

The press release announcing the profit warning should contain enough explanations, in a straightforward and concise manner:

- What exactly happened? Is this a one-time or a recurring issue?
- Are the causes internal to the company or external?
- What is the financial impact of the problem?
- What measures and action plan has the company implemented to remedy the situation?

The company may not readily offer revised targets, only if it is necessary to do so: These revised targets may be delivered to the market at a later date, for instance, upon the initially scheduled reporting date, once the company has gathered all the information it needs to revise its targets in a credible manner. This, however, is likely to create overhang in the stock until new objectives are made available.

In the vast majority of cases, warnings and pre-announcements refer to a negative performance: results are not going to be what was expected. But positive pre-announcements do happen, though rarely (in other words, the company may decide to announce that its performance is going to exceed its initial projection or analysts' estimates, ahead of the initially scheduled reporting date). They are usually called earnings surprises. That says it all!

Mergers and Acquisitions

Mergers and acquisitions (M&A) must be announced in accordance with regulations governing insider information.

Takeovers often catch the market off-guard. Announcements should be carefully prepared and the IRO, duly organized, possibly with the assistance of investment banks, legal and other advisors if the Investor Relations team has little or no experience in this field. In particular, provisional statements will have to be drafted for every eventuality, in case rumors of the deal are leaked early, the deal itself collapses or is pulled off.

M&A communications are conducted in accordance with the following principles:

- All parties should keep the transaction confidential until the last minute. At least one press release should nonetheless be kept on hand, for example, in case the market gets wind that a transaction is imminent.
- The justification given should be solid, credible, and perfectly in keeping with the company's strategic messages. You don't want to leave stakeholders to draw their own conclusions.
- The valuation applied should be clearly laid out, as should the projected financial impact and the anticipated benefits such as synergies along with when they can be expected to feed through. A detailed integration roadmap should also be provided. These are the most challenging messages to prepare and the ones the market will be most interested in. Unfortunately, most press releases issued to announce acquisitions fail to provide this information, let alone disclose the acquisition price. True, this may be because full details are not yet available because the completion of the transaction remains subject to a number of conditions. While quantifiable synergies are always a strong positive in this investment case, management may exercise caution before committing to precise figures before becoming the actual owners of the business. In some cases, the evaluation process is still underway, or the working assumptions still contain too many variables. The financing terms may not be finalized. Be that as it may, the more quantitative data analysts have to assess the consequences of a transaction on the company's future profitability, the better the chances that the market will welcome the deal.

Investor Relations should also address any impact in terms of human resources and corporate culture insofar as the deal can affect operations management, staff levels, or the values of the companies involved. The announcement will benefit from the input of both the corporate and internal communications teams.

If not properly marketed, even acquisitions that are strategically beneficial for the buyer will put pressure on the share price for a long time. All communications relating to acquisitions should, therefore, be prepared in advance with the IRO, the person who can most effectively help management anticipate the market's reaction. Brought into the process as early on as possible, the IRO can offer crucial advice on shaping the messages that will be released to the market.

If the transaction is large enough, the press release may be followed by a conference call or information meeting with appropriate visuals and support materials, such as questions and answers (Q&A) documents.

The same timing and transparency apply when a key business is sold. Assuming the acquisition is not a hostile takeover, buyers and sellers should try to agree on their respective messages.

Below is a summary of other key recommendations for M&A communications

- Consider a dedicated section on your website for significant transactions;
- Educate the market about the "new" business/geography;
- Provide a sustainable M&A rationale, how it fits your strategy and how it will create value over time;
- Be realistic about profit enhancement and integration challenges;
- Think twice before providing quantitative synergy targets;
- Be clear from the very beginning about what type of pro forma financial statements you will provide and for how long;
- Update on integration progress;
- If appropriate, provide an updated guidance;
- Reach out to the sell-side to ensure their models accurately reflect the change in the scope of consolidation.

Other Special Situations

Crisis situations—whether financial, operational, geopolitical, or reputational—test the coherence of an Investor Relations strategy more severely than routine disclosure cycles. In such moments, IR's role is not to reassure at all costs, but to preserve trust through factual, timely, and coordinated communication. This requires close alignment with legal, corporate communications, and senior management, as well as discipline in distinguishing what is known, what is uncertain, and what will be updated. Companies that prepare for crisis communication as part of their ongoing IR framework are better positioned to avoid credibility gaps when stress events occur.

Leadership Change

The materiality of leadership changes depends as much on the title involved as on the individual's role in capital allocation, guidance setting, strategy formulation, and external representation. The event becomes disclosure-relevant when it raises questions about strategic continuity, execution capacity, or accountability toward the market.

Investor Relations should focus disclosure on the rationale for the change, the governance process underpinning succession, the timeline and structure of the transition, and—in most cases—the extent to which strategic priorities and financial policies remain unchanged. The objective is to reassure markets about continuity of direction and decision-making authority, not to personalize the narrative.

Distinguishing Materiality by Leadership Role

Not all leadership changes carry equal market impact or trigger identical disclosure obligations.

CEO and CFO transitions trigger mandatory disclosure requirements in most jurisdictions. Markets expect immediate clarity on:

- Whether the departure was voluntary or involuntary
- The governance process that identified the successor
- Interim leadership arrangements if a permanent successor has not been named
- Any implications for previously issued financial guidance
- The transition timeline and knowledge-transfer mechanisms.

Credit rating agencies typically reach out proactively for CFO changes, and IR should anticipate questions about financial controls, reporting quality, and treasury/capital allocation continuity.

Other C-suite and senior operating roles require materiality assessment. The disclosure threshold is whether a reasonable investor would view the change as significantly altering the company's strategic execution or operational capability. Consider:

- Does this executive represent the company in investor meetings or earnings calls?
- Is this role central to a key strategic initiative currently underway?
- Does the market associate this individual with the company's recent performance trajectory (positively or negatively)?
- Would analyst models or investor theses be disrupted by this change?

If the answer to any of these is "yes," proactive disclosure is warranted—either through press release, inclusion in the next earnings disclosure, or targeted investor outreach. If "no," the change may be handled through standard organizational announcements without separate investor communication.

Timing and Messaging

Leadership changes create inherent disclosure tension between legal requirements, competitive dynamics, and market perception management.

Planned transitions (retirements, board-managed successions) offer maximum control. Announce after formal Board approval but before market rumors develop. The disclosure timeline should allow for:

- Coordination between regulatory filing and investor-facing communications
- Pre-briefing of major shareholders where legally permissible and strategically valuable
- Preparation of the IR team with talking points addressing guidance continuity, strategic direction, and search/succession process.

Abrupt departures (termination, resignation amid strategic disagreement, health crises, or unforeseen events) compress preparation time dramatically. In these scenarios:

- Legal disclosure obligations take precedence; work with counsel to determine required timing
- A brief regulatory filing may precede detailed market explanation—reserve fuller context for an earnings call, investor update, or management statement
- Distinguish between what must be disclosed immediately and what strategic messaging can follow once governance decisions (interim leadership, search process) are finalized.

- Speed becomes paramount—disclosure should occur within hours of confirmation rather than the standard 24-hour window when circumstances are particularly sensitive or likely to leak
- Consider requesting a trading halt if the departure occurs during market hours and involves CEO
- Where circumstances dictate coordinate disclosure timing with affected parties (family members, law enforcement, or medical authorities) while balancing urgency of market notification.

Contested or performance-related exits require particular care. Markets will interpret vague language ("pursuing other opportunities," "mutual agreement") as deflection if recent performance has been poor or if strategic disagreements are known. In these cases, factual directness preserves more credibility than euphemism.

What to Disclose—and How

Depending on the nature of the transition, effective disclosure includes:

- Rationale for the change: Retirement, strategic evolution of the role, Board decision to seek different capabilities, or (if applicable) performance-related factors. Clarity here prevents speculation.
- The governance and succession process: Was the search for a new CEO internal versus external? What criteria did the Board use? How long has succession planning been underway? This demonstrates governance quality and preparedness.
- Transition structure and timeline: Is there an overlap period for knowledge transfer? Who holds interim authority if the role is unfilled? When will leadership formally transfer? Clear timelines reduce uncertainty. In sudden departures, immediate identification of interim leadership is the most material investor concern—this must be addressed in the initial announcement.
- Strategic and financial continuity: Explicitly address whether strategic priorities, financial policies, capital allocation frameworks, or guidance remain unchanged. If the transition signals strategic evolution, explain what is changing and why—without creating the impression of directionless drift.
- Board oversight during transition: If interim leadership is in place, clarify what Board-level governance mechanisms ensure continuity and accountability during the search period. In challenging circumstances, the Board voice should be prominent—statements should come from the Board

Chair or Lead Independent Director, not IR alone, to signal governance engagement and authority.
- In sensitive situations, balance transparency with dignity—factual confirmation without unnecessary detail serves both legal requirements and organizational respect.
- Acknowledgements when appropriate: In circumstances involving loss or hardship, a brief, professional acknowledgment is appropriate before pivoting to governance continuity. Avoid overly emotional language, but recognize the human dimension before addressing business continuity. One or two sentences acknowledging contributions and expressing appropriate sentiment suffices.

Critical Pitfalls to Avoid

Leadership transition disclosure failures typically stem from the following mistakes:

- Euphemistic or evasive language. Using boilerplate phrases like "pursuing other opportunities" or "spending more time with family" when the departure is clearly performance-related destroys credibility. Markets are sophisticated; vague language invites speculation that is often more damaging than the truth. If someone was terminated for cause or resigned amid strategic disagreement, factual acknowledgment—within legal boundaries—preserves trust better than obfuscation. However, avoid speculation about circumstances that are unconfirmed or under investigation. Phrases like "sudden departure" or "unexpected change" are sufficient when full details are not yet available or appropriate to disclose.
- Announcements ahead of the weekend to "minimize impact." The instinct to announce difficult news immediately before non-trading days often backfires. It signals fear of market reaction and prevents IR from engaging with concerned investors. It also maximizes weekend speculation in the absence of context. Unless legally required to announce immediately, consider waiting until the first morning the market reopens when your team can actively manage investor questions. In urgent situations requiring immediate disclosure regardless of day or time, ensure the IR team is prepared for extended availability.
- Failing to pre-brief major shareholders before public announcement. Where legally permissible (after Board approval but before public filing), informing top institutional holders of an imminent leadership announcement—particularly for CEO or CFO roles—demonstrates respect for key

stakeholders and allows you to control the narrative before media or sell-side research interprets it for them. This is not about selective disclosure of material nonpublic information; it is about relationship management within appropriate disclosure windows. In sudden or sensitive departures, this window may be extremely compressed or impossible—in such cases, prepare for immediate post-announcement outreach to key stakeholders.

- Allowing executive compensation details to dominate the narrative. Severance packages, retention bonuses, and equity acceleration provisions are material information but should not become the primary storyline. If compensation details are disclosed in regulatory filings concurrent with the leadership announcement, prepare a separate investor narrative that focuses on strategic continuity and governance quality. Otherwise, proxy advisory firms and media coverage will frame the transition around "golden parachutes" rather than future leadership capability.
- Over-relying on successor credentials without addressing strategic continuity. A detailed biography of the incoming leader is necessary but insufficient. Investors care less about résumé line items than about whether the new executive will sustain the strategy and relationships that drive their investment thesis. The communication should explicitly connect the individual's capabilities to the company's strategic priorities and reassure investors that their understanding of the business model and forward expectations remains valid.
- Delaying to craft "perfect" messaging in time-sensitive situations. When circumstances require rapid disclosure, speed and factual accuracy matter more than polish. A brief, direct statement can be followed by more comprehensive Board commentary hours or days later. Delayed disclosure to refine language creates rumor vacuums and erodes control of the narrative.
- Making the announcement solely about investor reassurance when human acknowledgment is warranted. In situations involving personal hardship or loss, immediate focus exclusively on "business as usual" messaging can appear insensitive. The first statement should recognize the human dimension of the event, then pivot to governance continuity. This balance demonstrates organizational maturity and respect while still addressing market stability concerns.

Treating the announcement as the end of the process rather than the beginning. Leadership transitions require sustained investor engagement. The announcement is simply the opening of a multi-month credibility test. IR should plan for:

- Immediate availability to answer investor questions
- Introductory meetings or calls between the new executive and major shareholders
- Roadshows schedules that allow the incoming leader to build relationships with the investment community
- Monitoring of sell-side research for factual errors or misinterpretations, with rapid correction where warranted
- Extended engagement if the transition involves a founder or iconic leader closely identified with the company—expect disproportionate market reaction and questions about "life after [name]" that require visible Board leadership.

Failing to prepare the IR team with consistent messaging. In the hours and days following a leadership announcement, the IR function will field dozens of inquiries from investors, analysts, media, and proxy advisors. Without clear, pre-approved FAQs and messaging discipline, inconsistent answers will emerge—creating confusion about guidance, strategy, or the circumstances of the departure. The entire investor-facing team (IR, CEO, CFO, and in some cases Board members) must operate from the same script on key questions: Why now? Why this person? What changes? What stays the same? In sensitive or sudden transitions, explicitly instruct the IR team not to speculate beyond the official statement—"I can only confirm what's in the announcement" is an acceptable response when circumstances remain fluid.

Employees should be informed simultaneously with public disclosure, never after markets or media learn of the change. This is particularly critical in sudden transitions where morale and organizational stability are at stake. Internal and external communications must be sequenced carefully to maintain employee trust while meeting disclosure obligations.

Key customers, strategic partners, and major lenders may warrant proactive outreach, particularly if business relationships were closely tied to the departing executive. In sudden or unexpected departures, a brief call to critical stakeholders can help prevent relationship disruption, competitive opportunism or partnership instability.

Underestimating the impact on credit markets. Equity investors are not the only constituency watching leadership changes. Credit rating agencies, bond investors, and lenders closely monitor CFO and CEO transitions—particularly at companies with significant debt, upcoming refinancing needs, or covenant compliance sensitivities. Failure to proactively communicate with these stakeholders can result in rating downgrades or increased borrowing costs that compound equity market volatility.

Leadership Transition Checklist for IR Teams

When a leadership change is imminent, the following actions help maintain control and credibility:

- Legal and regulatory review: Confirm disclosure requirements and mandatory timing; distinguish between required content and strategic messaging. In sudden departures, determine whether trading halt is warranted.
- Board approval and coordination: Ensure Board has formally approved announcement content, timing, and any forward-looking statements about strategy or guidance. In unexpected situations, confirm Board has determined interim leadership before announcement.
- Coordinate with affected parties: Where circumstances involve family members, medical authorities, or law enforcement, coordinate disclosure timing appropriately while balancing urgency of market notification.
- Stakeholder pre-briefing: Where legally permissible, inform top institutional shareholders of the forthcoming announcement to maintain relationship trust and control initial interpretation. In time-compressed situations, prepare for immediate post-announcement outreach instead.
- FAQ and message discipline: Prepare comprehensive FAQs for the IR team covering: rationale, succession process, guidance implications, strategic continuity, timeline, and interim governance. In sensitive situations, explicitly instruct team not to speculate beyond official statement.
- Cross-functional coordination: Align timing and content with corporate communications to ensure internal (employee) and external (investor, media) announcements are sequenced appropriately and consistently. Employees should never learn from external sources.
- Credit and rating agency outreach: Alert credit rating agencies and key lenders if the change involves CFO or CEO roles, particularly in companies with material debt. Prepare for rapid engagement—agencies often respond within hours.
- Key relationship outreach: Identify critical customers, partners, or lenders whose relationships were tied to the departing executive; plan proactive communication to prevent competitive opportunism.
- Investor presentation updates: Modify standard IR presentation materials to reflect interim leadership structure or new executive profiles as appropriate.
- Monitoring and rapid response: Track sell-side analyst research, proxy advisor commentary, and media coverage for factual inaccuracies; correct errors promptly to prevent narrative distortion. In sensitive transitions,

monitor for speculation and address factual errors without engaging with rumors.

- Post-announcement engagement plan: Schedule introductory calls or meetings between the new executive and major investors; plan NDRs or roadshows to build credibility. In founder or iconic leader transitions, prepare for extended engagement addressing strategic vision beyond the individual.
- Extended availability: Ensure IR team has capacity for immediate and sustained investor engagement following the announcement, including potential weekend or after-hours communication in urgent situations.

Leadership Disclosure as Governance Signal

Leadership transition disclosure should be understood as the visible output of ongoing Board succession planning and governance quality—topics that sophisticated investors increasingly probe during normal-course engagement. A well-managed transition announcement signals that the Board has been actively preparing for continuity, has clarity on required capabilities, and maintains control over strategic direction even amid executive change. Conversely, reactive or poorly communicated transitions raise questions about Board effectiveness, governance oversight, and organizational stability that extend well beyond the individual departure. In situations involving sudden loss, health crises, or unexpected events, the quality of disclosure becomes a real-time test of governance maturity and succession planning discipline. Investors increasingly view how a Board manages unplanned transitions as evidence of its broader strategic oversight capacity.

Macro-Geopolitical Shocks

The COVID-19 pandemic represented an unprecedented stress test for Investor Relations. Unlike previous financial or sector-specific crises, it simultaneously disrupted operations, supply chains, labor markets, and capital markets worldwide—while offering little initial visibility on duration, magnitude, or financial impact. Neither listed companies nor regulators had established precedents for disclosure under conditions of such extreme uncertainty and operational disruption.

In the absence of clear regulatory guidance, many companies felt compelled to communicate early and frequently. The first wave of communication was largely non-financial in nature, focusing on employee safety, business continuity, and social responsibility. For many issuers—particularly those traditionally limiting disclosure to periodic financial reporting—this marked a profound shift. It underscored a lasting evolution in Investor Relations: the recognition that credibility, trust, and valuation are not built on numbers alone, but on how companies behave under stress.

This first phase also introduced compassion and solidarity as legitimate—and, in extreme circumstances, necessary—components of capital markets communication. Expressions of concern for employees, customers, suppliers, and communities were not peripheral to Investor Relations; they became signals of leadership quality, governance maturity, and long-term orientation. In moments of systemic shock, investors do not assess companies solely on financial resilience, but also on whether management demonstrates responsibility, empathy, and alignment with societal expectations. When authentic and proportionate, such communication reinforces credibility rather than undermining it.

COVID-19 also strengthened the case for de-siloed, integrated communications under conditions of systemic stress. As employees, customers, investors, regulators, and communities were simultaneously affected, fragmented or function-specific messaging quickly proved untenable. Companies that spoke with one coherent voice—aligning Investor Relations, corporate communications, legal, human resources, and executive leadership—were better able to preserve credibility and avoid inconsistency. The crisis underscored that, in extreme circumstances, Investor Relations cannot operate in isolation: message discipline, timing, and tone must be governed centrally to ensure that financial disclosure, stakeholder communication, and leadership signaling remain coherent and mutually reinforcing.

These circumstances also dramatically intensify inbound information flows toward Investor Relations. Periods of heightened uncertainty trigger a surge in investor, analyst, creditor, and intermediary inquiries, placing IR under immediate operational pressure. At the same time, they create a unique opportunity: such interactions provide real-time insight into market expectations, fears, and emerging narratives. When structured and filtered appropriately, this intelligence becomes a critical input for executive management and the board—informing disclosure decisions, capital allocation priorities, and risk assessment. In this sense, Investor Relations acts not only as a transmission channel, but as an early-warning system translating capital-market signals into actionable internal insight.

A second wave of communication followed as companies gradually gained operational visibility. This phase, which often prompted stock market authorities to issue specific disclosure requirements, focused on preliminary assessments of business disruption, liquidity preservation, and early financial sensitivities. Where uncertainty remained high, many companies appropriately suspended or withdrew guidance. This was not a failure of forecasting discipline, but an exercise of governance judgment—acknowledging that precision without visibility would have been misleading rather than reassuring.

The enduring lesson from COVID-19 is not that companies should communicate more, but that they must communicate differently under macro-systemic stress. Investor Relations must be able to distinguish clearly between:

- expressions of empathy and responsibility,
- operational updates grounded in observable facts and measurable impacts, and
- price-sensitive disclosures subject to regulatory constraints.

Blurring these categories risks either under-disclosure or over-communication—both of which erode trust.

Since then, geopolitical risk has moved decisively from the background into the core of corporate valuation narratives. The invasion of Ukraine, conflicts in the Middle East, sanctions regimes, trade fragmentation, and renewed sovereign risk have reintroduced macro-geopolitics as a persistent, structural variable rather than an episodic disruption. In many cases, investors and companies alike have had little prior experience to guide interpretation.

In this context, disciplined disclosure becomes critical. Investor Relations must resist pressure to speculate or provide premature scenario analysis that cannot be substantiated. The priority is to distinguish exposure from impact, and to anchor communication in verifiable facts. In addition to assessing the human impact, effective disclosure should focus on:

- geographic revenue and cost exposure,
- operational dependencies and supply-chain sensitivities,
- mitigation levers within management control, and
- clearly identified financial transmission mechanisms.

Where uncertainty remains elevated, explicitly acknowledging limits to visibility is preferable to offering speculative reassurance—provided this stance is consistent with previously communicated assumptions and governance principles. Markets are generally more tolerant of uncertainty than of later reversals. The appropriate scope for empathy in IR communication depends on context. In systemic health or humanitarian crises affecting all stakeholders (such as COVID-19), expressions of concern for employees and communities signal leadership quality and strengthen credibility. In adversarial or conflict-driven contexts involving sanctions, military action, or diplomatic tensions, however, Investor Relations must remain strictly factual and avoid moral positioning that could create legal, reputational, or geopolitical complications beyond the company's control.

Macro-geopolitical shocks are no longer exceptional events. They are a recurring feature of the capital markets environment. Investor Relations strategy must therefore be designed to operate credibly under prolonged uncertainty—protecting trust, maintaining internal discipline, and ensuring that disclosure remains factual, coherent, and valuation-relevant even when predictability is fundamentally impaired.

In practice, effective execution under macro-geopolitical stress depends less on specific tools than on governance readiness. Clear escalation protocols, defined decision authority, disciplined internal information flows, and structured feedback loops between Investor Relations, executive management, and the board are prerequisites. The quality of Investor Relations in such periods is reflected not in the absence of volatility, but in the consistency of messaging, the avoidance of corrective disclosures, and management's ability to make capital markets decisions informed by real-time investor intelligence.

Shareholder Activism

Shareholder activism does not, in itself, constitute a disclosure event. It becomes one when public campaigns emerge, board processes are materially affected, or strategic alternatives are formally under review. In such cases, disclosure discipline lies in explaining governance frameworks, decision-making processes, and fiduciary responsibilities—without engaging in reactive or defensive messaging. Investor Relations should reinforce that market feedback is considered, but that strategy remains the prerogative of the board and management.

At that point, fragmented or reactive communication creates a vacuum that activists are uniquely skilled at exploiting—often at significant financial and reputational cost to the company. The principal disclosure risk is therefore not silence, but loss of narrative control through misalignment between strategy, performance, governance, and messaging.

Investor Relations plays a central role in managing this risk—not by debating activists or countering individual claims, but by ensuring that shareholders can assess competing perspectives through a fact-based, governance-anchored lens. Communications should emphasize decision-making processes, fiduciary responsibilities, capital-allocation discipline, and long-term value creation, rather than personalities, motives, or tactical moves. Evidence shows that defensive postures, personalized responses, or attempts to discredit activists tend to reinforce their credibility rather than undermine it.

Disclosure discipline during activist situations requires restraint and internal alignment. Attempts to rebut every argument, introduce new strategic initiatives mid-campaign, or accelerate governance changes often weaken credibility and create additional vulnerabilities. Similarly, undertaking major strategic or financial actions during a campaign—unless strictly mission-critical—risks being interpreted as reactive or coercive, particularly by proxy advisors and long-term institutional investors. Markets tend to reward companies that remain measured, consistent, and focused on execution, even under sustained pressure.

Ultimately, activist campaigns rarely create weaknesses; they expose those that already exist. Underperformance relative to peers, unclear capital-allocation priorities, governance misalignment, insufficient linkage between executive pay and performance, or poorly articulated ESG policies are recurring fault lines. From a disclosure perspective, the objective is not to "win" the argument, but to demonstrate that the company's strategy, governance framework, and performance trajectory can withstand sustained external scrutiny. Where this is the case, shareholder support is more likely to consolidate around management and the board—regardless of the activist's visibility, persistence, or tactical sophistication.

Restructuring and Turnaround

Restructuring programs test management credibility particularly acutely. Unlike M&A transactions—where outcomes are influenced by counterparties and market conditions—or financial guidance, which is exposed to macroeconomic uncertainty, restructuring is largely within management control. The ability to identify inefficiencies, design corrective actions, and execute them with discipline is therefore a direct measure of executive capability.

From an expectations-management perspective, restructuring effectively redefines the reference point against which future performance will be assessed. Cost savings, margin ambitions, and execution timelines become new anchors in investor models. Once disclosed, these anchors are difficult to reset without damaging trust.

Failure to deliver stated restructuring objectives typically signals weak execution, insufficient cost discipline, or poor diagnosis. Conversely, transparent disclosure combined with consistent delivery builds a track record of credibility that investors reward over time. As with guidance, restructuring narratives cannot substitute for performance: credibility is earned through measurable delivery against explicit commitments, not through intent alone.

Restructuring initiatives require clear, disciplined, and structured disclosure to prevent erosion of confidence. Typical trigger events include plant closures, asset disposals, company-wide reorganizations, large-scale cost-savings programs, workforce reductions, post-acquisition integration roadmaps, and potentially large asset impairments.

Once such measures become material—typically when they affect more than 5% of operating costs, involve facility closures, or require workforce reductions above 10%—the company is no longer operating under normal disclosure conditions. Information asymmetry risks increase, internal decision-making timelines compress, and investor tolerance for ambiguity declines. In this respect, restructuring disclosure shares important characteristics with activist situations and other stressed-market conditions discussed above: communication is evaluated not only for accuracy, but for coherence, consistency, and governance quality.

While disclosure requirements vary by jurisdiction, the core Investor Relations challenge remains consistent across markets: coordinating regulatory obligations, internal consultation processes, and capital markets expectations without creating credibility gaps or selective disclosure risk.

Investor Relations must articulate the objectives, scope, timing, and financial implications of the restructuring program with precision, clearly distinguishing between cash and non-cash, one-off effects and structural, recurring improvements.

Investors need to understand not only *what* management intends to achieve, but *how*, *by when*, and *against which baseline* success will be measured.

Core disclosure elements include:

- Strategic rationale: why restructuring is necessary and how it supports long-term strategy and capital allocation priorities
- Scope and actions: the businesses, geographies, or functions affected and the concrete measures being implemented
- Financial framework:
  - cost (cash and non-cash), phased over time
  - annualized run-rate savings once fully implemented

  - cash-flow and liquidity implications
  - margin impact, where credible

- Timeline and phasing: program duration and key execution milestones
- Governance and accountability: named executive ownership and board oversight
- Baseline definition: a clear reference point against which savings are measured.

Cost-savings targets are the most frequently disclosed metric, typically expressed as annualized and cumulative run-rate savings. Common levers include reductions in headcount and selling, general and administrative expenses, footprint consolidation, procurement efficiencies, organizational delayering, and digital or process improvements. Margin expansion targets are often disclosed as a secondary metric, particularly where savings are expected to translate directly into profitability.

In larger or multi-year programs, companies may formally brand restructuring initiatives to reinforce accountability.

Managing Disclosure Across the Life of the Restructuring Program

Restructuring disclosure is not a single event but a process that unfolds over time.

Announcement Phase

At launch, disclosure should present a complete framework: rationale, scope, costs, savings, timeline, and governance. This moment establishes the assumptions investors will carry forward into their models.

Execution Phase

During implementation, disclosure intensity increases. Progress should be tracked consistently through regular reporting cycles, focusing on:

- costs incurred versus plan
- savings realized versus target
- tangible execution milestones
- explanations for any material deviations from the original plan.

As in activist or crisis situations, credibility during execution depends on early acknowledgment of issues rather than delayed or selective disclosure.

Completion and Normalization

When the program is substantially complete, companies should clearly signal the transition back to normal disclosure conditions. This includes confirming recurring savings embedded in the cost base and explaining how performance will be assessed going forward without restructuring serving as a recurring explanatory overlay.

Companies that establish track records of transparent, consistent communication—even when delivering difficult news—preserve investor confidence and valuation support.

Credible disclosure patterns include:

- Quantified targets supported by clearly defined baselines
- Explicit separation of cash and P&L effects
- Distinction between gross savings and net savings after reinvestment
- Consistent metrics applied throughout the program lifecycle
- Visible executive accountability with named program ownership
- Early acknowledgment of deviations with remediation plans

Disclosure practices that undermine credibility:

- Qualitative claims without quantification ("significant," "substantial")
- Shifting definitions of success or changed baselines mid-program
- Inconsistent or selective progress reporting (updates only when convenient)
- Reliance on narrative to offset missed milestones
- Delayed disclosure of material challenges or scope changes
- Changed metrics or methodologies without transparent explanation

The cumulative effect of these patterns is substantial. Over time, weak disclosure practices erode trust, increase valuation discounts, widen credit spreads, and in extreme cases trigger activist intervention or governance challenges—even when headline savings targets are eventually delivered. Conversely, companies that maintain disclosure discipline through restructuring cycles build institutional memory and market reputation that creates measurable advantages in cost of capital and strategic flexibility.

A critical question for investors—and a frequent source of confusion or frustration—is whether identified savings will flow through to reported earnings or be partially reinvested in growth, transformation, or resilience initiatives.

This allocation decision should be disclosed explicitly at program launch. Ambiguity creates misaligned expectations: investors model full earnings uplift, management reinvests a portion, and the resulting "disappointment" triggers negative reactions despite successful execution.

Transparent articulation of how savings will be allocated—between margin expansion, growth investment, debt reduction, or shareholder returns—aligns expectations upfront, enables accurate investor modeling, and demonstrates strategic clarity. It also signals whether management views restructuring as purely defensive (survival-focused cost reduction) or as a foundation for repositioning (creating financial capacity for strategic investment). Both can be legitimate, but the choice must be made clear and defended credibly.

The effectiveness of restructuring disclosure can be assessed through both quantitative market signals and qualitative stakeholder feedback:

Market-based indicators:

- Relative stock performance during announcement and execution phases (credible programs typically recover initial announcement declines within 3–6 months)
- Trading volume and volatility patterns (transparent communication reduces information asymmetry and volatility spikes)
- Analyst rating and target price revisions (incorporation of savings into forward models signals credibility)
- Institutional ownership stability (retention of long-term holders despite short-term uncertainty)

Stakeholder feedback indicators:

- Analyst research commentary on execution confidence and management credibility
- Investor meeting feedback on clarity, trackability, and governance quality
- Sell-side and buy-side perception surveys comparing restructuring communication to peer practices
- Board and audit committee assessment of disclosure process effectiveness

Ultimately, however, the defining test remains delivery. Restructuring programs are largely controllable events, and sustained credibility is built when commitments are met, normalized into the cost base. As with financial guidance and stressed disclosure more broadly, the currency of trust in restructuring is earned through consistent execution against explicit, measurable commitments.

Bankruptcy, and Other Going-Concern Events

Situations involving acute liquidity pressure, covenant stress, or material going-concern uncertainty represent some of the most sensitive disclosure environments an Investor Relations function will ever face. In these circumstances, disclosure is no longer primarily about valuation optimization; it becomes a matter of legal compliance, credibility preservation, and orderly stakeholder management under severe constraints.

Once solvency risk becomes credible—through deteriorating cash positions, lender negotiations, covenant breaches, rating actions, or auditor emphasis of matter—normal disclosure practices are suspended. Legal and regulatory obligations dominate the communication framework, and Investor Relations must operate within a tightly controlled perimeter defined by securities law, insolvency regimes specific to each jurisdiction, and contractual confidentiality provisions. Judgment remains essential, but discretion narrows materially.

Early, factual communication is critical, even when visibility is limited. Attempts to delay disclosure in the hope of securing financing or concluding negotiations often prove counterproductive, accelerating loss of trust and increasing volatility once information inevitably enters the market. Conversely, premature or speculative communication can trigger unnecessary alarm and undermine negotiations with creditors and counterparties. The balance lies in disciplined, principle-based disclosure: timely, precise, and narrowly focused on what is known, what is uncertain, and what governance processes are in place to manage the situation.

Investor Relations must work in lockstep with executive management, legal counsel, auditors, and—where relevant—financial advisors. Messaging authority typically shifts upward, with board-level oversight and, in some jurisdictions, formal sign-off requirements. In this context, IR's role is not to "shape the story," but to ensure internal coherence, factual consistency, and compliance across all disclosure channels.

Disclosure should clearly articulate:

- the nature and origin of the liquidity or solvency stress;
- the status of lender, creditor, or restructuring discussions, where disclosure is legally permissible;
- the hierarchy of stakeholder priorities implied by the capital structure;
- the implications for shareholders, including dilution risk, suspension of dividends, or potential loss of value.

What must be avoided—without exception—are false reassurances, selective disclosure, or optimistic forward-looking statements unsupported by firm commitments. Markets are highly intolerant of credibility gaps in distressed situations, and any perception of obfuscation can irreparably damage management's standing with investors, creditors, regulators, and—in restructuring scenarios—judges or administrators.

Equally important is consistency across stakeholder groups. While disclosure obligations differ, contradictory messaging to investors, employees, customers, or suppliers quickly erodes confidence and may expose the company to legal and reputational risk. Investor Relations plays a central coordination role here, ensuring that capital markets disclosures align with internal communications and external stakeholder messaging without extending beyond what regulations allow.

Handled correctly, disclosure during solvency stress does not eliminate downside risk—but it can preserve trust, reduce uncertainty premiums, and maintain a foundation for future re-engagement should the company stabilize or emerge from restructuring. In complex cases, restructuring or insolvency proceedings can extend over multiple years, requiring sustained disclosure discipline and stakeholder engagement throughout protracted uncertainty—often under materially constrained resources.

In practice, this requires pre-cleared messaging protocols, unified stakeholder mapping, and real-time coordination between IR, legal, and restructuring advisors. This discipline reflects core Investor Relations principles: accuracy, completeness, timeliness, and respect for the market's capacity to process difficult truths.

ESG-Related Incidents

ESG-related incidents—including climate events, industrial accidents, pollution, social controversies, or governance failures—represent a distinct category of disclosure risk. While such events are often discussed through a sustainability or reputational lens, Investor Relations must approach them first and foremost as potential value drivers or value destroyers, assessed through their financial materiality and implications for the company's risk profile, strategy, and cost of capital.

The first question is whether the incident triggers immediate disclosure obligations. Presumption of material disclosure typically applies when: fatalities or serious injuries occur; operations are substantially disrupted at a material facility; regulatory enforcement or criminal investigation is initiated; or the company anticipates financial impact exceeding internal thresholds.

When uncertainty exists, the safer course is to disclose and update as facts develop, rather than delay and risk appearing reactive or evasive.

When an ESG incident becomes known, disclosure should focus on four core dimensions: the nature and scope of the event; the immediate and potential operational disruption; the legal, regulatory, or contractual consequences; and the possible implications for long-term value creation. Investors will seek clarity on whether the incident affects asset integrity, production capacity, supply chains, licenses to operate, insurance coverage, capital expenditure requirements, or future cash flows. Where relevant, the hierarchy of risks—operational, regulatory, financial, and reputational—should be made explicit, rather than implied through narrative.

Investor Relations must also ensure strict consistency with previously disclosed ESG metrics, targets, and commitments. Incidents should be framed against what the company has already told the market about its environmental exposure, safety record, social practices, or governance controls. Ad hoc narratives, moral positioning, or value-based justifications that are not anchored in measurable impact undermine credibility and invite skepticism. The role of IR is to explain how an incident affects the investment case, risk assumptions, and long-term cost of capital.

In many cases, the full financial impact of an ESG incident is not immediately known. In such circumstances, disciplined restraint is essential. Disclosure should prioritize verifiable facts, clearly distinguish between confirmed information and areas of uncertainty, and avoid speculative estimates. At the same time, it is appropriate—and often expected—to acknowledge the human, environmental, or social dimension of the event. Expressions of compassion for affected employees, communities, or stakeholders, combined with a clear outline of remedial and corrective measures, reinforce leadership credibility without straying into advocacy or premature conclusions. Process transparency—investigations underway, authorities engaged, governance oversight activated—is often more valuable than numerical precision at early stages.

Here is an example of a listed company that experienced an uncharacteristic environmental incident: it acknowledged the event promptly, framed it as serious but atypical, and focused its initial disclosure on immediate containment, regulatory engagement, and mobilization of independent experts rather than causation or blame. Early communications emphasized leadership accountability and "doing what is right," while explicitly noting that investigations and impact assessments were ongoing and that conclusions would evolve.

Over the following months, the company shifted from crisis statements to a structured disclosure cadence, embedding progress updates into ESG and results reporting rather than relying on reactive media commentary. Remediation, monitoring, and governance oversight were described in increasing detail, with milestones communicated selectively to avoid re-amplifying risk. By the second year, the incident was normalized into regular risk and ESG disclosures, with management emphasizing progress made, controls strengthened, and lessons incorporated into operating practices.

The approach worked because it prioritized early acknowledgment and action-oriented facts over completeness, used independent validation to sustain credibility, and maintained disciplined follow-through until the issue could be integrated into the long-term investment narrative.

ESG incident disclosure commonly fails when companies: minimize the event initially, then must later disclose larger impacts—destroying credibility; provide different details across channels (regulatory filing vs. press release vs. investor calls)—triggering regulatory scrutiny; disappear after initial disclosure despite material developments—fueling speculation and volatility; or lead with values statements rather than operational facts—signaling lack of control over the situation.

Importantly, disclosure around ESG-related incidents cannot be treated as a one-off exercise. As facts evolve, investigations progress, or remedial actions translate into measurable outcomes, the market must be updated in a timely and disciplined manner. Investor Relations should proactively assess when new information becomes material and ensure that subsequent disclosures remain consistent with prior statements, clearly explain what has changed, and why. Regular, factual updates—rather than reactive or fragmented communications—help prevent speculation, reduce volatility, and reinforce confidence in management's control over both the situation and the disclosure process.

ESG incidents require tight coordination between Investor Relations, corporate communications, and internal communications. While tone and emphasis may differ by audience, the underlying facts, timelines, and commitments must remain identical. Investor Relations plays a central role in ensuring that market-facing disclosure stays compliant, coherent, and firmly anchored in financial relevance—protecting trust at precisely the moment it is most at risk.

5.5 Attracting Analyst Coverage

Equity research remains one of the most powerful mechanisms through which capital markets form expectations, allocate attention, and price securities. Research demonstrates that analyst coverage enhances liquidity by reducing information asymmetry and improving the dissemination of firm-specific information—creating favorable market conditions through reduced bid-ask spreads and increased trading volumes. In today's environment, however, high-quality analyst coverage has become both scarcer, more selective. Coverage is no longer a given outcome of listing; it is an earned consequence of liquidity, investor demand, and strategic coherence over time.

Effective analyst coverage does more than restate company messaging. It improves visibility among both active and passive allocators, contributes to informed trading and liquidity, anchors valuation expectations, and reinforces management credibility by amplifying signals already validated by the market. Analyst coverage is therefore best understood not as a communications objective, but as an outcome of sustained Investor Relations discipline.

For the purpose of this book, we are only discussing sell-side analysts and sponsored research in the following sections and not buy-side analysts whose reports are only available to the investment management firms they work for.

Understanding Sell-Side Economics

Sell-side analysts operate under clear economic constraints. They are not paid by issuers, but by trading commissions and corporate-access revenues generated with buy-side clients. Coverage decisions are therefore driven by liquidity, investor interest, sector relevance, and the analyst's ability to monetize attention—not by the issuer's desire to be covered.

Before initiating coverage, analysts implicitly assess whether a stock can generate client interest, trading activity, and a credible investment case over a multi-year horizon. Companies cannot dictate this decision. They can, however, influence it by making their equity relevant, understandable, and investable.

A critical implication follows: buy-side demand precedes sell-side supply. Companies that attract one or two credible institutional investors often trigger a validation effect, encouraging further buy-side engagement, followed by analyst attention, broader visibility, improved liquidity, and additional institutional ownership. This self-reinforcing dynamic—the "circle of influence"—is foundational to sustainable coverage.

Sponsored Research

For many small- and mid-cap issuers, traditional sell-side coverage is structurally difficult to secure. Independent research providers can partially bridge this gap by offering third-party validation to paying subscribers, particularly within specific sectors or regions. While such research rarely matches the visibility of bulge-bracket coverage, it can support early market understanding as liquidity and investor interest develop.

Sponsored research, where the issuer pays for coverage, should be approached with caution. Institutional investors heavily discount it, and its primary value lies in raising awareness rather than credibility building. Used selectively and transparently, it may serve as a temporary solution—not a substitute for genuine market demand.

Meanwhile, AI-driven research tools are reshaping how investors screen and analyze companies. Structured, consistent, and machine-readable disclosure increasingly affects discoverability. While AI does not replace analyst judgment, it raises the bar for disclosure quality and consistency.

Analyst Coverage and Company Size

Analyst coverage remains closely correlated with market capitalization and trading volume. Large-cap companies may attract dozens of analysts; for smaller issuers, securing coverage from even three to five credible firms is a meaningful achievement. Regulatory changes such as MiFID II have further reduced coverage breadth, particularly in Europe, intensifying competition for analyst attention.

Small-cap companies should therefore calibrate expectations and target boutique or regional firms whose economics and client base align with earlier-stage issuers. These relationships often prove more durable and can evolve as the company grows.

While companies cannot change analyst economics, they can materially improve their attractiveness by focusing on three fundamentals.

First, reporting discipline. Timely, predictable, and internally consistent financial reporting is non-negotiable. Analysts must be able to model the business with confidence. This includes stable formats, clear reconciliations, and explanatory commentary on variances and drivers.

Second, strategic clarity. Analysts engage more readily when a company articulates a credible three-to-five-year strategic trajectory. This does not require granular guidance, but it does require coherence: a clearly defined value proposition, a plausible path to sustainable returns, and transparent discussion of opportunities and risks. In practice, this means answering: What market need are we addressing? What are our sustainable competitive advantages? What are the key operational and financial milestones over the next three to five years? What could derail the plan?

Third, market visibility. Consistent engagement—through earnings calls, investor meetings, roadshows, and news flow—keeps the company visible and relevant. Visibility alone does not generate coverage, but invisibility guarantees its absence.

Smaller issuers can further differentiate themselves by becoming reliable sources of sector insight and by offering direct access to senior decision-makers. For analysts, unfiltered access to CEOs and CFOs is often an advantage, not a liability, when evaluating emerging companies. Implementation requires discipline: consistent quarterly check-ins, industry primers published proactively, and responsiveness to model-building questions—none of which require large IR budgets, but all of which require executive commitment. The challenge intensifies post-IPO, when expanding coverage beyond the lead underwriters requires 12–24 months of demonstrated execution—a reality that makes early IR discipline essential.

Building Relationships Before Coverage

One of the most effective long-term strategies is to engage analysts before they formally cover the company. Familiarity lowers the threshold for initiation. Analysts are more likely to launch coverage on businesses they already understand, trust, and can explain to clients.

Pre-coverage engagement should be educational rather than promotional: a mid-cap industrial might brief a sector analyst on emerging supply-chain trends, regulatory shifts, or customer concentration dynamics—providing context that aids sector understanding without pressing for initiation. Over time, as liquidity improves and investor demand grows, these relationships often convert naturally into formal coverage.

Coverage Quality over Quantity

Not all coverage adds equal value. Five respected analysts with deep sector expertise and strong institutional distribution are more valuable than broad but superficial coverage. Analyst targeting should therefore align with the company's investor-base objectives, geographic priorities, and liquidity strategy.

Equal access to information remains a regulatory imperative. Companies must refrain from commenting on analyst ratings or price targets, threaten to withhold access, or provide selective disclosure to favorable analysts—practices that violate regulations and damage credibility. Within those boundaries, however, engagement depth can be differentiated based on analytical quality and strategic relevance—not on favorability of opinion.

In this way, analyst coverage both reflects and reinforces the shareholder base a company ultimately attracts—a dynamic with particular implications for emerging-market issuers seeking international capital.

The International Coverage Challenge of Emerging and Frontier Market Issuers

Attracting international sell-side coverage presents distinct challenges. International analysts apply the same economic calculus—liquidity, trading volume, investor demand—but with higher thresholds. They assume weaker governance, less transparent disclosure, and greater execution risk until proven otherwise. Client education requirements are higher. Currency and settlement friction reduce attractiveness for many mandates.

The credibility imperative comes first. Before pursuing international coverage, emerging-market issuers must establish baseline credibility that developed-market companies take for granted:

- Voluntarily adopt stricter standards (e.g., quarterly reporting if home market requires only semi-annual)
- Engage leading accounting and auditing firms recognized in target investor markets.
- Use professional translation services with financial specialization.
- Consider an American Depositary Receipt (ADR) or equivalent structure to simplify investor access.
- Engage European or US IR advisory firm to enhance credibility.

Governance excellence must be demonstrated proactively: strong independent board oversight, robust risk management frameworks, ethical culture embedded in operations, and transparent executive compensation aligned with long-term value creation are prerequisites.

Deliver on guidance and commitments consistently; achieve stated strategic objectives; demonstrate disciplined capital allocation; and learn from mistakes transparently.

The strategic sequence matters: establish credibility (governance, disclosure, execution track record) before building international investor demand, which in turn precedes analyst coverage.

Buy-side demand precedes sell-side supply—this principle applies with greater force to emerging-market issuers.

Institutional investors can increasingly access foreign companies through depositary receipts, cross-border trading platforms, and index products without a formal secondary listing. In many cases, targeted, well-executed international IR—roadshows, conferences, virtual meetings—provides better cost–benefit than a full cross-listing.

Analyst targeting should prioritize sequentially: emerging-market specialists at international banks who already understand regional context, then regional boutiques with emerging-market focus, and only later bulge-bracket global sector analysts (typically requiring $5B + market cap).

Common pitfalls include: insufficient preparation before international outreach, poor translation quality, home-market-centric framing unfamiliar to international investors, time-zone inaccessibility signaling low priority.

Realistic timeline: Building international credibility and coverage typically requires 18–36 months. Companies that rush this process rarely succeed. Those willing to build investor demand systematically, and engage analysts patiently—while maintaining execution discipline—position themselves to attract coverage as markets recognize emerging-market opportunities.

Measuring Success of Coverage Expansion

Coverage success should be assessed through both quantitative and qualitative lenses: number and type of analysts, estimate quality and dispersion, investor feedback, and the contribution of research to meaningful investor engagement. For example, tracking whether estimate dispersion narrows over time (indicating convergence around a shared understanding), or whether analyst-initiated investor meetings produce higher-quality prospects than other sourcing channels, provides evidence of coverage value beyond the number of firms covering the company.

Practical discipline matters as much as strategy. Companies that succeed in attracting and maintaining quality coverage typically implement quarterly analyst tracking (coverage gaps, estimate changes, research quality), maintain updated analyst materials accessible on the IR website, and assign clear ownership—whether to the IRO, CFO, or in smaller companies, the CEO—for relationship continuity.

Analyst coverage is not an end in itself. It is a by-product of strategic clarity, reporting credibility, and sustained investor demand. When approached deliberately, it becomes a powerful amplifier of Investor Relations effectiveness and a visible marker of trust earned over time.

5.6 Shareholder Identification

Before a company can shape its shareholder base, it must first understand who actually owns its stock—and what it can realistically know. Shareholder identification is neither uniform across markets nor unlimited in scope; it is constrained by regulation, intermediaries, market structure, and IR budgets. Yet, when used thoughtfully, ownership data, voting patterns, and changes in holdings provide critical intelligence for Investor Relations. Beyond mere identification, this insight helps IR to anticipate investor behavior, detect shifts in sentiment, and distinguish between transient flows and long-term conviction.

A listed company that does not seek to identify its shareholders runs the risk of not reaching its audience. Knowing precisely who owns your stock, and why, are the keys to building a secure shareholder base. At the same time, increasing investor activism is making shareholder identification more important and more difficult.

It is not an easy task, and sometimes a nearly impossible one, to draw up an exhaustive list, unless the stocks are held in a "registered" form. In this case, the shareholder's identity is recorded in a specific share registrar maintained by the issuer or a dedicated depositary bank. Yet the most common form of share ownership is the "anonymous" bearer form, as allowed under certain regulations, and in systems where shares have been dematerialized and are traded in an electronic form.

This makes the identification process all the more challenging and requires resources and systems that can do the following:

- Track and quantify holdings as well as categories of investors (individual shareholders, institutional investors) from a variety of sources;
- Provide senior management team with a strategic analysis of who end-owners, also known as "beneficial owners" of the company's shares actually are.

There are different legal and technical ways to discover your shareholder base. This high-cost and time-consuming effort is worth undertaking only if you have a clear idea of what your objectives for doing so are, if you conduct the analysis on a regular basis, and if you want to proactively manage your free float.

Furthermore, companies are not the only ones interested in knowing who owns their shares. Institutional investors are also very keen to be informed, as it gives them valuable insight into the potential evolution of the shares. For instance, the presence of many hedge funds as shareholders can result in higher risks of volatility, while a large portion of the shares held by employees can indicate long-term stability.

Legal Means

Share-ownership disclosure regulations vary from one country to another. For instance, some may require shareholders to officially declare their holdings in a company when they pass a certain threshold, expressed either in nominal value, as a percentage of the share capital, or as a percentage of the voting rights. There are also countries where no such obligation exists. Furthermore, in certain jurisdictions the power of investigation is given to the companies, while, in others, the local regulator has the power to dictate shareholder identification.

- Notification of threshold crossing

Depending on applicable regulations in the country where the shares are listed and the company's bylaws, shareholders may be required to disclose the number of shares or voting rights they hold when threshold limits are crossed (generally fractions of 0.5 percent of the capital). Stock market law strictly regulates the crossing of legal and statutory thresholds: the latter are approved by shareholders and included in the bylaws. Failure to make the required disclosure can result in lawsuits and deprivation of the voting rights attached to the shares. This, for instance, would prevent voting rights from being exercised in the event of a hostile takeover bid.

- Identification by a central securities depositary

Securities on the world's major stock markets have largely been dematerialized, meaning they now exist in electronic rather than paper form. In a number of countries, central securities depositaries and clearing agencies exist which are responsible for maintaining register of securities, issuing international securities identification numbers (ISIN) for all issues of securities, and clearing and settlement of securities. In addition, they provide additional services to the issuers, such as securities ownership identification. This allows an issuer of bearer securities to request and obtain a list of all, or part of, the securities' holders registered on the custodians' books.

Issuers may regularly request (once a year or more often) that the agency make inquiries based on thresholds as set out in their bylaws, for instance, upward of 10,000 shares per custodian bank and 500 shares per shareholder. They may also ask for full identification of all shareholders, even those with only one share, although this is a costly undertaking for companies with millions of shareholders, and the content analysis process is quite complex. In addition, while significant progress has been made over past years in certain legislations, it is still often extremely difficult to identify individual foreign shareholders as opposed to the custodian banks where these shares are deposited. This is an important factor if we consider that in certain markets, foreign or "non-resident" investors may hold more than half of an issuer's shares.

At the end of this process, the issuer obtains a file, which includes the name and address of all identified shareholders, be they corporations or individuals, along with the number of shares owned, and their location. While unique of its kind, the information contained there must be expanded through other online search, possibly via the acquisition of specialized databases.

- Analysis of voting results

This type of analysis is much more varied and the findings depend, in large part, on the thresholds and means of convening shareholder meetings. The proxy ballot cards sent by mail, or brought in person by shareholders attending the annual general meeting (AGM), are legally the property of the company. To perform the analysis, these are captured and stored in a well-customized Investor Relations contact database and provide additional information about, or confirm the identity of, the shareholders identified by the issuer during the process described above.

The exercise is also very helpful when it comes to planning the annual meeting for the following year. You will want to compare the number of printed proxy ballots versus the number of shareholders who returned them and those who actually came to attend the AGM. Useful cross-analysis should also be conducted to do the following:

- Calculate the average number of shares held by retail investors: This is valuable information if the issuer plans a capital increase and wants to estimate the subscription rate for this category of shareholder;
- Assess the sensitivity of individual and institutional shareholders to different kinds of resolution based on how they vote;
- Adjust the size and, consequently, the budget of the event to actual presence of shareholders.

Technical Means

- Free shareholder identification techniques
  - Resourcefulness. There is nothing to prevent IROs from directly asking the institutional or retail investors they are in contact with whether they own shares in the company and, if so, how many. Even if no specific answer is given, the question will rarely be dismissed outright. This can, in fact, be a valuable opportunity to discover what it would take to convince those who do not already own shares to invest. A shift in strategy? Lower valuation multiples? Any information thus gathered should be shared with company management.
- Fee-based identification tools
  - Standard mailing techniques. When a contact database already exists, issuers can rely on traditional investigation and marketing methods. For instance, they may send out questionnaires, anonymous if so desired, including questions about the number of shares owned. It is wise to plan this type of undertaking well in advance and to inform the relevant authorities in the country in question, ahead of time, of any plans to create a contact database that will be used to this end, to update a contact data base to distribute a shareholders' newsletter, for instance.
  - Databases. There are numerous databases and platforms that list international institutional investors and provide a breakdown of their portfolios by geography, size, and the nature of the holdings, investment policy, and so on. In some countries, institutional investors must disclose the content of certain portfolios such as the mutual funds, unit trusts, and collective investment vehicles they manage on an annual, half-yearly, or quarterly basis. Many such databases are publicly available. They can also be developed specifically for issuers. Information is available on the number of shares held, changes made to the portfolio since the

previous reporting period, the name and contact information of the fund manager, the buy-side analyst covering the country in which the shares are issued, specifically the one in charge of the sector in which the issuer is active. Moreover, databases also mention the competitors or peers in which shares are owned, the amount of funds under management, and a breakdown between domestic and foreign investments (this gives an indication of how familiar foreign investors are with the stock exchanges and economies of other countries).

- Financial intermediaries

Financial intermediaries have privileged access to listed companies' shareholder bases:

- Investment banks and brokers. Through the transactions they execute for institutional clients and retail investors, these intermediaries can tell IROs whether particular fund managers own a large enough number of shares for the issuer to plan a meeting or whether they recently added to or liquidated their holdings. This information may not always be as accurate or current as the issuer would like, but it does nonetheless tend to be highly valuable.
- Retail banks. In certain countries, large retail banking networks can provide a different kind of information. While issuers cannot gain access to the names of those who own shares through securities accounts, they can inquire about the possibility of obtaining a breakdown of the bank's customers by the number of shares owned (for instance, less than 5, 5–10, 10–20, and so on) along with other types of information, usually about the place of residence, socio-professional category, and age of stockholders. Assuming it is legally permitted, the results will depend on the degree of sophistication of the bank's information systems. Data pertaining to share ownership is particularly valuable for the issuer. For instance, understanding the average value of shareholders' investment in your company's shares can provide you with a valuable indication the amount of shares that could be subscribed in the event of a capital increase. It is also useful in planning meetings with retail investors in specific regions, which can in this case be substituted for the identification process described earlier.

5.7 Diversifying the Shareholder Base

A well-diversified shareholder base is one of the most valuable strategic assets a public company can build. Much like diversifying a customer base, an appropriately balanced shareholder structure enhances resilience and optionality. It contributes to trading liquidity and price stability, mitigates concentration risk, and provides management with greater freedom to execute strategy across cycles.

Shareholder diversification is not a passive outcome of market trading. It is the result of deliberate Investor Relations strategy, grounded in a clear understanding of who owns the stock, why they own it, and how their behavior influences valuation dynamics over time.

Why Diversification Matters

Excessive shareholder concentration creates vulnerability. Dependence on a limited number of investors exposes the company to abrupt shifts in sentiment, strategy, or liquidity needs that may be unrelated to fundamentals. A more diversified shareholder base helps absorb these shocks and dampen their market impact.

Three structural benefits underpin the strategic importance of diversification:

1. Liquidity and price stability

A shareholder base composed of investors with differing mandates, time horizons, and decision triggers reduces the likelihood of synchronized buying or selling. This heterogeneity supports smoother trading patterns and moderates price volatility.

2. Risk mitigation

When one investor category exits—whether due to macroeconomic events, regulatory constraints, or portfolio rebalancing—other investor groups can provide stability. Diversification spreads exposure across investor behaviors rather than concentrating it within a single cohort.

3. Strategic flexibility

A balanced shareholder base reduces the influence of any single constituency, enabling management to pursue long-term strategic objectives without disproportionate short-term pressure.

Key Dimensions of Shareholder Diversification

- Investor Type

Most listed companies are predominantly institutionally owned, yet the presence of retail and other investor categories can materially influence market dynamics. Retail shareholders often contribute to ownership continuity and brand visibility, while different institutional profiles shape liquidity, engagement patterns, and governance expectations.

There is no universally optimal mix. The appropriate balance depends on market structure, listing venue, regulatory environment, and corporate maturity. Investor Relations must therefore assess shareholder composition in context, rather than against generic benchmarks.

- Investment Style

Shareholder composition should align with the company's economic profile and strategic trajectory. Growth-oriented, value-focused, quality-driven, and index-tracking investors respond to different signals and performance attributes.

Targeting investor styles that are incompatible with the company's fundamentals creates unstable ownership and recurrent disappointment. For instance, if a company seeks to attract pension funds but does not pay a dividend, its efforts are likely to prove unsuccessful. Realistic targeting is essential: not every business model can support every investment style at scale.

- Geographic Distribution

Geographic diversification of the shareholder base reduces exposure to country-specific capital flows, regulatory shifts, and macroeconomic shocks. In practice, international ownership often lags the geographic diversification of revenues and operations.

Investor Relations should regularly assess whether shareholder geography reasonably reflects the company's operational footprint and strategic priorities. Perfect symmetry is neither necessary nor achievable, but persistent misalignment warrants targeted engagement.

- Investment Horizon

Investment horizon is among the least visible yet most consequential dimensions of shareholder composition. Short-term and long-term capital each play distinct roles in market functioning. Liquidity often depends on the presence of investors with shorter decision cycles, while strategic stability is supported by holders with longer time horizons.

The objective is not to eliminate turnover, but to ensure that the shareholder base collectively supports both liquidity and long-term value creation. Excessive emphasis on stability can impair market depth, just as excessive turnover can undermine trust and valuation.

For example, a company in a multi-year transformation may benefit from anchor investors with 3–5 year horizons who provide stability during restructuring, alongside sufficient shorter-term holders to maintain daily liquidity for index inclusion and options market functioning.

- Employee Shareholders

Employee shareholders occupy a unique position in the shareholder base, combining economic interest with proximity to the company's operations and culture. While often overlooked in Investor Relations strategies, they can represent a stabilizing force. Communicating with employee shareholders requires careful coordination with internal communications and human resources, as well as sensitivity to information asymmetry and expectations. When approached strategically, employee share ownership can reinforce alignment, credibility, and long-term commitment—provided it is treated as a distinct audience rather than an extension of retail investors.

How to Achieve Shareholder Base Diversification

Shareholder diversification requires disciplined execution.

- Reference point

As previously mentioned, Investor Relations should conduct regular shareholder analysis to understand ownership concentration, investor types, styles, geographies, and turnover patterns. This assessment should be formalized in a shareholder mix strategy that articulates objectives, rationale, and time horizon, and is benchmarked against relevant peers.

- Definition of target profiles

Target investors should be defined by their investment philosophy, holding period, sector expertise, portfolio construction approach, engagement style, and geographic mandate. Clear targeting improves the quality of engagement and avoids indiscriminate outreach.

- Targeted engagement

Investor meetings should be selected deliberately. Accepting every meeting proposed by intermediaries dilutes strategic focus. Quality of engagement consistently outweighs quantity in shaping shareholder composition over time.

- Geographic expansion

For internationally competitive companies, building ownership across regions and currencies can reduce vulnerability to localized market dislocations. Priority should be given to markets where the company's industry, governance standards, and strategic narrative are well understood. Multilingual disclosure may be appropriate where international ownership is a strategic objective.

Measuring Diversification Effort

While no single metric defines success, Investor Relations can monitor diversification through a combination of concentration indicators, ownership mix analysis, geographic distribution, turnover patterns, and estimated holding behavior.

Shareholder composition should be reviewed at least annually and in connection with major corporate events. Progress against diversification objectives must be tracked and targeting adjusted as the company's strategy and market positioning evolve.

Progress toward diversification objectives can be tracked through:

- Ownership concentration
- Investor type distribution (institutional/retail/insider split)
- Investment-style composition (growth/value/blend/index/other)
- Geographic distribution by region
- Estimated holding period per category of investor
- Ownership turnover rate

Defining an "ideal" shareholder base is inherently company-specific. Industry characteristics, growth stage, capital intensity, governance profile, and liquidity constraints all shape what is appropriate. The objective is to balance market depth—the presence of buyers and sellers across price levels—with market breadth, which insulates the stock from event-driven disruption.

A further constraint: beneficial ownership visibility varies significantly by jurisdiction. In markets where shares are held through custodian banks, identifying foreign shareholders may be impossible, requiring IR teams to rely on proxy data, investor intelligence from meetings, and periodic perception studies.

A strategic review of shareholder composition is warranted following material changes such as mergers and acquisitions, restructuring, shifts in strategic direction, changes in capital allocation policy, geographic expansion, persistent valuation dislocations, or the emergence of unwanted activism.

Diversification addresses who owns the stock; retention determines who stays through cycles.

The former shapes market structure, while the latter determines long-term support—providing the natural transition to the discussion of shareholder loyalty and retention in the following section.

5.8 Enhancing Shareholder Loyalty and Retention

Attracting investors is a prerequisite for access to capital; retaining them is what ultimately stabilizes or enhances valuation through cycles. Shareholder loyalty is the cumulative result of trust earned over time, reinforced by predictable behavior, disciplined governance, and consistency between words and actions.

While acquisition is forward-looking and opportunity-driven, retention is judgment-based: investors continuously assess whether management has demonstrated sufficient reliability, coherence, and discipline to merit staying invested when conditions deteriorate or expectations are challenged.

Understanding Selectivity

No company can—or should—seek to satisfy every investor constituency. Capital markets are inherently pluralistic: investors differ in time horizon, risk tolerance, income expectations, governance priorities, and views on capital allocation. Attempting to appeal simultaneously to incompatible preferences inevitably leads to diluted messaging, strategic ambiguity, and weighs on valuation.

Effective shareholder retention therefore begins with strategic selectivity. Investor Relations must be anchored in a clear understanding of which shareholders the company is structurally positioned to serve—and which it is not. Loyalty is strongest when expectations are aligned upfront, not retrofitted through communication.

Selectivity is not exclusionary; it is clarifying. By articulating what the company stands for, how it allocates capital, and the principles that guide decision-making, Investor Relations allows investors to self-assess fit and commit with informed conviction.

Strengthening Reputation Through Trust and Consistent Execution

Trust is accumulated incrementally and depleted rapidly. Investors do not measure trust by the absence of adverse developments, but by the quality of explanation when outcomes diverge from expectations. Credibility is reinforced when management explains variance clearly, avoids narrative drift, and resists reframing setbacks as temporary anomalies without evidence.

Over time, trust becomes observable. Experienced IR teams monitor indicators such as shareholder turnover during company-specific volatility, the balance between strategic and tactical investor questions, the stability of proxy advisor recommendations, and the ease with which the company can access capital when needed.

Conversely, early signs of trust erosion often include a shift in investor dialogue toward procedural or governance mechanics, increased demand for reassurance meetings from historically stable holders, divergence in proxy voting patterns, or a change in sell-side narrative tone that cannot be explained by results alone.

Investor Relations plays a critical role in detecting these signals early and ensuring that explanations remain factual, proportional, and consistent with prior disclosures.

Long-term investors do not require flawless forecasting; they seek behavioral consistency. Predictable companies exhibit stable disclosure rhythms, recurring analytical frameworks, and continuity in how performance drivers are explained.

Strategic evolution is often necessary. What matters is how change is framed. Credible evolution is characterized by an explicit rationale, continuity of underlying principles, and clear forward-looking guardrails. What undermines predictability is not change itself, but unexplained drift.

By maintaining consistency in how strategy, risks, and capital allocation are discussed over time, companies reduce interpretive risk and allow investors to focus on fundamentals rather than second-guessing management intent.

Financial Strategy as a Shareholder Filter

Financial policy is one of the most powerful—and often underappreciated—determinants of shareholder composition and retention. Dividend policies, share buyback programs, leverage targets, and cash reinvestment priorities act as implicit signals that attract certain investors while discouraging others.

Income-oriented investors, such as pension funds or insurance-driven mandates, tend to value predictability and cash return visibility. Other investor segments may prioritize capital appreciation through share repurchases or reinvestment-led growth. Neither preference is inherently superior; each reflects a distinct investment logic. What matters is coherence between financial strategy, disclosed priorities, and the shareholder base the company seeks to cultivate.

Clarity around capital allocation philosophy strengthens retention by ensuring that investors self-select into the equity for the right reasons.

Company-Shareholder Alignment

Long-term shareholder loyalty is not achieved by continuous adaptation to shifting investor demands. It is achieved when investors recognize that management decisions follow a consistent financial logic—even when those decisions are not universally popular.

By articulating capital allocation choices transparently and applying them consistently over time, companies create a natural alignment mechanism. This discipline reduces friction, limits expectation gaps, and reinforces investability across market cycles.

Regional Retention Dynamics

Retention strategies are shaped not only by company behavior, but also by market structure.

In relationship-driven markets—such as Germany, Japan, and parts of Asia and the Middle East—ownership structures often include family-controlled shareholders, cross-shareholdings, or long-standing strategic investors. These features tend to result in longer holding periods but increase sensitivity of external shareholders to governance credibility, board behavior, and process integrity. In such contexts, retention depends heavily on continuity, consistency of messaging across formats and languages, and confidence in oversight rather than short-term performance.

In index-driven markets—most notably the United States and the United Kingdom—passive ownership provides baseline stability but limited discretionary support during periods of stress. Retention is shaped primarily by analytical consistency, transparent capital allocation logic, and credibility with active managers who influence market sentiment. Shareholder bases can shift more rapidly, making disciplined targeting essential.

In emerging markets, additional complexity arises from currency volatility, geopolitical exposure, and divergent behavior between domestic and international shareholders. Investor Relations must often address different risk perceptions while maintaining a coherent core narrative.

Effective retention strategies recognize these structural differences without fragmenting the equity story. The principles of trust, predictability, and alignment remain universal; their expression does not.

Mastering Shareholder Retention

Retention must be actively monitored and governed. A practical approach is a periodic retention review that connects what the company said it would do with what it actually did—and how shareholders responded.

Such a review typically examines expectation alignment, behavioral consistency in financial and governance decisions, and changes in shareholder composition and engagement patterns over time. When documented and discussed with senior management and the board, this discipline helps distinguish temporary dislocation from structural misalignment in the shareholder base.

Retention Strategy Under Activist Pressure

Shareholder loyalty matters most when it is tested. Activist situations reveal whether retention has been built structurally or relied solely on goodwill.

Crucially, retention cannot be improvised once activist pressure emerges. A resilient retention strategy is established well in advance, through regular engagement with core long-term holders, documented rationale for capital allocation decisions, consistent execution of strategic priorities, and a clear understanding of governance expectations.

During activist situations, disclosure discipline becomes even more critical. Selective disclosure rules apply fully, and any adjustment to engagement cadence must be coordinated closely with legal counsel.

Retention strategies fail less often from lack of effort than from inconsistency. Common red flags include adjusting strategic narratives depending on the audience, incremental capital allocation changes driven by individual investor preferences, governance communication disconnected from operational reality, or continual introduction of new adjusted metrics to sustain narrative momentum.

Such practices may reduce short-term friction, but they systematically erode long-term.

Retention as Resilience Factor

A loyal shareholder base functions as strategic insurance. It does not prevent adverse events, but it mitigates their impact by reducing volatility, shortening recovery periods, and preserving management's freedom to execute a defined long-term strategy.

Diversification determines who owns the stock; retention determines who stays through the cycle. Together, they contribute to the resilience of the shareholder base and the company's capacity to lead rather than react when markets are least forgiving.

Investor Relations operates within a framework of governance, authority, and control. The next section focuses on the internal architecture that protects credibility and ensures consistency under scrutiny. It addresses the IR-Board interface, coordination with legal and governance functions, proxy situations, and the discipline required to maintain message coherence across stakeholder channels. The emphasis is less on decision rights than on IR's authority to flag risk, enforce consistency, and safeguard the company's standing in the capital markets.

5.9 Investor Relations Working with the Board

Investor Relations operates at the intersection of governance and capital markets—a junction under growing pressure. Activist campaigns now target companies of all sizes and share ownership structures; institutional investors demand direct Board access on ESG and capital allocation; retail shareholders mobilize on social platforms. In this environment, IR's authority to manage the investor-Board interface is no longer administrative—it is integral to corporate governance.

This sub-section addresses how IR exercises its authority in investor-Board interactions: determining when such engagement is appropriate, preparing directors for market scrutiny, and ensuring that governance dialogue reinforces—rather than undermines—the company's long-term investment case.

The emphasis is practical and decision-oriented. IR's role is to act as guardian of consistency and disclosure discipline when governance enters the investor arena.

When Investor-Board Meetings Make Strategic Sense

Investor requests to meet Board members should never be treated as routine access or relationship currency. They are governance signals and must be evaluated as such. IR plays a central role in advising whether such meetings serve the company's interests at a given point in time.
A request merits consideration when:

- The investor holds material ownership (typically > 2%) with demonstrated long-term holding behavior,
- The request concerns governance oversight—CEO succession, capital allocation discipline, Board composition, or material ESG risk—not operational performance, and
- The company's disclosures are current and the governance narrative is stable.

IR should recommend declining when:

- The request is driven by short-term trading positions or recent underperformance dissatisfaction
- The investor is not yet a shareholder and seeks information asymmetry (early access to guidance, deal specifics, competitive intelligence)
- The company is in a disclosure-sensitive period (pending transaction, activist defense, material non-public information overhang)
- Granting access would create precedent the company cannot sustain.

Ownership size alone is not determinative. A 1% owner with a 20-year governance track record may warrant engagement; a 4% position accumulated in two months does not.

Timing matters. Investor-Board meetings are most effective when governance narratives are stable, disclosures are current, and the company is not in a reactive posture. Poorly timed engagement can amplify uncertainty rather than resolve it.

Governance Roadshows: Purpose and Protocols

Governance roadshows represent a structured form of investor-Board engagement. Their purpose is to listen, ask questions, not to market. When executed well, they provide the Board with unfiltered insight into investor expectations and concerns while reinforcing the company's governance maturity.

Appropriate triggers include:

- A shift in ownership profile toward stewardship-oriented investors.
- Anticipated proxy contests or heightened voting scrutiny.
- Strategic repositioning that raises governance questions.
- Post-crisis or post-activism restoration of investor trust.

Governance roadshows should be tightly scoped. Participation is typically limited to the Chair or relevant committee chairs, with clear agreement on objectives and boundaries. Messaging must remain consistent with public disclosures, and discussions should focus on governance oversight rather than operational execution.

When executed poorly, governance roadshows create more risk than they resolve. Directors who speak without coordination may inadvertently disclose material non-public information, contradict management messaging, or signal divisions within the Board. Investors interpret these meetings as governance signals—if the Chair appears defensive, uncertain, or unfamiliar with market concerns, the engagement damages credibility rather than building it.

IR's role is to design the engagement architecture, ensure coherence across meetings, and capture investor feedback in a structured manner for Board consideration.

The IRO's Role in Investor-Board Meetings

The Investor Relations Officer should attend all investor-Board meetings. IR's presence serves three critical functions:

First, IR acts as guardian of consistency, ensuring that discussions align with the established investment narrative and previously disclosed information. Second, IR mitigates selective disclosure risk by maintaining situational awareness and intervening when necessary. Third, IR provides continuity—bridging individual meetings into an engament strategy rather than a series of isolated conversations.

IR is not there to script directors or to dominate the dialogue. Its authority lies in facilitation, contextualization, and discipline. When discussions approach disclosure-sensitive territory—unreported guidance revisions, merger speculation, succession timelines not yet disclosed—IR must intervene in real time: "That's an area we haven't publicly addressed yet; let me note it for formal consideration." This is not procedural caution; it is IR exercising its mandate to protect institutional credibility.

Preparing Directors for Investor Engagement

Effective investor-Board interaction begins well before the meeting. Preparation is not only about rehearsed answers, but also about shared understanding.

IR should brief participating directors on:

- Investor context: Who they are (ownership %, holding period, voting history), what they care about (governance philosophy, ESG priorities), and why they're asking now (portfolio transition, proxy concern, sector repositioning).
- Market context: Current sentiment on the company's governance (proxy advisor views, peer governance controversies, recent voting results), and emerging themes the investor is likely to raise (say-on-pay trends, climate disclosure expectations, Board refreshment pressure).
- Boundaries: Topics where public disclosure is complete and discussion is appropriate (Board committee structure, director independence criteria, governance philosophy) versus topics that are disclosure-sensitive or management's domain (specific succession candidates, deal negotiations, operational targets).

Directors need context, more than scripts. Equally important is alignment on boundaries: what can be discussed and what cannot IR's role is to ensure that directors engage with confidence while remaining anchored in disclosure discipline.

IR's Annual Board Presentation

At least once a year, IR should make a formal presentation to the Board.

The purpose of this session is to position market perception as a governance input and to surface risks the Board cannot see from financial reports alone: Where is investor confidence eroding before it shows up in the share price? Which governance practices are falling behind peer standards? What questions are investors asking that the company isn't answering well?

Boards need insight into how the company is understood, where expectations are forming, and where risks to credibility may emerge. This is very different from a catalogue of IR activities.

An effective IR Board presentation focuses on:

- Shifts in investor expectations and valuation narratives. Where is consensus forming around assumptions the company hasn't validated (growth trajectory, margin expansion, capital intensity)?
- Ownership trends and engagement quality. Which significant holders have reduced positions, and what does their stated investment thesis reveal about perception gaps?
- Emerging governance themes relevant to the company. What proxy advisor policy changes, peer controversies, or investor coalition themes will affect the company in the next 12 months?
- Forward-looking risks to trust, consistency, or market confidence. Are investor questions becoming more skeptical, meeting requests declining, or sell-side analysts shifting coverage posture?

This reinforces IR's authority to discuss risk and challenge assumptions, while supporting the Board in its oversight role.

The IR Board Report

The IR Board report should be concise, analytical, and forward-looking.

A well-designed report highlights:

- Key investor themes, recurring questions.
- Signals from proxy advisors and stewardship.
- Areas of weakness or strength, where governance, strategy, or disclosure may come under pressure, or, on the contrary, need to be emphasized.
- Indicators of credibility strength or erosion in the market.

Effective reports lead with forward-looking risk assessment, not historical activity. A clear executive summary should answer: What governance issue is most likely to surface in the next six months, and what does the Board need to consider now?

By framing investor feedback in governance-relevant terms, IR enables the Board to anticipate issues rather than react to them.

Handled with discipline, the Board-IR interface strengthens institutional credibility. Handled carelessly—access granted without criteria, directors engaging without preparation, IR excluded from conversations—it creates selective disclosure risk, message inconsistency, and governance doubt. In these moments, IR's authority derives not from hierarchy but from its singular accountability: to ensure that when the Board speaks to the market, the company's credibility is protected, not put at risk.

Corporate Governance and Internal Control

Corporate governance is a separate legal requirement that must be addressed via financial communications. It covers the following areas:

- The organization, composition, role, and operations of the board of directors;
- Special committees (such as risk, investment, ompensation, audit, nominations, strategy, ESG, digital transformation);
- Assessments of the board and committees' work.

Some companies use Investor Relations collaterals such as presentations, annual reports, to highlight the excellence of their corporate governance, notably focusing on the following:

- The high proportion and competence of independent board members;
- The existence of a code of ethics or code of conduct, notably governing the trading of company shares by directors and management;
- The transparency of the executive compensation policy;
- How shareholders are allowed to submit resolutions to the AGM, ask for representation on the board, and prevent a dilution of their holdings in the event of a hostile takeover bid.

  IROs work closely with the company's legal department in this area. They may suggest, for example, that a press release be issued to announce the appointment of an independent board member. All are jointly involved in the preparation of the AGM.

5.10 Integrated Communications: The Convergence of Investor Relations and Corporate Communications

The convergence of Investor Relations and corporate communications is a structural reality of global capital markets. What once appeared as separate disciplines—financial communication on one side, corporate and media relations on the other—now operate within a shared information environment where messages circulate instantly across audiences, channels, and geographies.

Historically, Investor Relations was largely the domain of finance professionals speaking to analysts and investors, while corporate communications addressed the media and broader stakeholders. This separation created recurring problems that compromised credibility and effectiveness: no single point of contact within the company, mixed messages issued from different areas of the organization, and an artificial distinction between shareholders and other stakeholders. In practice, these groups were never mutually exclusive. Employees are often shareholders. Customers and suppliers follow financial news. Media articles shape investor perception.

In today's environment, fragmented communication is not just inefficient. It is a source of reputational, regulatory, and valuation risk.

Integrated Communications as a Leadership Discipline

Integrated communications should not be driven by the organization chart, but by leadership mindset. At its core lies a simple principle: the company must speak with one voice.

This does not imply uniform messaging for all audiences. Different stakeholders require different levels of detail and emphasis. However, the underlying strategic narrative—how the company creates value, allocates capital, manages risk, manages human capital, and positions itself for the future—must remain consistent across all communications.

From this perspective, integrated communications operates as a system. Strategy sits at the center. The CEO orchestrates coherence. Investor Relations acts as the interface between the company and the capital markets, translating strategy into valuation-relevant language and feeding market intelligence back into decision-making. Corporate communications amplifies and contextualizes that same strategy across broader stakeholder groups. Crisis communications then becomes an accelerated expression of the same system under stress.

Alignment Across Stakeholder Groups

One of the enduring lessons of integrated communications is that there is no hierarchy of stakeholders. All are important, and all are interconnected.

A strategic decision may be welcomed by investors while creating anxiety among employees. A product innovation may excite customers while raising questions about capital allocation or execution risk. Integration does not seek to eliminate these tensions. It ensures they are addressed within a coherent framework that explains the rationale behind decisions, acknowledges impact, and preserves reputation across constituencies.

When companies fail to do this, messages become blurred at best and contradictory at worst. When they succeed, they build trust precisely because stakeholders recognize consistency of intent, even when outcomes affect them differently. This trust, sustained across stakeholder groups over time, increasingly drives corporate valuation in an environment where intangible assets—reputation, relationships, and strategic credibility—represent a significant share of enterprise value.

Integrated Communications and Consistency Challenges

Integrated communications alone is not sufficient. Consistency is mission-critical.

Seemingly non-financial announcements—press releases, speeches, sustainability statements—can carry price-sensitive implications. Without coordination, such communications risk contradicting previously disclosed information or creating unintended signals.

This is why Investor Relations must be positioned as an integral part of the overall communications discipline. IR does not "own" the message, but it plays a central role in assessing materiality, ensuring alignment with disclosed strategy and outlook, and safeguarding equal access to information.

Companies that communicate their objectives, performance, and constraints consistently across stakeholder groups are better placed to withstand periods of volatility and to and to earn stakeholder understanding when it matters most. Over time, this discipline strengthens reputation, supports valuation, and reduces the cost of capital.

Crisis as the Ultimate Proof Point

Crisis situations—whether operational, financial, governance-related, or geopolitical—represent the ultimate test of integrated communications capability.

Under stress, stakeholder boundaries collapse. Investors read employee messages. The media influence analyst interpretation. Regulatory scrutiny intensifies. In such moments, any lack of coordination is immediately exposed.

Companies that have embedded integrated communications into their day-to-day operations respond more effectively in crises. They are able to establish facts quickly, align messages across audiences, and communicate with clarity even when uncertainty remains. Those that rely on siloed communication structures often amplify confusion and erode trust at precisely the wrong moment.

Making Integration Work in Practice

There is no single organizational model for integrated communications.

Corporate Affairs and Investor Relations must operate as allies, not enemies. When treated as competing functions, communication becomes fragmented and reactive. When aligned as strategic partners, they form a powerful architecture that serves the company's interests. Supports resilience, and long-term value creation.

Cooperation opportunities between Investor Relations and corporate communications abound and recur throughout the corporate calendar, including:

- the development and governance of the disclosure policy, including disclosure committees where applicable;
- participation in strategic communications committees to align narrative, timing, and positioning;
- joint ownership of the annual report or integrated report;
- coordination of the financial calendar and disclosure milestones;
- management of newsflow, including content development, sequencing, and distribution;
- preparation and execution of the Annual General Meeting of shareholders; and
- major corporate events, such as capital markets days, restructurings, transactions, or leadership changes.

When these touchpoints are managed collaboratively, companies benefit from continuous intelligence gathering and feedback, shared resources, and full alignment across stakeholder groups. Most importantly, they become crisis-ready—prepared to respond under pressure with speed, consistency, and discipline.

Beyond risk mitigation, this partnership enables productivity, cross-fertilization of skills and perspectives. Investor Relations contributes market discipline, valuation sensitivity, and investor intelligence. Corporate Affairs brings narrative expertise, media awareness, and stakeholder context. Cost-sharing emerges naturally from this alignment—not as an end in itself, but as a consequence of eliminating duplication and reinforcing coherence.

Integrated communications enhances strategic clarity, improves decision-making, and supports long-term access to capital. By reducing information asymmetry and reinforcing consistency, it limits volatility arising from confusion caused by fragmented or heterogeneous messaging.

Companies that fail to integrate communications experience valuation discounts as investors price in "communication risk" as a proxy for execution risk. They expend resources producing high volumes of communication that confuse rather than clarify. They attract short-term investors focused on exploiting information inefficiencies.

Ultimately, integrated communications is an expression of leadership maturity. It reflects an understanding that credibility is built over time, across cycles, and across stakeholders—not through isolated disclosures, but through the disciplined alignment of words, actions, and strategy.

In that sense, integrated communications is not a function. It is a discipline—and a responsibility that sits squarely at the top of the organization.

5.11 Anticipating Change

An Investor Relations strategy is only effective if it remains credible as conditions change. Capital markets evolve continuously: disclosure expectations expand, market structures shift, and technology reshapes how information is produced, analyzed, and challenged. The task for IR is therefore not only to communicate well in the present, but to ensure that the investment case remains coherent, trusted, and intelligible as the environment evolves.

Anticipation is the discipline that enables this. It means identifying inflection points early and developing messaging content, governance dialogue, and communication discipline accordingly. Anticipatory IR works upstream. It ensures that when change becomes explicit, the company is not explaining itself for the first time.

Regulatory, structural, and technological changes rarely arrive as isolated events. They unfold gradually and tend to expose weaknesses in alignment long before they crystallize. These are the moments when silos reappear, messages drift, and credibility is lost fastest. Anticipation is therefore not an optional refinement of Investor Relations; it is a core capability and the highest expression of integration.

Regulatory Changes

Regulatory change matters to Investor Relations not only because it adds disclosure requirements, but also because it reshapes how investors interpret performance, risk, and long-term value creation. Integrated reporting, expanded sustainability disclosure, new accounting standards, and evolving definitions of materiality all change the analytical lens through which companies are assessed.

Integrated reporting is a useful stress test. It forces companies to explain how strategy, capital allocation, risk management, and non-financial factors connect into the business model to generate a single value-creation story. Where these elements have been developed separately—by function, by report, or by audience—regulation exposes fragmentation.

Anticipatory IR addresses this well before compliance becomes mandatory. It works with the Board and management to ensure that financial and non-financial content reinforce each other and that new disclosures confirm an existing logic rather than forcing a reactive rewrite.

As definitions of materiality continue to evolve, IR's role is to understand how investors incorporate non-financial information into valuation and to shape disclosure accordingly. This requires dialogue, judgment, and prioritization—not box-ticking.

Structural Changes

Structural changes—such as delisting, index inclusion or exclusion, or shifts in ownership concentration—directly affect how investors access the company and how it is valued. These are not technical transactions; they are strategic capital markets decisions with reputational consequences.

Delisting illustrates this clearly. It takes two distinct forms, each with different implications for Investor Relations.

Going private may result from an acquisition or from a deliberate decision to exit public markets. In either case, assuming that delisting ends the need for Investor Relations is a serious mistake. Even without a public listing, the company retains a reputation, a stakeholder base, and ongoing capital-market interactions—through debt issuance, private placements, banking relationships, or a potential future return to public markets.

Anticipatory IR ensures that the strategic rationale for a possible delisting is prepared well in advance. Arguments such as the need for longer-term decision-making, reduced regulatory burden, or misalignment between public-market valuation and intrinsic value should already be familiar to investors. When the decision is announced, it should read as confirmation, not shock. Importantly, governance discipline, transparency, and regular communication should not disappear post-delisting. Maintaining them preserves optionality and credibility.

Foreign delisting presents a different challenge. In today's electronic markets, a secondary listing is no longer a prerequisite for foreign investor access. Institutional investors routinely hold shares through home-market trading venues. For many companies, the costs of maintaining foreign listings for this sole objective now outweigh the benefits. (Visibility considerations may however have to be taken into account when evaluation whether to delist).

Here again, anticipation is decisive. IR must clearly establish that some form of investor access, disclosure quality, and engagement will be maintained despite the change in listing structure. A strong equity story, consistently communicated, allows a company to navigate foreign delisting without reputational damage.

Index inclusion or exclusion raises similar issues. Forced buying or selling by passive investors can create volatility unrelated to fundamentals. Anticipatory IR ensures that index mechanics do not become the dominant narrative by preparing investors for both outcomes and anchoring expectations in strategy and execution.

Technological Changes

Technology—particularly AI—has transformed Investor Relations in two fundamental ways. First, it has created genuine productivity gains for IR teams. Second, it has shifted the balance of information power decisively in favor of investors.

On the productivity side, technology can materially improve IR effectiveness when used with discipline. Advanced shareholder identification and investor targeting allow teams to focus effort where it matters most. Real-time peer benchmarking provides better insight into how competitors frame narratives and metrics. Automation reduces the cost and effort of certain recurring deliverables. Improved analytics make it easier to assess the effectiveness and return on investment of IR activities. Used well, these tools free time for higher-value work: analysis, judgment, and meaningful investor dialogue.

At the same time, technology has created a structural asymmetry. Most investors now operate with far more sophisticated data, tools, and analytical capability than Investor Relations teams. Buy-side firms analyze disclosures, earnings calls, peer data, alternative datasets, and macro indicators simultaneously. They may arrive at meetings better informed about the sector and competitive landscape than the company itself.

This reality has important consequences. The traditional idea that IR "controls the narrative" through managed information flow is no longer viable. Investors test claims instantly. Inconsistencies are flagged automatically. Vague language is compared across peers. The cost of imprecision has risen sharply.

Technology also introduces real risks. Over-automation can erode authenticity and corporate voice. Generic, AI-generated messaging flattens differentiation and weakens trust. Poorly governed use of technology across functions can fragment identity, producing inconsistent definitions and competing narratives, misinformation, data-quality issues. Security risks, including earnings release manipulation or unauthorized publication, deepfake videos or audio impersonating executives, and data breaches involving shareholders, employees, or customers, may further undermine the company's reputation and valuation.

Anticipatory IR uses technology to enhance productivity and insight, while preserving human judgment as non-negotiable. It insists on precision in claims, consistency across channels and time periods, and transparency about uncertainty. It protects corporate voice by ensuring that technology supports, rather than replaces, thoughtful communication.

In this environment, IR's role evolves. As data becomes widely available, the scarcity is no longer information, but credible interpretation. Investors do not need more numbers; they need help understanding what matters, why it matters, and how it connects to long-term value creation. IR becomes curator and interpreter, no longer the information gatekeeper. This role cannot be automated.

Regulatory, structural, and technological changes often converge.

This is where the integrated communications mindset described earlier becomes operational. When IR works closely with the Board, when strategy and communication are aligned, and when governance discipline is visible across all disclosures, the company can absorb multiple changes without losing coherence.

Anticipation transforms integration from a steady-state concept into a resilience mechanism. It ensures that disclosures confirm strategy, structural decisions reinforce long-term logic, and technological scrutiny validates rather than undermines reputation.

Effective Investor Relations is ultimately judged by how consistently it preserves credibility as conditions evolve. When financial and corporate communications are truly aligned, when strategy is coherently explained, and when the Board is an active partner in IR, change validates the investment case.

In the architecture of this book, this chapter served as the strategic synthesis chapter. It bridges the structural foundations of IR strategy with the executional focus of Chapter 6, providing the strategic logic that informs how Investor Relations is practiced, adapted, and governed across the corporate lifecycle.

Practical Implications

Execution discipline

- Build repeatability and resilience before pursuing sophistication or volume.
- Protect message consistency, decision authority, and escalation discipline under all circumstances.

IR infrastructure and continuous improvement

- Use IR infrastructure to enforce processes, preserve institutional memory, and enable learning.
- Ensure budgets, tools, and events are aligned with strategic priorities ahead of visibility objective.
- Conduct structured debriefing reviews after major events to drive continuous improvement.

Perception as intelligence

- Use perception studies and feedback-gathering mechanisms to inform strategic judgment.
- Focus on persistent perception gaps that affect valuation, access to capital, or trust.
- Use IR-Management-Board feedback loops to refine future disclosure and engagement.

6

Executing Investor Relations in Practice

Chapter 5 presented the core Investor Relations strategies—defining what IR seeks to achieve, how it creates value, and why it matters to corporate performance. Strategy defines what IR seeks to achieve and why. This chapter addresses: how Investor Relations operates under real conditions, how discipline is maintained when pressure builds, and how execution quality is sustained across market cycles.

This chapter sits deliberately between strategy and measurement. It translates the strategic principles established in Chapter 5 into repeatable operating disciplines and builds the execution infrastructure that makes the measurement frameworks in Chapter 7 possible. Without disciplined execution, strategy remains aspirational. Without credible measurement, execution cannot improve. This chapter is the bridge between the two.

Execution quality determines long-term IR effectiveness. Message consistency therefore takes precedence over speed, structural discipline over flexibility, and long-term credibility over short-term convenience.

For this reason, perception and measurement come last, not first. Before IR can assess how the market perceives the company, it must establish what the company says, how it says it, and through which mechanisms communication is delivered, governed, and refined. Perception tracking without execution discipline encourages reactivity.

Measurement without operational rigor produces noise rather than insight. Sections 6.1 through 6.5 therefore establish how Investor Relations runs—around an IPO, day to day, through structured engagement, across a disciplined operating cycle, and supported by robust infrastructure. Only then do Sects. 6.6 and 6.7 address continuous improvement and perception tracking.

A. Guimard, *Investor Relations Strategy*, https://doi.org/10.1007/978-3-032-21679-3_6

This sequencing reflects a central argument of the book: Investor Relations is a management discipline, not a communications function. Its effectiveness depends on structure, repeatability, and resilience—not on sophistication, volume of activity, or sensitivity to market mood. This chapter makes that discipline explicit and operational.

6.1 Executing Investor Relations Around an IPO

An initial public offering (IPO) is a defining moment in the life of a company. It is the point at which a private narrative becomes public, informal communication gives way to regulated disclosure, and internal assumptions are tested against external scrutiny. While banks, legal advisers, and market conditions shape the transaction itself, Investor Relations determines how the company is understood, valued, and trusted once the transaction is over.

Investor Relations around an IPO is therefore not limited to the offering process. Over time, and once valuation mechanics and transaction dynamics have faded, the quality of Investor Relations becomes the primary driver of sustained IPO success. It is IR that sets expectations, builds credibility, and ensures that strategy, performance, and risk are explained consistently to the market.

This section examines IPO execution through four distinct but connected phases. Each phase has its own objectives, risks, and execution priorities. Together, they form a blueprint for building Investor Relations as a durable management capability rather than a temporary transaction function (Fig. 6.1).

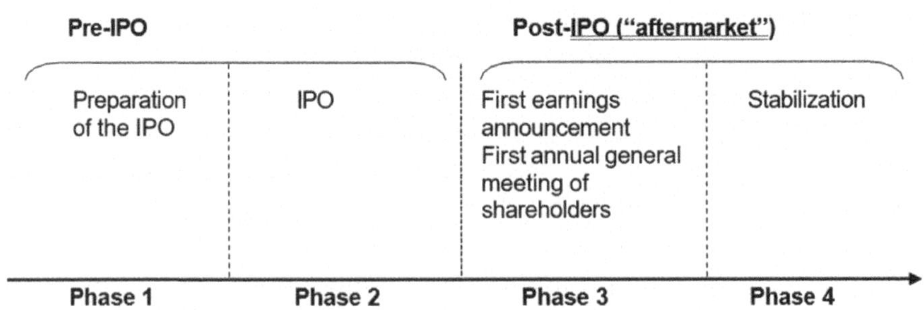

Fig. 6.1 The four phases of Investor Relations in an IPO

Phase 1—Pre-IPO: Readiness, Discipline, and Rehearsal

Investor Relations does not begin with the filing of a listing prospectus. It begins when a company starts to behave like a listed company—often 18 to 24 months before the IPO (Fig. 6.2).

The primary objective of the pre-IPO phase is to ensure internal readiness. This is where disclosure discipline is established, reporting routines are built, and management learns to operate under continuous market scrutiny. Many IPO disappointments originate here, not during pricing or trading, but in underestimating the organizational and cultural shift required to function as a public company.

From an IR perspective, this phase is about rehearsal rather than active promotion. Companies begin to:

- Structure a coherent and repeatable equity story;
- Align strategic, financial, and operational narratives;
- Define what can and cannot be communicated;
- Establish internal processes for information flow, validation, and escalation.

Management and the board must also be prepared for their new role. Executives need to understand how investors think, how analysts model the business, and how market expectations are formed and sustained. Investor Relations plays a central role in educating leadership teams, exposing them to investor questioning, and instilling message discipline well before the IPO.

Key execution priorities in this phase include:

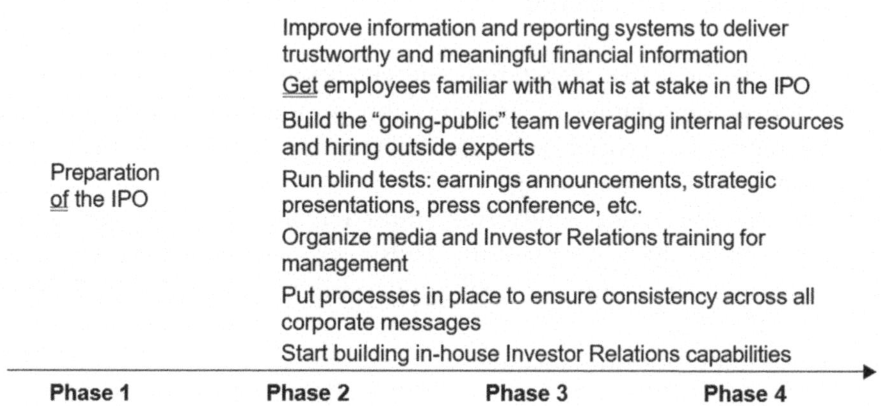

Fig. 6.2 Preparation of the IPO (Phase 1)

- Information systems readiness: Reporting processes must be capable of delivering reliable, auditable data within regulatory timelines. A practical test is whether the company would be able to meet quarterly reporting requirements and deadlines if it were already listed and, if not, what and how long it would take to become compliant.
- Governance and disclosure discipline: Internal codes of conduct, disclosure policies, and spokesperson rules should be established or updated to reflect public-company obligations.
- Market intelligence: Peer benchmarking analysis, guidance practices, reporting frequency, analyst coverage, and investor behavior should be studied early. This intelligence shapes the future equity story and helps avoid misalignment with market norms.
- Organizational preparation: A clear IR working group should be established, typically involving the CEO, CFO, finance, legal, communications, and external advisers. Roles and decision rights must be defined and tested before pressure builds.
- Early IR practice: "Dry runs" of earnings materials, presentations, and Q&A sessions allow management to test messages, identify weaknesses, and gain confidence. These rehearsals are invaluable learning tools but must be conducted with increasing regulatory discipline as the IPO approaches.

The objective of Phase 1 is therefore credibility readiness.

Phase 2—IPO Preparation and Execution: Message and Interaction Discipline

Phase 2 covers the active preparation and execution of the IPO. This phase is characterized by compressed timelines, intense scrutiny, and strict regulatory constraints. The central execution challenge is discipline—in messaging, interaction, and ambition setting.

During this phase, the equity story must remain fully consistent across the prospectus, analyst presentations, roadshows, and management interactions. Any divergence, however small, undermines confidence and damages credibility (Fig. 6.3).

Core execution priorities include:

- Equity story articulation: Working with advisers such as investment banks, IR and PR firms, legal counsel, management learns to articulate a clear, credible investment case that explains strategy, differentiation,

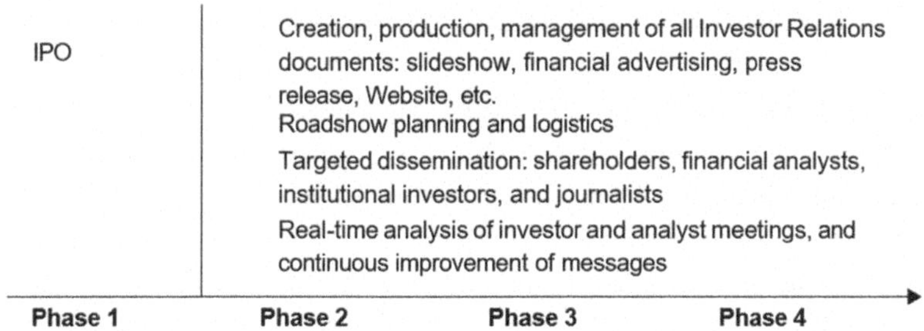

Fig. 6.3 The IPO (Phase 2)

growth drivers, and risks. Conflicting incentives inevitably arise during this process. Investor Relations plays a critical role in protecting coherence and long-term credibility, rather than optimizing short-term enthusiasm.
- Guidance and ambition setting: Decisions about outlook, targets, and strategic objectives made at IPO often anchor the initial shareholder base and market expectations for years. Investor Relations will ensure that ambition is balanced with deliverability, and that commitments made during the transaction can be sustained once the company is public, assuming underlying conditions remain unchanged.
- Tool and material consistency: Presentations, press releases, website content, and roadshow materials must form a coherent whole. Some tools are mandatory; others are discretionary. Selection should prioritize consistency, clarity, and regulatory compliance over volume.
- Roadshows and investor meetings: These interactions are more than sales exercises. They are structured learning opportunities. Questions asked, concerns raised, and points of confusion provide critical input for post-IPO strategy. Systematic capture of feedback is essential.
- Interaction discipline: Demand signals during roadshows can be seductive. Experienced IR teams resist the temptation to adjust messaging opportunistically. Their role is to protect long-term credibility, not to optimize short-term demand.

Throughout this phase, the IR team must be organized to handle increased workload, ensure equal access to information, and maintain rigorous documentation. By the time trading begins, IR should already have:

- A clear picture of the initial shareholder base;
- A structured investor and analyst contact database;
- An initial understanding of analyst consensus and key assumptions;
- A record of recurring questions and themes emerging from meetings.

Phase 3—Immediate Post-IPO Stabilization

Phase 3 begins on the first day of trading. At this point, the company is listed and effectively "on its own", given that investment banks and legal advisers have left. This phase is often underestimated, yet it is where credibility is either reinforced or eroded.

Once trading starts, analyst coverage initiates, consensus forms, and market expectations crystallize. Investor Relations will have to shift rapidly from transaction-driven execution to aftermarket management (Fig. 6.4).

Execution priorities in this phase include:

- Monitoring how the equity story is interpreted in practice;
- Identifying early misunderstandings or unrealistic assumptions;
- Managing the transition from prospectus language to regular reporting;
- Maintaining disclosure discipline under heightened scrutiny.

The first results announcement as a listed company is particularly sensitive. Any disconnect between IPO messaging and early performance is magnified. Investor Relations must ensure continuity of explanation, even when performance deviates from initial expectations.

By the end of this phase, the company should have:

- A reliable shareholder base analysis by category and geography;
- A functioning investor and analyst database;

Fig. 6.4 Beginning of the aftermarket (Phase 3)

- An initial sell-side consensus and understanding of its drivers;
- A structured Q&A repository reflecting real market concerns.

The objective of Phase 3 is stabilization.

Phase 4—Transition to Life as a Listed Company

Phase 4 typically begins 18 to 24 months after the IPO. Companies that succeed treat the IPO as the foundation of their Investor Relations identity (Fig. 6.5).

By this stage, the company has settled into regular reporting, held its first AGMs, and experienced changes in share price, ownership, and analyst coverage. Lock-up expiries and shareholder turnover may have altered the free float. Visibility may fade as IPO attention dissipates.

The execution challenge now is to institutionalize discipline. Practices tolerated during the IPO—exceptional disclosure effort, intensive management availability, heavy adviser support—will gradually evolve into a steady-state operating model without creating a perception of reduced transparency.

Key priorities include:

- Establishing a reliable annual financial calendar;
- Reinforcing consistent messaging across reporting cycles;
- Defining long-term engagement priorities;
- Embedding IR as a permanent management function rather than a transaction tool.

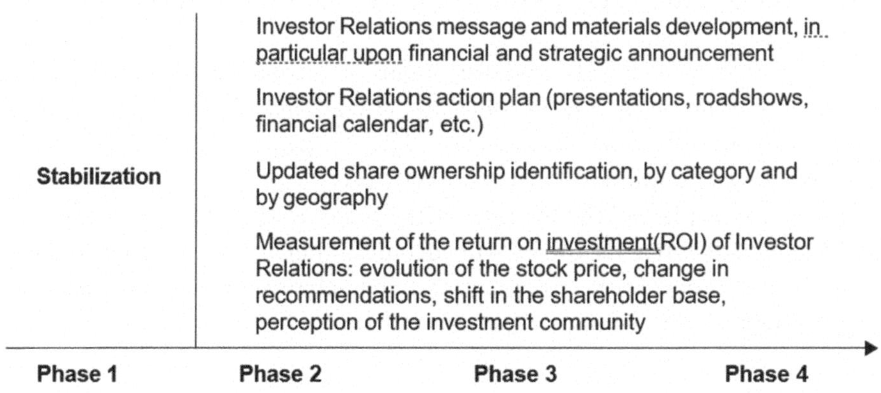

Fig. 6.5 Stabilization (Phase 4)

This phase is where many companies struggle. A perceived drop in transparency after listing is one of the most common early credibility failures. Investor Relations must actively manage this transition, ensuring continuity without excess.

The four phases of Investor Relations around an IPO illustrate more than a transaction process. They show how execution discipline is built, tested, and institutionalized. Behaviors established before, during, and immediately after an IPO often persist for years.

This is why IPO Investor Relations deserves to be treated as foundational rather than exceptional. It is where discipline is learned, credibility is earned, and long-term relationships with capital markets begin.

Executing Investor Relations Around an IPO—Practical Implications

- Treat Investor Relations as a **multi-year management capability**, not a transaction workstream
- Begin behaving like a listed company well before the IPO; disclosure discipline and reporting routines cannot be improvised under pressure
- Protect message consistency relentlessly across the prospectus, roadshows, presentations, and management interactions
- Use IPO roadshows and investor meetings as **learning mechanisms**, not sales exercises
- Anchor guidance and ambition setting in long-term deliverability; commitments made at IPO define credibility for years
- Prepare explicitly for the transition from transaction-driven IR to steady-state IR to avoid a perceived drop in transparency after listing

6.2 How Investor Relations Is Run Day to Day

Once a company is listed, Investor Relations stops being a project and becomes a permanent operating function. The quality of execution no longer depends on one-off effort, but on how IR is organized, how decisions are made, and how discipline is enforced over time.

This section explains how Investor Relations is actually run in steady state. It makes explicit what IR owns, who decides what, how coordination with internal stakeholders works in practice, what changes under pressure, and how experienced teams prevent execution drift.

What Investor Relations Owns

Investor Relations owns market expectations.

Not valuation.
Not performance.
Not the share price.

IR is accountable for how the company is understood, interpreted, and assessed by capital markets over time. That responsibility translates into very concrete ownership.

Investor Relations owns:

- the consistency of the equity story across time and channels,
- the sequencing of information to the market,
- the framing of results, outlook, and strategic developments,
- the interface with investors and analysts, and less frequently, with the media,
- the discipline of what is said, when, and by whom.

Investor Relations does not own:

- business performance,
- strategic decisions,
- capital allocation outcomes, or
- market reactions.

In practice, execution breaks when IR is treated as a delivery channel rather than an owner. When IR is asked to "just communicate" decisions it did not help frame or sequence, credibility suffers. IR must therefore have authority over *how* information reaches the market, even when it does not control *what* management decides.

When priorities clash, message consistency wins over speed. When internal pressure builds, market credibility wins over internal convenience.

The IR Decision Model

A functional IR operating model makes decision rights explicit **before** pressure hits.

At a minimum, the following must be clear:

- Who decides the message
  Investor Relations decides how strategy, performance, and outlook are explained to the market, within the boundaries set by management decisions and disclosure rules.
- Who decides timing and sequencing
  Investor Relations decides when and in what order information is released, unless regulatory obligations dictate otherwise.
- Who speaks externally
  IR controls access and spokesperson roles. Management participation is planned, not improvised.
- Who escalates—and when
  IR escalates when information may be market-sensitive, inconsistent, or legally complex. Escalation thresholds must be predefined.

When there is disagreement, the rule is simple:

IR arbitrates execution; management arbitrates substance.
Execution failures almost always stem from blurred authority. If no one knows who decides under time pressure, the loudest voice wins—and consistency is lost.

IR and Internal Coordination

Internal alignment does not happen through goodwill alone; it happens through routine.

In steady state, Investor Relations works in a predictable rhythm with finance, legal, and communications:

- Before results
  IR drives preparation timelines, message alignment, and Q&A development. Inputs are collected early. Late changes are the exception, not the rule.
- During disclosure windows
  IR controls external communication flow. Parallel messaging is avoided. Key internal stakeholders know what has been said and what has not.
- After-market interactions
  IR captures feedback, filters noise, and reports insights internally. Not every comment is escalated. Patterns matter more than anecdotes.

Coordination fails when it is informal. Informality works when teams are small and calm. It collapses under pressure. A good operating model formalizes routines just enough to ensure predictability without creating bureaucracy.

Handling Pressure

Pressure is not the exception in Investor Relations. It is the norm.

Under earnings pressure, market volatility, activist approaches, or unexpected events, some things must adapt, while others must remain unchanged.

What changes:

- response speed,
- internal availability,
- frequency of interaction,
- intensity of monitoring.

What must not change:

- message coherence,
- disclosure discipline,
- decision authority,
- escalation rules.

Under stress, discipline beats creativity.

IR execution must become tighter.

IR execution rarely collapses overnight. It erodes gradually.

Warning signs include:

- growing inconsistency in explanations,
- expanding agendas without reprioritization,
- increasing reliance on individuals rather than structure,
- reactive changes driven by single investor comments.

Experienced IROs:

- revisit decision rights regularly,
- reset priorities after major events,
- reinforce routines after periods of stress, and
- resist incremental scope creep.

The rule is simple: *what is not actively maintained deteriorates.*

An IR operating model only works if it is treated as a living system, not a one-time design.

Practical Implications for Running Investor Relations Day to Day

- Be explicit about what IR owns—and stop accepting accountability for outcomes it cannot control.
- Define decision rights and escalation rules before you need them.
- Make coordination routine, not personality-driven.
- Under pressure, tighten discipline instead of improvising.
- Actively prevent execution slippage; it will not correct itself.

6.3 Building and Running the Investor Engagement Program

Investor engagement is one of the most visible parts of Investor Relations—and one of the most frequently mismanaged. Too often, it is treated as a succession of meetings rather than as a structured program with clear objectives, priorities, and discipline.

In practice, investor engagement is how Investor Relations organizes and manages ongoing interaction between the company and the investment community. It is through this interaction that understanding is built, expectations are managed, and the composition of the shareholder base evolves over time.

This section focuses on how to run investor engagement in practice, following a deliberate progression: how to define target shareholders, how to prioritize access, how to structure engagement over time, and how to allocate management attention where it matters most. It assumes familiarity with the strategic rationale discussed earlier in the book and concentrates exclusively on execution.

The Seed, Harvest and Lock approach, introduced in the second edition of this book, remains the most practical way to organize investor engagement. In this chapter, it is used as an operating logic for planning, prioritizing, and managing investor interactions day to day.

Defining the Target Shareholder Base

Companies cannot please every investor—but they alone determine whether investors like them.

Rather than passively enduring an ineffective or hostile free-float structure, Investor Relations should treat shareholder composition as a deliberate strategic outcome. Just as companies define their target customers, they can—and should—define their target shareholders.

There is no one-size-fits-all model. An "ideal" shareholder base depends on the company's size, liquidity, growth profile, capital needs, ownership history, and geographic footprint. The objective is not perfection, but intentionality: building a free float of investors who stay with the company through good periods and difficult ones, because they trust it.

It is equally important to be explicit about which shareholders the company does not want to attract—either because of disproportionate maintenance costs, misaligned time horizons, or investment behaviors that conflict with the company's long-term interests.

An optimally diversified shareholder base brings tangible benefits: greater price stability, better liquidity through cycles, and strategic flexibility when capital needs arise. One of the simplest rules of effective Investor Relations is to maintain a standing pool of potential buyers who can absorb stock when existing shareholders reduce positions.

There are limits to this ambition. The notion of a permanently loyal, long-term shareholder base is often more aspiration than reality. Markets evolve, mandates change, and capital reallocates. Investor Relations does not eliminate turnover but manages it intelligently.

This definition becomes the practical filter for investor targeting, access decisions, and management time allocation.

Intelligent Investor Targeting

Moving beyond a static list of existing shareholders requires a structured targeting process. This work is not optional, regardless of the actual size of the free float. It is the foundation on which all meaningful investor engagement rests (Table 6.1).

Investor Relations must identify:

- Who does not own the stock today (but owns that of your competitors, for instance);
- Why they do not (for instance because of limited liquidity);

Table 6.1 Investor landscape and ownership mapping framework

Key dimensions to map
• **Investor type**
• Active, passive, sovereign, retail, credit, private capital
• **Investment horizon**
• Long-term holders versus high-turnover capital
• **Economic exposure vs voting power**
• Influence on governance relative to ownership size
• **ESG and governance sensitivity**
• Drivers of voting and engagement behavior
• **Geographic concentration**
• Jurisdictional expectations and regulatory context
• **Proxy advisor alignment risk**
• Likelihood of ISS/Glass Lewis influence

- Under what conditions that could change (the "catalysts").

Targeting should never be outsourced blindly. Roadshow schedules and conference lists proposed by banks or other intermediaries must be challenged. Every meeting should be justified from the company's perspective, not the intermediary's.

Traditional investor segmentation remains useful, but insufficient on its own. More discriminating criteria include holding period, portfolio concentration, turnover, decision-making complexity, investment style, and proxy voting policies.

These criteria determine whether a meeting justifies CEO time.

Targeting in a Market Dominated by Passive Investors

Investor targeting today takes place in a market where a growing share of the free float is held by algorithms, passive and index-tracking investors. These investors do not buy or sell based on company-specific engagement, valuation views, or narrative alignment. Their ownership is driven by index inclusion, weighting methodologies, and flows beyond the company's control.

This has two practical consequences for Investor Relations.

First, passive investors are not a targeting audience in the traditional sense. No amount of engagement will cause them to initiate or exit a position outside index mechanics. Targeting efforts aimed at passive investors for ownership outcomes are therefore misplaced.

Second, passive investors still matter enormously. They influence liquidity, voting outcomes, and the stability of the shareholder base. If at all, engagement with passive managers should focus on stewardship priorities, governance, and long-term positioning—not on ownership expectations. Many of the largest firms associated with passive investing also manage actively managed funds alongside their index products. Examples include BlackRock, Vanguard, and State Street Global Advisors. This distinction is important in Investor Relations because ownership classified as "passive" at the firm level may still include actively managed portfolios within the same institution. Consequently, targeting assumptions based solely on the asset manager's overall reputation as a passive investor can be misleading.

Investor Relations is therefore going to separate:

- targeting for ownership change, and
- engagement for stability and governance alignment.

Confusing the two leads to wasted effort and disappointments.

Targeting in the Age of Data and Artificial Intelligence

Advances in data analytics and artificial intelligence have significantly changed how investor targeting is conducted. Modern tools can analyze holdings, trading patterns, mandate constraints, and historical behavior to identify investors with a higher statistical likelihood of buying, selling, or reallocating within specific timeframes.

Used well, these tools improve prioritization and efficiency. They help Investor Relations focus management time where it has the highest probability of impact and avoid unfocused outreach.

Algorithms, however, cannot overcome structural constraints such as insufficient liquidity, index exclusion, or mandate misalignment. They also cannot replace judgment about investor quality, time horizon, or strategic fit.

The role of Investor Relations is therefore to use AI and data as decision support.

The "Seed, Harvest and Lock" Approach to Investor Relations

Once the targeting exercise is complete, the IRO initiates the "seeding" phase. This is a proactive process in which the IRO contacts analysts and investors identified as potential shareholders to introduce the company's products, business model, historical financial and operational track record, strategy, and growth prospects. At this stage, the objective is not to secure immediate investment, but to establish relevance, credibility, and interest.

If the institution shows genuine intent to consider building a position, the process moves to the "harvest" phase. Here, the objective shifts from awareness to investment decision-making. Depending on the investor's focus, the CFO may need to be involved to address detailed financial questions, modeling assumptions, capital allocation priorities, or operational execution. This phase is about providing the depth and confidence required for a fund manager to initiate a position.

The "lock" phase focuses on strengthening and anchoring ownership. A meeting with the CEO is usually required by the investor's fiduciary mandate to convert an initial position into a larger or longer-term holding. At this stage, the emphasis is on strategic direction, leadership trustworthiness, and long-term value creation. The IRO should facilitate sustained relationships between the CEO—and where appropriate, the chairman—and chief investment officers at major institutions whose support matters through cycles.

This progression underscores why disciplined selection criteria during the targeting process are essential. The "seed-harvest-lock" approach is not only about investor conversion; it is also a mechanism for optimizing senior management time. As a rule, management involvement in Investor Relations should not exceed 20 to 25% of their time, although this allocation may vary depending on circumstances.

One principle, however, admits no exception: the CEO should never meet an investor or analyst whom the IRO has not met first. The allocation of senior management time is itself a core IR execution tool. The principle remains clear:

- the IRO is the primary point of contact for new investors and analysts;
- the CFO engages with financially focused institutions and detailed modeling discussions;
- the CEO meets with high-impact shareholders and strategic holders whose long-term support is critical.

Hedge Funds, Activists, and the Limits of Targeting

Hedge funds and activist investors sit at the boundary of traditional targeting logic. They should neither be categorically avoided nor naïvely embraced.

Management time is scarce. The IRO has full legitimacy to determine who meets whom, and under what conditions. Dialogue must be reciprocal.

As a rule, debates with activists are best conducted privately. Public escalation consumes time, polarizes positions, and reduces strategic flexibility.

Building and Running the Investor Engagement Program—Practical Implications

- Treat investor engagement as a structured program, not a series of meetings
- Define a target shareholder base deliberately
- Maintain a live, prioritized targeting list that guides management access decisions and management time allocation
- Distinguish clearly between targeting for ownership change and engagement for stability and governance
- Allocate CEO, CFO time as carefully as you would allocate capital

6.4 The Investor Relations Operating Cycle

An operating schedule gives Investor Relations control over time. Without an explicit schedule, IR becomes reactive, management time is consumed inefficiently, and market expectations go unmonitored until valuation damage has already occurred.

A professional Investor Relations function operates simultaneously across three schedules: annual, quarterly and/or half-yearly, and continuous. Each serves a distinct purpose.

The Annual Schedule

The annual schedule, or annual IR calendar, is the backbone of Investor Relations execution. It is one of the few moments in the year when the function can step back and reassess whether the shareholder base, engagement priorities, and messaging architecture remain fit for purpose.

At least once a year, Investor Relations should conduct a structured review of the shareholder base. It is an indispensable analytical exercise that examines who owns the stock, why they own it, how stable those positions are, how they have evolved over time, and which parts of the free float may be at risk.

Changes in ownership concentration, geographic balance, investor type, turnover, and voting behavior should be analyzed in relation to liquidity, valuation sensitivity, and governance outcomes.

The conclusions of this review must feed directly into an annual IR plan. As Chapter 7 will show, they also form a set of key reference points against which the return on investment in Investor Relations can be assessed. This plan is fundamentally different from a communications calendar. It is an execution document that sets priorities, timelines, and constraints. It defines which investor segments matter most in the coming year, where management time should be concentrated, which forms of engagement add more or less incremental value the level of budget required.

Within this framework, several moments anchor the year: full-year and half-year or quarterly results, the Annual General Meeting, and the engagement periods immediately before results announcements (until the quiet period begins) and immediately thereafter, through analyst meetings, roadshows, one-on-one meetings, and other forms of direct interaction with the investment community.

Results announcements are the primary moments when market expectations are recalibrated. Preparation discipline is therefore non-negotiable. Investor Relations must own narrative development and lock its content well ahead of the announcement, ensure internal alignment on tone and emphasis, and rehearse management responses to the questions that will inevitably arise. This preparation extends beyond scripts to include agreement on language, framing, sensitivities, boundaries, and role-play between the CEO, CFO, and other executives where relevant. Some companies have adopted a 'pre-close call' practice whereby management or the IRO updates the market on recent trading trends before the quiet period begins. The practice remains debated, however, as some market participants view it as a useful expectations-management tool while others question its consistency with disclosure discipline and equal access principles.

Following results, engagement is when investor attention is highest and feedback is most informative. Meetings should prioritize existing shareholders and high-priority targets identified in the annual IR strategy. Post-results roadshows may, however, prove inefficient when dozens of companies report simultaneously and compete for the attention of the same investors. As a result, CEOs and CFOs may end up meeting with junior analysts or portfolio managers whose priorities have been allocated elsewhere. Since the results are already public by that stage, it may be more advisable and effective to schedule roadshows later in the year and focus discussions on strategy, capital allocation, and longer-term positioning, unless specific circumstances require immediate post-results engagement.

The Annual General Meeting requires equal discipline. It should be treated as a governance and credibility checkpoint, not as a procedural obligation. It is also, albeit indirectly, a corporate communications event and should be managed as such, given that retail shareholders may be in attendance—a rarity for earnings webcasts. The AGM is one of the moments where integrated communications works best.

Voting dynamics, sensitive resolutions, and likely shareholder concerns must be anticipated well in advance. Ideally, they will already have been discussed during a governance roadshow. AGM messaging must be fully consistent with prior disclosures, with particular care taken to ensure clarity and readability, avoiding legalistic language wherever possible.

The Quarterly Schedule

The quarterly or half-yearly discipline is when market expectations are formed, reinforced, or corrected. If analysts' earnings estimates—the "consensus"—drift away from the company's underlying reality, the consequences are predictable: volatility around results, erosion of credibility, and persistent valuation gaps. In some jurisdictions, tracking earnings estimates is also a regulatory requirement.

Managing consensus is therefore not a tactical exercise; it is a core Investor Relations responsibility. Because it is, it reinforces the necessity for IR to have full access to budgets, forecasts, and internal reporting. The objective is to ensure that the market's working model of the company—the assumptions embedded in analyst forecasts and investor expectations—remains aligned with what the company has disclosed and can credibly deliver.

After each reporting cycle, Investor Relations should run a structured consensus-management review. The first step is diagnosis. This involves analyzing not only headline consensus figures, but the assumptions underneath them: revenue drivers, margin drivers, capital intensity, cash generation, and the way the market interprets management's priorities and constraints. Shifts in analyst language and dispersion of recommendations, target prices, and estimates often matter more than changes in the midpoint.

Consensus monitoring should extend beyond the current year. Each results announcement provides an opportunity to help the market adjust its longer-term forecasts without immediately triggering revisions to target prices or investment recommendations that could trigger sharp share-price reactions.

The second step is structured feedback capture. Investor Relations aggregates questions and concerns raised across earnings calls, post-results meetings, follow-up conversations, and written research. Repeated questions, recurring misunderstandings, and systematic differences in interpretation are signals. These signals indicate where consensus is fragile or wrong and therefore requires timely correction.

The third step is internal alignment. Investor Relations translates these signals into a concise internal brief that makes the situation explicit: where consensus is aligned, where it is drifting, and which assumptions are driving divergence. Management should not receive raw commentary such as the latest analyst reports attached to an email without appropriate contextualisation; it should receive a clear diagnosis and a proposed course of remedial action.

The fourth step is corrective action, executed strictly within disclosure discipline. When market assumptions are wrong, Investor Relations corrects them through clearer disclosure, tighter language, consistent repetition of priorities, and, where appropriate, explicit clarification of constraints and sensitivities. This must be done within the regulatory boundaries governing price-sensitive information. Corrective action may take place through results materials, follow-up Q&A, targeted investor conversations, or dedicated events, depending on the scale of the gap.

This process requires sound judgement, communication and persuasion skills. At the same time, because it is conducted through dialogue, it is also a powerful way to gather market intelligence and inform strategic decision-making.

The objective is to ensure that the market is modeling the company accurately. Two boundaries remain absolute: Investor Relations never uses inside information to correct consensus, and it never encourages assumptions the company cannot sustain. Analysts remain responsible for the quality and defensibility of their own forecasts.

Continuous Information Dissemination

Beyond formal reporting cycles, Investor Relations operates continuously. This does not imply constant communication; it implies constant awareness.

The purpose of continuous monitoring—and listening—is operational control. It enables IR to detect early signals of misunderstanding, misinformation, or execution risk and to decide—calmly and consistently—whether intervention is warranted.

Investor Relations should therefore maintain ongoing visibility on:

- share-price movements relative to peers and key indices;
- abnormal trading volumes;
- changes in analyst recommendations and estimates;
- media coverage and informal market narratives such as "finfluencers".

Where ownership data is available, changes in holdings should be monitored to identify emerging patterns rather than isolated transactions. It is both acceptable and often advisable for an Investor Relations Officer to contact an investor who has sold a significant position, in order to understand the reasons for the sale, and identify which catalysts might support re-entry. The objective is insight, not persuasion.

Escalation must remain disciplined and selective. It should be reserved for clearly defined situations:

- when incorrect or misleading information is circulating;
- when market interpretation diverges materially from disclosed facts;
- when trust is at risk.

These escalation thresholds must be explicit internally and applied consistently, so that decisions are not driven by emotion, market noise, or short-term pressure.

It is important to distinguish continuous monitoring from formal perception intelligence. The former supports day-to-day execution discipline and early warning. The latter, formal perception studies, addressed in Sect. 6.7, serve a different purpose. They are structured, periodic diagnostic tools used to assess how the company is understood over time, typically ahead of a Capital Markets Day, or in connection with strategic change, leadership transition, or major capital markets decisions.

Perception studies should be deployed deliberately—only when internal signals are ambiguous or conflicting, or when management requires structured, independent insight into market understanding.

Continuous monitoring provides awareness and judgment; formal perception analysis, discussed later, provides depth and context. Confusing the two undermines both.

Internal Cohesion Around the Operating Cycle

The effectiveness of the Investor Relations operating cycle depends on internal alignment. Without it, even the best-designed structure collapses under pressure.

Management must clearly understand when IR intensity peaks, which periods require concentrated availability, and when engagement is deliberately constrained. The board should be briefed regularly on how market feedback is collected, how it is filtered, how consensus is assessed, and under what conditions escalation occurs. This transparency builds confidence in the IR function and ensures that directors receive actionable insight.

Practical Implications

- Treat the annual IR calendar as a strategic resource, with explicit discipline around when Investor Relations plans, engages, and monitors.
- Plan Investor Relations activity annually, using a structured shareholder-base review and a clear IR execution plan to set priorities and constraints.
- Manage market consensus deliberately on a quarterly or half-yearly basis, focusing on the assumptions underpinning expectations rather than headline numbers.
- Concentrate investor engagement where it has the greatest impact, rather than dispersing effort evenly throughout the year.
- Correct incorrect or drifting market assumptions through disciplined, compliant disclosure, not informal negotiation.
- Escalate selectively, and resist pressure to react to day-to-day market fluctuations.
- Use quarterly feedback to identify recurring patterns and emerging expectation gaps.
- Rely on continuous monitoring to inform judgment and early warning.
- Commission perception studies strategically, with a clear intention to act on the findings.

6.5 IR Infrastructure: Tools, Events, and Budgets

Without supporting infrastructure, IR strategic priorities remain aspirational, consistency deteriorates under pressure, and execution drifts toward reactive engagement. Infrastructure, led by strong IR leadership, makes priorities real, enforces consistency over time, and prevents that drift.

Investor Relations infrastructure is therefore more than the sum of its systems, processes, and responsibilities. It should be understood as the set of resources, mechanisms, and constraints through which execution discipline is operationalized. It encompasses four inseparable dimensions—talents, tools, events, and budget management—through which disclosure is delivered with consistency, engagement is structured with discipline, and market confidence is built over time.

The most robust IR infrastructures are those that continue to function optimally when budgets are reduced, management attention is constrained, and scrutiny is highest. They also enable systematic learning, making it possible to measure what matters and refine execution over time.

Within this framework, three categories of infrastructure matter most. Budget management anchors priorities in reality. Events, including investor days, roadshows, and recurring engagement moments, create the controlled, scheduled settings in which disclosure discipline, targeting, and consensus management are tested in public. Core publications and technology enable repetition, consistency, and institutional memory, reducing dependence on individual relationships or improvisation. Continuous training and up-skilling ensure that Investor Relations capabilities evolve alongside market expectations, regulatory requirements, disclosure practices, and technological change.

This section focuses on how to resource and operationalize the execution disciplines established earlier in the chapter. It addresses practical choices: how to allocate limited budgets, how to design events that deliver execution, visibility and enhanced valuation, and how to build infrastructure that continues to function when conditions deteriorate. The objective is not to accumulate tools, but to ensure that Investor Relations remains credible, coherent, and effective across cycles.

Investor Relations Budgets

Budget discipline underpins all other disciplines.

IR budgets are typically treated as cost centers—departments that do not directly generate revenues. Yet this framing obscures their actual contribution: an efficient Investor Relations strategy can measurably reduce a company's cost of capital, improve valuation multiples, and enable access to capital on favorable terms. The question is whether resources are allocated to activities that genuinely support those outcomes.

IR teams face a permanent tension: containing costs while delivering increasing value to shareholders, management, and the board. The answer is to align every budget decision with strategic priorities established in Chapter 5 and execution disciplines defined in earlier sections.

IR Budget Design

An effective IR budget must be explicitly linked to:

- The company's strategic objectives and capital allocation priorities;
- Its capital markets profile (listing status, sector, geography, complexity);
- Its current and target shareholder structure;
- Upcoming milestones (earnings cadence, transactions, leadership changes, strategy updates, regulatory filings).

Budgeting should therefore not be incremental—"last year's budget plus or minus a few percent." At key inflection points (IPO, major acquisition, strategic repositioning, leadership transition), it should be zero-based, forcing explicit choices about which activities truly matter and which can be deferred or eliminated.

This approach mirrors the resource allocation discipline required when building IR infrastructure from scratch, as private companies must do when preparing for public markets. Even established public companies benefit from periodically asking: *If we were designing this IR function today, what would we spend money on, and why?*

IR Minimum Budget Prerequisites

IR budgets vary widely by company size, market capitalization, and sector, but they typically include:

- Disclosure and distribution infrastructure: Regulatory filings, earnings materials production, newswire services, translation (where required);
- IR website and webcasting: Hosting, design, live event streaming, replay archiving;
- Ownership intelligence and targeting tools: Shareholder identification services, CRM platforms, targeting databases, position tracking;
- Events: Non-deal roadshows, investor conferences, analyst and investor days, AGMs, and other shareholder meetings;
- IR staff, external advisers and consultants: IR counsel, perception studies, transaction support, specialist expertise (ESG, governance, restructuring).

IR leaders should think in terms of progressively increasing budget needs as Investor Relations move from foundational tools to strategic integration.

IR Budget Priorities

Economic downturns, leadership changes, and corporate restructurings inevitably put pressure on IR budgets. When constraints tighten, priorities must be clear:

- Disclosure reliability and regulatory compliance are non-negotiable. Any savings that compromise timely, accurate, or legally compliant disclosure create existential risk.
- Tools and processes that optimize management time come next. Ownership monitoring, investor targeting, interaction tracking, and preparation infrastructure enable the CFO and CEO to engage effectively without wasting time on low-priority meetings or repetitive questions.
- Visibility-enhancing initiatives are discretionary. Activities that increase awareness or expand reach—additional conferences, broader roadshow

coverage, supplementary webcasts—may be scaled back or postponed or replaced by lower-cost alternatives when resources are constrained, provided core engagement with priority shareholders and analysts continues.

This hierarchy reflects the principle established throughout this chapter: execution quality depends on discipline, repeatability, and cost effectiveness—not on sophistication or volume of activity.

Maintaining IR Quality on a Reduced Budget

Maintaining IR quality on a reduced budget requires identifying genuine efficiency opportunities rather than making across-the-board cuts:

- Recycle content systematically across channels. The same strategic narrative, financial updates, and operational milestones should flow through earnings materials, presentations, website updates, and one-on-one meeting preparation—reducing duplication of effort, and inconsistency risks.
- Favor digital formats over travel where appropriate. Virtual roadshows, webcasts, and video meetings eliminate travel costs and expand geographic reach. Not all engagement requires physical presence; reserve in-person meetings for high-priority shareholders and complex discussions.
- Consolidate events. Rather than holding multiple small investor meetings throughout the year, consider a single well-executed investor day that serves both existing and prospective shareholders.
- Leverage technology to replace manual processes. Automated tracking of interactions, template-based preparation materials, and structured CRM workflows reduce administrative burden and improve consistency.
- Eliminate low-impact activities. Rigorously evaluate which conferences, meetings, and publications genuinely advance strategic objectives. If an activity cannot be linked to improved understanding, analyst coverage, or shareholder alignment, it should be reassessed.

Taking AI and Automation into IR Budget Considerations

Artificial intelligence and automation increasingly support IR productivity through:

- Shareholder targeting and monitoring,
- Earnings call transcription and sentiment analysis,
- Content management and distribution,
- Interaction tracking and follow-up workflows.

But technology must be deployed pragmatically. AI should reduce workload and improve consistency, not create new layers of complexity, dependence, or compliance risks. Unless developed internally within secure environments, AI tools are generally not appropriate for handling material, confidential, or inside information. Any AI-generated content used in investor communications should therefore be reviewed by experienced Investor Relations professionals before dissemination.

The test is simple: Does this technology make the IR function more efficient, or does it introduce new points of failure? Does it enable better judgment, or does it replace judgment with automation?

Measuring IR Budget Effectiveness

Budget discipline is reinforced by measurement. IR teams should track outcomes that connect spending decisions to strategic impact:

- Engagement quality: Are interactions with priority shareholders becoming deeper, more strategic, and better informed? Are they resulting in larger positions?
- Analyst coverage evolution: Are you expanding coverage in target markets or among sector specialists?
- Shareholder composition changes: Is your investor base evolving toward your target structure?
- Consensus alignment: Are analysts' models and expectations converging with management's view of the business?
- Event outcomes: Are investor days, roadshows, and earnings calls reducing perception gaps?

The objective is not about proving short-term causality between specific budget items and share-price movements. It is to demonstrate long-term contribution to valuation credibility, market access, and cost of capital—the core outcomes that justify IR as a strategic function.

As discussed further in Chapter 7, IR measurement should focus on whether the function is fulfilling its strategic mandate: building long-term, trust-based relationships with the investment community, supporting the company's access to capital, and protecting credibility across market cycles.

Treating IR as an Investment, Not a Cost Center

When budget decisions are explicitly linked to strategic priorities, shareholder targeting, calendar and other execution frameworks established earlier in this chapter, IR stops being a cost center and becomes a strategic enabler: reducing cost of capital, improving valuation, expanding market access, and protecting credibility when conditions deteriorate.

The most effective IR budgets are those designed to continue functioning—delivering disclosure reliability, protecting management time, and maintaining key relationships—even when resources are reduced. That resilience is not achieved through sophisticated tools or expensive events.

Investor Relations Events

Events are where Investor Relations strategy meets the market in real time. They concentrate disclosure, management exposure and engagement, targeting, and consensus management into defined moments that test execution publicly. For that reason, events are among the most powerful—and most risky—tools available to IR teams.

Investor days and roadshows are scheduled enforcement points for execution disciplines defined earlier in this chapter: narrative consistency (preventing message drift), management alignment (preventing internal lag), targeting (operationalizing shareholder segmentation), and expectation setting (supporting consensus management). When poorly designed, they waste management time and amplify volatility.

A professional IR program deploys different event formats, each serving a specific execution purpose. One-to-one meetings with priority investors and prospects support targeting objectives. Non-deal roadshows reinforce message consistency across geographies and investor segments. Analyst and investor days deepen understanding and correct perception gaps at scale. Conferences expand visibility within target investor segments without consuming disproportionate management time. Public shareholder meetings, including AGMs, fulfill statutory obligations while showcasing corporate governance, reinforcing strategic direction and engaging retail investors, in particular. Earnings calls and webcasts synchronize disclosure with market dialogue.

Each event must be justified against a specific execution objective. Activity for its own sake introduces execution failures such as message fragmentation and inconsistency, and reactive behavior. Roadshows—whether deal-related or non-deal—must therefore be driven by targeting logic, not by broker convenience. The IRO retains full authority over who is met, where, and why.

Supporting Infrastructure for Event Execution

Events function as execution instruments only when supported by reliable infrastructure. Calendar integration ensures that events are locked into the financial calendar early, and most importantly in the CEO's schedule, with dependencies such as board approvals, quiet periods, and blackout windows clearly mapped. Targeting and CRM systems ensure that investor day invitations and roadshow participant lists are drawn from structured relationship management and targeting work, tracked systematically, and refined based on prior engagement quality. Message libraries and preparation materials provide centralized access to approved narrative, financial assumptions, and Q&A guidance, ensuring consistency across events. Interaction tracking, and follow-up protocols capture investor feedback systematically, enabling pattern recognition and continuous refinement. Compliance and documentation processes ensure that all events involving material disclosure or selective engagement are properly recorded for audit trail and regulatory purposes. Honest debriefing improves the quality and effectiveness of future events.

These IR systems are addressed in the next section. In their absence, events quickly degrade from strategic execution tools into one-off activities, undermining the repeatability and resilience principles established earlier in this chapter.

Investor Days and Capital Markets Days

Investor Days—also referred to as Analyst Days or Capital Markets Days—are among the most effective tools available to Investor Relations when used correctly. They are structured capital markets engagements, initiated by the issuer, designed for analysts and institutional investors, and executed without reliance on intermediaries.

When well prepared, investor days deepen understanding of the business model and strategy, support valuation and potential re-rating, expand analyst coverage, and strengthen management credibility. In many cases, they can replace multiple roadshows at a lower overall cost. For mature IR programmes, they are no longer optional.

There is no fixed frequency. Investor days are company-specific and should be held only when there is something meaningful to explain—typically when preparing for or following an IPO, presenting a new strategic roadmap, introducing new leadership, updating long-term objectives, completing transformational acquisitions, or addressing perception gaps. Holding an investor day simply because peers do is a mistake. Avoiding one when expectations require recalibration is equally costly.

Execution discipline is essential because investor and analyst expectations are exceptionally high. Investor days should be run in project mode, typically starting six to nine months in advance. They require clarity of purpose and management endorsement, rigorous preparation, disciplined agendas, and structured post-event takeaways. Detailed planning guidance—including timelines, agenda design, budgeting frameworks, and post-event assessment tools—is provided in the Resources section.

Across all event types—investor days, roadshows, conferences, and one-to-one meetings—execution quality depends on the same foundational disciplines: clear strategic objectives, targeting rigor, message consistency, flawless execution. When integrated with budget discipline and enabling systems, events become repeatable mechanisms for the execution principles established throughout this chapter.

IR Publications

Core publications and technology, when designed correctly, reduce reliance on individuals, preserve institutional memory, enforce consistency across cycles, and allow the IR function to improve over time through continuous refinement.

Publications

Whether in print or digital form, the annual report remains the cornerstone of financial communication. It is the most complete and durable articulation of the company's strategy, performance, governance architecture, and long-term value creation logic. For investors, analysts, regulators, and boards, it is the reference document against which all other communication is implicitly tested.

The annual report anchors the narrative used across earnings calls, investor meetings, roadshows, and analyst models, preventing message inconsistencies. Formats may evolve, but the quality of writing, structure, and presentation signals organizational maturity.

Other core materials—investor presentations, factbooks, ESG publications, capital markets slideshows —should be treated as extensions of this foundational document.

Electronic or digital distribution should be maximized to control costs and improve accessibility, but never at the expense of clarity, completeness, or auditability.

CRM and Interaction Tracking

Customer Relationship Management ("CRM") and interaction-tracking systems allow Investor Relations to arrange and document meetings, questions raised, commitments made, and follow-up actions required. They ensure that targeting guidelines are applied consistently, that management access decisions are informed by past interactions, and that engagement quality improves over time.

Without systematic tracking, Investor Relations quickly becomes reactive: meetings are repeated with the wrong investors, questions are answered inconsistently, and management time is misallocated. With disciplined tracking, the IR function can prioritize access, tailor preparation intelligently, and identify which relationships are progressing—and which are not. CRM systems for IR often come with investor identification and targeting platforms.

They enable better judgement and create the foundation for the continuous improvement approach addressed later in this chapter and for the measurement frameworks developed in Chapter 7.

Financial Calendar Integration and Workflow

Calendar rigor is a core execution principle established earlier in this chapter.

Calendar integration tools allow Investor Relations to lock key disclosure moments, engagement windows, and preparation periods well in advance. They help manage dependencies such as board approvals, quiet periods, blackout windows, and internal review cycles. This protects preparation time and reduces last-minute pressure, while clearly identifying project owners.

Monitoring, Analytics, and Feedback Systems

Monitoring tools—covering ownership changes, analyst reports, consensus evolution, investor feedback, and market commentary—provide essential signals about how the company is understood and valued.

Analytics and feedback systems should support systematic learning, identify patterns, test assumptions, and inform judgment over time.

Effective monitoring requires structured processes:

- Structured capture protocols (recording investor questions, analyst concerns, emerging themes immediately after interactions);

- Regular reviews (weekly IR team debriefs, monthly consensus reviews, quarterly or annually shareholder base assessments);
- Clear escalation criteria (when does a pattern warrant management attention or strategy adjustment?);
- Documented refinement decisions (what changed, why, and when—enabling accountability in particular).

Used properly, these systems enable Investor Relations to refine execution —correcting misunderstandings through disciplined disclosure rather than reacting to every market fluctuation. They also create the foundation for continuous improvement and perception tracking, addressed in the sections that follow.

IR Board Reporting and Compliance

Investor Relations infrastructure must also support upward communication. Beyond defining what is reported to the board, effective IR requires systems and processes that allow market intelligence to flow reliably and consistently to senior management and directors.

Structured reporting tools enable IR intelligence—investor sentiment, ownership dynamics, emerging concerns—to be consolidated, documented, and escalated without distortion. This ensures that capital markets feedback informs decision-making in a timely and traceable manner. In practice, this often takes the form of a concise monthly or quarterly summary for senior management and, where appropriate, the board. Such summaries typically synthesize:

- current sentiment and positioning trends;
- key positive and negative themes;
- consensus evolution, changes in estimates and investment recommendations;
- priority issues or actions requiring CEO, CFO, or board-level attention.

Equally important are documentation and compliance systems. Audit trails, and access controls are not simply administrative burdens; they protect credibility. In stressed or contested situations such as investigations by stock market authorities, the ability to demonstrate what was disclosed, when, to whom, and on what basis becomes a strategic asset rather than a compliance formality.

IR Technology Selection

The most effective IR infrastructure is rarely the most sophisticated. It is the most robust.

Tools should be selected based on their ability to support repeatable processes, integrate with existing systems, function with limited resources, and remain usable during periods of stress. Complex solutions that require full-time staff, constant maintenance or specialist intervention often fail precisely when they are most needed—during transactions, leadership transitions, or market disruption.

A simple rule applies: if a tool cannot be maintained during a budget reduction or team change, it is a liability, not an asset. This reinforces the budget rigor established earlier in this Chapter: infrastructure investments must be justified by their contribution to repeatability, productivity and resilience, not by sophistication or novelty.

Social media monitoring tools fit within this logic. While not primary disclosure channels, they enhance situational awareness by highlighting emerging narratives and misinformation. Used with structural consistency, they inform judgment without driving reactive behavior. This is also an investment that can be shared with Corporate Communications, for instance.

Publications, systems, and technology therefore all contribute to ensure that execution consistency will endure beyond individuals and market cycles.

Critically, robust infrastructure creates the conditions for systematic improvement. Regular process reviews—asking where friction, risk, or errors occur—should feed back into template updates, system configurations, approval workflows, and training. This operational feedback loop ensures that data captured through IR systems is reliable, integrated, and routinely used for decision-making.

The sections that follow address how to leverage this infrastructure for continuous improvement, structured perception tracking, and ultimately for the measurement frameworks developed in Chapter 7. You can only measure what you track. The infrastructure established earlier is what makes credible, actionable IR measurement possible.

IR Infrastructure: Tools, Events, and Budget Discipline—Practical Implications

- Treat IR infrastructure as an execution enabler, not a catalogue of tools
- Align budgets explicitly with strategic priorities, target shareholder structure, and execution disciplines

- Protect disclosure reliability and management time before investing in visibility-enhancing activities that you may be unable to sustain
- Design events as strategic milestones and building blocks of a coherent capital-markets strategy
- Select technology for ease of use, versatility, robustness—especially under budget or resource constraints
- Ensure systems support compliance

6.6 Continuous Improvement

Investor Relations operates on a recurring operating cycle: quarterly earnings, annual reporting, roadshows, investor days, board presentations. The same activities recur predictably, creating a choice: repetition can lead to either gradual improvement or slow degradation.

Continuous improvement in IR is about systematically refining how the function executes its core responsibilities—ensuring that each repetition is sharper, faster, and more reliable than the last.

This section addresses how a disciplined IR function gets better over time. It focuses on execution reviews, process refinement, and the governance of change.

Execution Reviews

The purpose of execution reviews is far from being limited to the review of share-price movements. On the contrary, it aims to assess how well IR delivered on its commitments to maximize valuation. This implies moving away from considering share-price movements, analyst rating changes, and consensus revisions as execution measures—they reflect market interpretation, competitive dynamics, and macro conditions beyond IR's direct control.

What IR can and should assess is:

- Did disclosure happen on schedule and without leak or error?
- Was management prepared for the interactions that followed?
- Did messaging remain consistent across formats and audiences?
- Were internal approval workflows efficient, or did they introduce delays and distortions?

These are execution questions. They require structured review after major events.

Post-Earnings Debriefs

Within 48–72 hours of an earnings release and call, the IR team should conduct an internal debrief covering:

- Preparation quality: Were materials ready on time? Were there last-minute changes that could have been avoided?
- Disclosure completeness: Did the release and call address expected questions? Were there gaps that surprised management during Q&A?
- Message consistency: Did the CFO, CEO, and written materials align? Were there any contradictions or ambiguities that required post-call clarification?
- Process friction: Where did approvals slow down? At the Board level? Which systems or templates or language caused problems?
- Follow-up discipline: Were investor and analyst questions logged systematically? Were commitments to provide additional information tracked and fulfilled?

These reviews should be brief, structured, and action-oriented. A one-page summary is sufficient. The objective is not exhaustive critique, but rapid identification of what must be corrected before the next cycle.

The objective is to identify process weaknesses that can be corrected before the next cycle.

Post-Roadshow and Post-Investor Day Reviews

Roadshows and investor days generate substantial qualitative feedback—investor questions, analyst observations, recurring concerns. But feedback is useful only when it is captured systematically and assessed purposefully.

Post-event reviews should address:

- Targeting accuracy: Did the right investors attend? Were there participants who should not have been prioritized?
- Message comprehension: Which elements of the presentation were well understood? Which generated confusion or pushback?

- Management performance: Were presenters prepared? How well did they handle difficult questions? Were there moments where credibility was weakened?
- Logistics and infrastructure: Did webcasting, registration, and materials distribution function reliably? How efficient were services providers?
- Follow-up execution: Were post-event follow-ups documented and tracked?

The review process exists to distinguish patterns from noise: A single investor expressing confusion about capital allocation policy is data. Ten investors raising the same concern across multiple meetings is a pattern that may require attention.

Continuous improvement requires identifying where execution becomes difficult, slow, or unreliable—before these issues become structural.

Typical sources of friction include:

- Late data deliveries (financial data arriving too close to disclosure deadlines, forcing rushed reviews);
- Repeated errors in materials (inconsistent figures across presentations, outdated boilerplate in legal disclaimers);
- Bottlenecks in approvals (multiple sequential sign-offs creating delays and encouraging last-minute compromises on quality);
- Gaps in meeting follow-up (investor questions not logged in CRM, commitments not tracked, follow-up actions unclear).

These are operational weaknesses that degrade execution quality and reputation over time if left unaddressed.

Regular process reviews—conducted quarterly or after major events—should ask:

- Where are we experiencing pressure or risk?
- Which processes or interactions rely too heavily on individual knowledge?
- Which tools or templates are creating more work than they save?
- Where are approvals adding delays without improving quality?

Observations from these reviews should feed back into:

- Template updates (improving clarity, removing outdated language, standardizing formats);

- System configurations (adjusting CRM workflows, calendar automation, compliance documentation);
- Training (ensuring new team members understand procedures, conducting refreshers on core processes and tools);
- Approval workflow redesign (consolidating reviews, clarifying decision authority, reducing sequential bottlenecks).

The purpose is to reduce unnecessary effort and increase reliability.

Since Investor Relations repeats the same core activities every quarter and every year, repetition can lead to complacency, and gradual erosion of standards.

Continuous improvement ensures that:

- Repetition leads to higher quality;
- Lessons are not lost when people change roles;
- Small errors are corrected before they become structural weaknesses.

This requires documentation. IR teams should maintain:

- Playbooks for recurring events (earnings preparation checklists, investor day planning guides, roadshow logistics protocols);
- Post-event summaries (what worked, what did not, decisions made, changes implemented);
- Updated templates and message libraries (reflecting current guidance, recent Q&A themes, approved language on sensitive topics);
- Decision logs (documenting why certain processes were changed, ensuring future teams understand the rationale).

A practical test of whether learning has been institutionalized is whether the IR function would behave the same way if the IRO changed tomorrow. If execution quality depends entirely on individual memory and relationships, you have a problem.

Closing the Internal Feedback Loop

Continuous improvement depends on a structured internal feedback loop—the mechanism through which observations become decisions, and decisions become improved processes and deliberate action.

Starting with observation and leading up to decisions, the loop has four stages:

1. ***Structured feedback collection***

Feedback from earnings calls, investor meetings, roadshows, and internal reviews should be captured systematically:

- Investor questions and concerns logged in CRM immediately after interactions;
- Analyst report themes summarized and tracked over time;
- Internal debrief notes documented within 48 hours of major events, including message absorption rates;
- Event execution issues recorded when they occur.

Without structured capture, feedback is lost, patterns are invisible, and decisions are made based on memory rather than evidence.

2. ***Regular reviews***

Feedback must be reviewed at defined intervals:

- Weekly IR team debriefs (reviewing recent interactions, flagging emerging questions, adjusting near-term preparation, budget updates);
- Monthly consensus reviews (tracking analyst estimate changes, identifying anomalies, assessing alignment with guidance);
- Quarterly (ideally) shareholder base assessments (evaluating ownership composition relative to target structure, assessing engagement quality);
- Annual program reviews (comprehensive assessment of execution effectiveness, infrastructure reliability, quality of providers, resource allocation, budget planning).

Regular review rhythms prevent feedback from accumulating unexamined and ensure that patterns are detected early.

3. ***Clear escalation to management criteria***

Not all feedback requires escalation to senior management or changes to strategy. Continuous improvement requires clear thresholds for when patterns warrant action:

- Disclosure gaps: If multiple investors or analysts ask questions that current disclosure does not address, escalate to CFO/legal for review.

- Message comprehension failures: If a core element of strategy is consistently misunderstood across meetings, escalate for messaging review, suggesting refinements.
- Process failures: If the same execution problem recurs across multiple cycles despite previous attempts to fix it, escalate for governance or resource review.
- Expectation misalignment: If consensus assumptions diverge materially from management's view despite clear guidance, escalate for strategic communication decision.

4. ***Documented IR decisions***

When changes are made—to disclosure formats, messaging emphasis, event structure, approval workflows—they should be documented with clear rationale:

- What changed: specific adjustment made (e.g., "added quarterly cash flow bridge to earnings presentation");
- Why it changed: pattern or issue identified (e.g., "six analysts asked for cash flow detail in last two quarters");
- When it changed: effective date (e.g., "implemented Q3 2026 earnings");
- Who approved: decision authority (e.g., "CFO sign-off on enhanced cash flow disclosure").

Documentation ensures accountability, enables future teams to understand the evolution of IR practice, and prevents "incremental deviation"—the gradual, undocumented erosion of standards that occurs when small changes accumulate without control.

The Governance of Improvement

Continuous improvement implies alignment on who decides what. For instance:

- IRO: Adjustments to logistics, templates, CRM workflows, meeting preparation protocols;
- CFO: Changes to disclosure content, financial presentation formats, guidance frameworks;

- CEO/Board: Strategic shifts in IR approach, free float management, major changes to engagement model, responses to significant perception gaps.

Before escalating feedback or proposing change, IR should assess:

- Frequency: How often has this issue appeared?
- Consistency: Is it raised by different investors/analysts, or by the same one repeatedly?
- Materiality: Does it affect understanding of core strategy, financial performance, or risk?
- Actionability: Is there a clear change that would address the concern without creating new problems and damaging valuation?

Proposed changes should be reviewed through the same structured rhythm used for execution:

- Quarterly IR reviews: Present observations, patterns, and proposed refinements to CFO/CEO;
- Annual strategic review: Comprehensive assessment of whether IR operating model, resource allocation, and engagement approach remain fit for purpose;
- Ad hoc escalation: For urgent issues (crisis response, major expectation gap, regulatory change requiring immediate adaptation).

Continuous improvement establishes process maturity, execution reliability, and data discipline. These are prerequisites for meaningful measurement of IR effectiveness.

Without systematic capture of interactions, structured review rhythms, and documented refinement decisions, IR cannot reliably assess:

- Whether engagement quality is improving over time;
- Whether messaging is enhancing valuation;
- Whether resource allocation is optimized;
- Whether perception gaps are narrowing, thereby reducing volatility.

If IR cannot improve its own execution systematically, measuring how the market perceives the company is premature. Perception tracking becomes a diagnostic without remedies.

Continuous improvement comes first. Perception tracking follows. The next section addresses how IR systematically assesses how the company is understood and valued by the market.

Continuous Improvement—Practical Implications

- Review execution quality after major events, focusing on delivery, preparation, and process, and market outcomes
- Distinguish patterns from market chatter; avoid reacting to isolated comments or short-term signals
- Identify and correct process dysfunctions before they become structural
- Institutionalize accumulated insight through documented playbooks, templates, and decision logs
- Lead change deliberately, with clear decision authority and escalation criteria
- Ensure continuous improvement strengthens discipline and cross-functional alignment

6.7 Understanding How the Market Sees the Company

Continuous improvement ensures that Investor Relations refines its own execution over time.

Perception tracking answers a different question: How does the financial community understand our strategy, assess management execution, and value our performance?

This section addresses how IR systematically captures, interprets, and acts on market feedback—through perception studies, sentiment monitoring, and structured qualitative research.

Why Perception Matters

Investor Relations exists to ensure that the market's understanding of the company is grounded in accurate information and clear strategic context.

Perception gaps—where investor understanding diverges from operational reality—create three specific risks:

1. Valuation risk: Misunderstood strategy or underestimated execution capability can compress valuation multiples and inflate the cost of capital;

2. Access risk: Governance concerns or insufficient investor confidence can constrain participation in capital raises or M&A processes;
3. Reputation risk: Persistent perception gaps erode trust, making future communication less effective and crisis response more difficult.

Between two companies with similar economic and financial performance, investors will choose the one with superior Investor Relations. Understanding and managing market perception is not optional—it is foundational to credibility and valuation support.

Importantly, perception tracking is much more than validation. The objective goes well beyond confirming that the market agrees with management. You will want to understand where confidence is strong, where weaknesses exist, and which aspects of the equity story are misunderstood or undervalued.

When to Assess Perception

Perception tracking should occur on two timelines: continuously (through real-time monitoring and quarterly feedback reviews) and periodically (through formal perception studies conducted every 18–24 months).

- **Continuous Monitoring**

  IR should track perception signals routinely:

- Ownership changes (institutional buying/selling patterns, new positions, exits);
- Analyst reports (ratings changes, revisions of estimates and investment recommendations);
- Consensus evolution (how aggregate expectations shift relative to guidance—whether it is provided qualitatively or quantitatively—to peers);
- Investor questions (recurring themes in meetings, calls, and roadshows);
- Media commentary (narratives gaining traction, emerging misconceptions).

This continuous monitoring provides early warning of perception shifts and enables IR to address concerns before they harden into entrenched views.

- **Perception studies**

Formal perception studies—typically conducted by independent third parties such as IR firms—provide the most robust assessment of investor sentiment. They are particularly valuable:

- When a new Chair or CEO is coming on board (establishing baseline perception and priorities);
- When a major strategic shift is being planned or executed (understanding investor confidence and potential concerns);
- During or after crisis resolution (evaluating the recovery of market confidence and the trust gaps that remain to be bridged);
- When simply wanting to understand market perception of the company's strategy, governance, and IR effectiveness.

Formal perception studies typically examine:

- Management credibility and reputation
  - Trust in CEO and CFO (integrity, transparency, follow-through on commitments);
  - Confidence in strategic vision and execution capability;
  - Assessment of governance quality and board oversight;
  - Quality of execution
- Strategic clarity
  - Understanding of business model and competitive positioning;
  - Confidence in growth strategy and capital allocation priorities;
  - Perception of innovation capability and adaptability to market changes.
- Disclosure quality
  - Completeness and clarity of financial reporting;
  - Transparency on risks, challenges, and strategic trade-offs;
  - Responsiveness to investor questions and concerns.
- IR effectiveness
  - Accessibility and responsiveness of IR team and management;
  - Quality of communication materials (presentations, earnings calls, investor days);
  - Effectiveness of engagement (one-on-ones, roadshows, conferences).
- Competitive positioning
  - Perception of company vs. peers on key value drivers and IR program;

- Awareness levels among target investor segments;
- Preference ranking within sector coverage universe.

The above criteria are far from being exhaustive and the perception study should be precisely tailored to the issues and opportunities it aims at identifying.

Perception studies are powerful diagnostic tools, but poorly executed, superficial studies create more risk than insight.

- Use independent third parties

Internal studies reduce candor and objectivity. Investors and analysts are more honest with independent researchers who guarantee confidentiality.

- Survey current and prospective investors, as well as sell-side analysts

Understanding why investors do not hold the stock is often more valuable than confirming why current holders do. Non-holders reveal perception barriers, competitive disadvantages, and suggest catalysts that existing shareholders may overlook.

- Include negative feedback

Negative feedback is the most valuable output of perception studies. The objective is to provide independent diagnosis.

- Do not conduct perception studies too frequently

Perception takes time to shift meaningfully. It requires a significant investment and is a time-consuming exercise, including for investors who will often say they'll provide feedback directly to management. Conducting studies more frequently than every 18–24 months risks measuring short-term noise rather than durable trends.

IR should ask:

- Is this a consistent pattern across multiple investors/analysts, or an isolated view?
- Does it reflect a genuine gap in disclosure or understanding, or a difference in strategic judgment?
- Is there a credible action that would address the concern responsibly?

- Would responding to this perception improve long-term market perception and support valuation?

Closing the external feedback loop means that perception insights will be acted upon.

When perception studies and continuous monitoring identify genuine gaps—misunderstandings that compromise valuation, or reputation—IR's response can include:

- Enhanced disclosure (adding detail to areas where understanding is weak—e.g., cash flow bridges, enhanced segment reporting, capital allocation frameworks);
- Targeted engagement (investor days focused on specific perception gaps, divisional deep dives, site visits to demonstrate operational capability);
- Message refinement (adjusting emphasis in earnings calls and presentations to address recurring questions proactively);
- Governance changes (if credibility gaps reflect legitimate concerns about board oversight, ESG transparency, or risk management).

Critically, responses should be documented and reviewed over time. Did the enhanced disclosure improve understanding? Did the investor day close the perception gap? This feedback loop—from perception diagnosis to action to reassessment—completes the cycle and enables continuous refinement.

Investor sentiment is intelligence. It reveals where the company is understood, what investor confidence is based on, and where trust is fragile.

It is important to distinguish the boundary between:

- Strategic response: Perception study reveals that investors do not understand capital allocation logic → IR develops enhanced capital allocation framework for next earnings announcement or investor day.
- Reactive response: Single analyst downgrades stock due to macro concerns → IR hosts ad hoc call to address downgrade.

The first is disciplined. The second undermines your standing.

Perception tracking completes the execution-to-learning loop established earlier and creates the foundation for the measurement frameworks to be addressed in Chapter 7.

Understanding How the Market Sees the Company—Practical Implications

- Treat perception tracking as a source of decision-useful intelligence
- Combine continuous monitoring with periodic, independent perception studies conducted at appropriate intervals on specific issues or themes
- Use perception insights to inform strategic disclosure and engagement decisions
- Focus on persistent perception gaps that affect valuation, access to capital, or management credibility
- Act on insights through disciplined disclosure, targeted engagement, or governance improvements

This chapter established how Investor Relations operates in practice: as a management discipline built on structure, repeatability, and resilience rather than sheer sophistication or volume. It demonstrated that execution discipline must precede measurement—you can only measure what you manage. Message consistency, decision authority, and escalation discipline must be protected under all circumstances. Infrastructure exists to enforce discipline, preserve institutional memory, and enable learning. Perception assessment follows execution discipline; without operational rigor, perception tracking is unlikely to produce actionable strategic insight.

This disciplined approach to IR execution creates a foundation—but quality execution alone does not demonstrate value, nor does it guarantee positive outcomes. Investor Relations is expected to create competitive advantage but also demonstrate measurable impact. Chapter 7 therefore addresses how to measure IR effectiveness: not by counting activities, but by assessing whether IR delivers the strategic outcomes that justify its existence as a management function.

7

Measuring the Effectiveness and Value of Investor Relations

Once Investor Relations strategy and execution disciplines are in place, the question naturally arises of how to assess whether the function is creating value. This chapter now addresses whether the competitive advantages expected from IR are being actually delivered. It introduces measurement frameworks that go beyond activity metrics and focus on capital-market outcomes, demonstrating return on investment and guiding continuous improvement.

The goal is to ensure that Investor Relations is measured in a way that reflects what IR is designed to achieve.

The measurement challenge is therefore strategic, as it provides answers to questions raised by Boards and CEOs such as:

- Is IR strengthening our competitive position for capital?
- Are we building valuation resilience and shareholder quality?
- Is consensus better aligned with our expectations?
- Is our standing among investors improving?
- Could the company raise capital efficiently if required?

They care less about whether the IR team conducted 180 meetings this quarter or published materials on schedule. Those activities matter—but they are inputs, not results.

If you measured IR against Chapter 5 strategies, you would know how well you executed your shareholder identification program, maintained your financial calendar, or deployed your communication channels. But you

A. Guimard, *Investor Relations Strategy*, https://doi.org/10.1007/978-3-032-21679-3_7

would not know whether this improved shareholder-base quality, narrowed consensus dispersion, or strengthened access to capital.

This chapter measures the latter—strategic outcomes—because they justify IR's existence as a strategic management function.

This also reflects the longstanding debate over whether share-price performance is the "ultimate arbiter" of Investor Relations effectiveness. While valuation and market performance cannot be ignored, they are influenced by many variables beyond IR alone. Measurement should therefore focus not only on market valuation, but also on the quality of the shareholder base, expectation alignment, and sustained access to capital. Measurement of Investor Relations therefore cannot be exact in the way accounting or operational KPIs are.

This chapter presents a three-tier measurement framework designed to:

1. Assess strategic impact by measuring progress toward Chapter 2's seven competitive advantages (Tier 3)
2. Evaluate market positioning by tracking how capital markets perceive, value, and trade the company relative to peers (Tier 2)
3. Monitor operational execution by confirming that Chapter 5's strategies and disciplines are being implemented with consistency and efficiency (Tier 1).

The framework treats Investor Relations as a strategic investment—deploying capital, management time, organizational capacity, and reputational capital to support long-term capital-market objectives—while avoiding the false precision and misattribution that often undermine IR scorecards.

Measurement ultimately answers a return-on-investment question. That investment includes direct financial cost (headcount, advisers, tools, events), senior management and board time, organizational attention, and reputational capital.

Measuring IR effectiveness is therefore inseparable from assessing whether resources—including management time—are being deployed where they create the greatest strategic return: the seven competitive advantages established in Chapter 2.

When an IR program conducts its annual review, the sequence should be:

1. Strategic assessment (Tier 3): Are we achieving the seven competitive advantages from Chapter 2?
2. Market positioning assessment (Tier 2): How are we positioned vs. peers?

3. Execution assessment (Tier 1): Are we executing Chapter 5's strategies effectively?

If Tier 3 shows weak results, this triggers investigation: Is Tier 2 positioning deteriorating (market context problem)? Is Tier 1 execution poor (strategy implementation problem)? Are the Chapter 5 strategies wrong for our context?

Measurement against Chapter 2's competitive advantages is the ultimate test.

The framework acknowledges that strategies evolve—technology platforms change, communication channels shift, investor targeting methodologies improve—but the seven competitive advantages are comparatively stable across market cycles, even as the methods and tools used to pursue them evolve. Companies will always need valuation resilience, shareholder quality, expectation alignment, management credibility, information efficiency, access to capital, and governance confidence.

Measuring against these stable outcomes, rather than evolving methods, creates a framework that remains relevant across market cycles, governance cultures, and stages of company maturity.

To treat IR as a genuine value driver, measurement must be:

- Strategic: Rooted in the equity story, aligned with corporate priorities, and focused on long-term value creation
- Actionable: Linked to decisions about targeting, messaging, disclosure, and resource allocation
- Balanced: Combining quantitative evidence with structured qualitative assessment
- Credible: Focused on what IR controls or influences.

This chapter operates from four guiding principles:

1. IR can and should be measured—far beyond the share price.
2. Measurement requires an explicit ROI mindset. IR spend is an investment, not overhead.
3. You can only measure what you track. Build tracking into everyday IR operations.
4. Distinguish execution from outcomes: measure what IR executes (Tier 1) and interpret what markets reflect (Tier 2) to assess strategic impact over time (Tier 3).

7.1 A Three-Tier Framework for Measuring Investor Relations

Investor Relations measurement must satisfy multiple audiences simultaneously: boards, executives, regulators, and internal management. Each requires different evidence of effectiveness.

The challenge is that IR can be measured too narrowly, or in ways that prioritize what is easy to count over what actually matters.

This chapter uses a three-tier measurement framework, designed to reconcile operational accountability with strategic impact assessment. All mature IR programs operate across all three tiers simultaneously, with emphasis shifting as strategy, governance culture, changes in leadership and company maturity evolve.

Tier 1: Measuring Operational Execution

Tier 1 focuses on whether the IR function operates effectively, looking at activity, capacity, and resource discipline. It demonstrates that Investor Relations is organized, responsive, and making disciplined use of resources.

Typical indicators include:

- Engagement volume and reach (investor meetings, roadshows, conferences)
- Analyst interaction and coverage maintenance
- Disclosure timeliness and consistency of content
- Management time allocation
- IR cost structure and efficiency.

Tier 1 indicators are essential for baseline accountability, budget and headcount justification, capacity planning, and operational credibility in scorecard-driven environments.

An IRO managing 200+ investor meetings annually alongside disclosure responsibilities, website management, and analyst relations has a quantifiable case for additional resources. Activity metrics make capacity constraints visible to CFOs who may not yet understand IR's strategic value.

However, they do not measure strategic impact. They measure whether IR is functioning properly. Volume is not quality—200 low-quality meetings accomplish less than 50 strategic conversations.

Tier 2: Measuring Capital Markets Outcomes

In order to answer the question "How is the company positioned in capital markets relative to strategy and peers?", Tier 2 tracks how the market perceives, values, and trades the company.

These indicators include:

- Analyst coverage, and dispersion of estimates, investment recommendations (e.g. buy, sell, hold) and target prices
- Shareholder composition and stability
- Liquidity and trading behavior, relative valuation positioning, market reaction patterns around disclosure.

These indicators are legitimate and necessary, but they are not measures of IR execution quality. They reflect the combined outcome of corporate performance, sector dynamics, macro conditions, peer developments, and capital flows—forces that IR influences but does not control.

Within this framework, Tier 2 indicators are treated as outcome measures requiring comparative and contextual interpretation over time, rather than direct attribution to IR actions.

Market reactions to external shocks—sector corrections, macro volatility, geopolitical events—are often used as implicit IR tests; within this framework they are interpreted as resilience signals (how the company performs vs. peers during stress), not execution scores.

A 20% share-price decline during a 40% sector correction demonstrates relative resilience. A 10% gain during a 30% sector rally demonstrates relative weakness. Absolute performance means little without comparative context.

They are most informative when:

- Assessed relative to peers and indices
- Tracked across market cycles
- Interpreted alongside qualitative context
- Used to evaluate resilience rather than absolute performance.

Analyst Coverage

Coverage breadth, recommendation distribution, and target price positioning provide visibility into market attention—but must be interpreted carefully.

Consensus estimate dispersion (standard deviation of analyst forecasts as % of consensus) is one of the most powerful proxies for market understanding and alignment with the company's expectations, whether stated qualitatively or quantitatively. Narrow dispersion indicates consistent modeling assumptions and clear communication by the company of its growth drivers. Wide dispersion signals fundamental uncertainty.

It us recommended to use coverage metrics to identify gaps in understanding and track whether analyst education efforts reduce modeling confusion. Do not hold IR accountable for coverage decisions driven by brokerage economics (firm restructurings, regulatory changes like MiFID II, firm-specific rating frameworks). Ten analysts who understand the business outperform twenty who don't.

Shareholder Base Composition

Shareholder quality is assessed through behavioral observation over time, not just static ownership data. The critical question is not simply "who owns the stock?" but "how do they behave?".

The IR team should track:

- Investment time horizon distribution (long-term fundamental investors vs. trading-oriented holders)
- Shareholder turnover rates by investor segment and, geography
- Ownership concentration among strategic holders
- Voting participation and alignment
- Stability of top 20 shareholders.

Strong signals include increasing ownership by investors whose mandates align with company strategy, stable or rising average holding periods, low turnover among key holders, and resilient ownership during sector volatility.

Valuation Positioning

Valuation reflects operational performance, market sentiment on upside potential, macroeconomic conditions, peer performance, and market structure—plus strategic clarity and credibility (where IR contributes).

The use of valuation metrics will help assess whether the market understands the company's differentiated positioning and to identify persistent valuation gaps that may signal communication failures. This should be supplemented by tracking positioning relative to peers over time.

Do not attribute valuation changes directly to IR activities, hold IR accountable for sector-wide multiple movements, or present short-term valuation shifts as evidence of IR success or failure.

Tier 3: Measuring IR Impact on Competitive Differentiation

Tier 3 assesses whether IR is delivering the competitive advantages that justify its role as a management function.

This includes:

- Expectation alignment and reduction of recurring misunderstandings
- Shareholder-base quality and stability
- Trust in leadership
- Access to capital preparedness
- Long-term investor alignment with governance.

Tier 3 measurement relies on structured qualitative assessment, supported by quantitative proxies, interpreted over multi-year horizons. Core tools include investor perception studies (conducted every 18–24 months), systematic meeting debriefs tracking understanding evolution, and board assessment of IR strategic contribution. Tier 3 indicators typically improve over 12–24-month horizons as credibility compounds.

It is here that return on IR investment becomes visible—not through activity volume or short-term market movements, but through improved resilience, credibility, and strategic optionality.

Tier 3 measurement is therefore organized around the seven competitive advantages from Chapter 2 because they define the durable strategic outcomes IR exists to deliver, namely: a more diversified and resilient shareholder base, a stronger corporate reputation through transparency and governance, stronger valuation support and lower perceived risk, greater commercial visibility, improved access to high-quality partners and suppliers, enhanced ability to attract and retain executive talent, sustained access to capital across market cycles.

- Advantage 1: A more diversified and resilient shareholder base

The assessment focuses on whether the shareholder base is diversified, stable, and aligned with the company's strategic time horizon, particularly during periods of market stress, through a set of metrics including:

- the distribution of investor time horizons,
- shareholder turnover by segment (e.g., institutional vs retail), and

- stability during volatility—specifically whether long-term holders maintain or increase positions during downturns.

Stability of the top shareholders over time and geographic diversification of ownership provide additional indicators of resilience.

- Advantage 2: Stronger corporate reputation through transparency and governance

This dimension assesses whether the company is perceived as well governed, transparent, and credible in its disclosures and decision-making. Evidence is drawn from:

- voting participation and approval rates
- the quality and frequency of governance-related engagement
- feedback gathered through perception studies.

Proxy advisor commentary and board-level assessments of investor confidence further inform this evaluation.

- Advantage 3: Stronger valuation support and lower perceived risk

Valuation and risk perception are best assessed comparatively and during periods of stress rather than in rising markets. In this case, what is measured is the company's ability to maintain or recover relative valuation positioning through sector corrections and broader market disruptions. Relevant indicators include:

- relative total shareholder return during stress periods
- the magnitude of share-price declines vs peers and indices
- recovery speed following corrections
- beta evolution across cycles (relative share-price sensitivity to market movements)
- the stability of valuation multiples over time.

- Advantage 4: Stronger external credibility

Greater commercial visibility reflects how well the market understands the company's business model, value drivers, and strategic positioning, as well as how efficiently new information is incorporated into market pricing. This is observed through:

- the breadth and quality of analyst coverage
- the level and evolution of consensus estimate dispersion and investment recommendations
- post-results volatility patterns
- bid-ask spread trends.

Beyond this, stronger external credibility means that the company's strategy, scale, and credibility are sufficiently clear and established in the market that it becomes easier for third parties to assess, engage with, and invest in the company.

- Advantage 5: Improved access to high-quality partners and suppliers

This advantage captures whether capital markets standing translates into broader strategic benefits beyond investors, whether capital markets visibility enhances the company's overall strategic attractiveness.

It is primarily assessed qualitatively through:

- management and board feedback on inbound interest from potential partners
- the caliber of counterparties in strategic transactions
- the company's position in commercial discussions. In some cases, supplier or partner perception surveys may provide additional insight.

- Advantage 6: Enhanced ability to attract and retain executive talent

A strong IR profile can also support leadership attraction and retention. This advantage evaluates whether the company's market reputation strengthens its appeal to senior executives. Evidence includes:

- feedback from the board and nomination committee
- recruitment outcomes
- workplace and employer reputation rankings.

- Advantage 7: Sustained access to capital across market cycles

This advantage measures the company's ability to raise capital efficiently when opportunities or needs arise, and to preserve strategic optionality through cycles. Quantitative indicators include:

- funding source diversification
- trends in the cost of capital
- subscription rates of past equity or debt issuances.

These seven advantages are interdependent:

- A diversified and resilient shareholder base reinforces governance confidence;
- High levels of transparency improves expectation alignment and risk perception.
- Management credibility and market understanding support valuation resilience and access to capital.

Measurement should therefore track progress across all seven dimensions over rolling 12–24-month horizons, prioritizing those most critical to the company's development stage, strategy, and capital markets objectives.

7.2 IR Scorecards

For readers operating in scorecard-oriented environments, the practical solution is to design effective IR scorecards that

- Are explicitly linked to strategy
- Combine a small number of quantitative indicators with structured qualitative input
- Track trends rather than point results
- Include interpretation and recommended actions
- Evolve as strategy and circumstances change (Table 7.1).

IR program effectively balanced operational excellence (Tier 1), maintained competitive market positioning (Tier 2), and delivered measurable strategic impact (Tier 3).

It could be recommended to continue with increased emphasis on ESG integration measurement for the next period.

Table 7.1 Practical example: Multi-Tier IR scorecard—Mid-Cap European Industrial Company

Tier	Metric category	Specific indicators	Current performance	Trend
Tier 1: Activity	Engagement volume	Investor meetings: 180 (target 150+)	✓ Exceeds target	→
	Analyst relations	Coverage maintained: 8 firms	✓ Stable YoY	→
	Management time	CEO: 15%, CFO: 25% of time	✓ Within policy	→
Tier 2: positioning	Analyst sentiment	Buy/Hold/Sell: 60%/30%/10%	Above peer average	↑
	Shareholder quality	Long-term holders: 45% (up from 38%)	Strong improvement	↑↑
	Liquidity	Avg spread: 0.24% (peer: 0.19%)	Improving	↑
	Relative valuation	EV/EBITDA premiusm vs peers: from + 3% to +12%	Significant improvement	↑↑
Tier 3: Strategic impact	Understanding quality	Estimate dispersion: -40% reduction	Excellent progress	↑↑
	Management credibility	Perception score: 7.8/10 (up from 7.2)	Measurable improvement	↑
	Capital access	Equity offering: 2.5x oversubscribed	Demonstrates credibility	✓

This shows boards how to use all three tiers simultaneously without creating dashboard overwhelm.

7.3 Measuring the Return on Investment in Investor Relations

IR measurement serves a governance function: demonstrating whether scarce resources—particularly senior management time—are being deployed where they create the greatest strategic return.

Three ROI questions frame effective measurement:

1. Resource allocation efficiency: Is management time concentrated among investors who matter most to the company's strategic objectives? Track time allocation by investor type, holding period, and influence on ownership decisions 2.
2. Strategic option preservation: Has IR maintained the company's ability to raise capital, attract strategic partners, or defend against activist pressure when needed? Assess preparedness, not just past transactions.
3. Credibility compounding: Is trust-building over multi-year horizons through consistent delivery, or eroding through volatility and disappointment? Track perception study trends during stress.

Avoid false precision: IR ROI cannot be calculated with accounting exactness, nor strictly based on IR budgets. But it can be assessed through peer benchmarking, improvement trend analysis, and qualitative validation through investor confidence outcomes.

Quantifying IR's Contribution to Capital Efficiency

IR investments—personnel, technology, events, advisors, research—create measurable returns through:

- Capital raising efficiency: Basis points saved on debt issuances (10–20 bps on a $500M issue = $500K-$1M annual savings), reduced underwriting discounts on equity offerings, oversubscription enabling better pricing and an upsized capital raise, speed of execution reducing market risk.
- Valuation improvements: Multiple expansion vs. peers (1–2 x P/E improvement on $2B market cap = $100-200 M value creation), reduced volatility lowering cost of equity, governance/ESG strength reducing risk premiums.
- Shareholder composition effects: Attracting long-term fundamental investors reduces volatility and cost of equity compared to portfolios dominated by short-term traders.

These examples illustrate economic sensitivity and their returns compound over time. A company that consistently executes capital transactions at 15–20 basis points better pricing than peers, maintains a P/E multiple 1.5 turns higher, and operates with 10–15% lower equity volatility demonstrates measurable IR contribution—even if those outcomes also reflect broader operational and market factors.

Measurement becomes strategic when it shifts resource allocation toward higher-return activities and away from commodity interactions that consume time without building advantage.

Quantitative Indicators and Their Limits

Market-outcome indicators (Tier 2) require disciplined interpretation:

Use peer-relative frameworks: A 15% share-price decline means one thing during a 5% sector correction (relative weakness) and something entirely different during a 30% sector sell-off (relative resilience). Absolute performance measurement needs to take into account the right comparative context as in the examples below:

- Assess across appropriate time horizons: Quarterly trends are more informative than weekly or monthly movements. Multi-year patterns reveal structural positioning.
- Acknowledge external factors explicitly: When presenting Tier 2 metrics to boards, state what drove outcomes: Valuation improved due to sector recovery (primary driver) and expectation alignment (IR contribution).
- Focus on resilience above all: The critical question is whether the company maintained or improved its positioning relative to peers during periods of stress. This mirrors procurement logic: success depends not only on lowering costs, but on lowering them more effectively than competitors.

7.4 Qualitative Assessment

Qualitative inputs are equally meaningful and require systematic discipline to become strategic (Table 7.2).

7.5 Applying the Measurement Framework in Practice

This section does not propose a rigid methodology or a universal timetable. It offers practical guidance on how companies that choose to measure the strategic impact of Investor Relations can do so in a disciplined and proportionate way, consistent with their maturity, objectives, and market

Table 7.2 Qualitative assessment framework

Practice	Purpose	Execution discipline	Strategic value
Perception study frequency	Track investor confidence, under-standing, and credibility over time	Comprehensive studies every 18–24 months for established IR programs; annually for companies rebuilding credibility. Results tracked longitudinally and segmented by investor type	Identifies shifts in trust, expectation alignment, and divergent investor views
Meeting debrief discipline	Capture qualitative insight from day-to-day investor interactions	After each meeting, document understanding level (1–5), key questions, concerns raised, and tone. Aggregate quarterly	Reveals recurring misunderstandings, emerging themes, and messaging gaps
Board feedback integration	Anchor IR assessment at board level	Annual board review covering shareholder-base quality, IR strategic contribution, management time allocation, and priority areas	Aligns IR focus with governance expectations and strategic oversight
Qualitative impact assessment	Assess strategic outcomes not captured by quantitative metrics	Focus on investor confidence, quality of understanding, and resilience	Captures investor confidence and resilience

context. The objective is ultimately to determine whether IR contributes to maximizing long-term valuation and strengthening the company's position in capital markets.

A Pragmatic Implementation Path

Early Phase

The first step is not measurement itself, but alignment. Management and the board should agree which of the seven IR advantages matter most at this stage of the company's development. From there, establish a clear starting point—understanding the current shareholder base and, where relevant, commissioning a perception study to capture how the market currently sees the company. Measurement cadence should be simple and realistic: regular quantitative tracking complemented by periodic qualitative review.

Building the Baseline

Over the following months, the emphasis should be on consistent tracking rather than exhaustive measurement. A small number of well-chosen indicators, such as shareholder base composition, analyst coverage, recommendation and estimate dispersion, liquidity metrics, and management time allocation—reviewed quarterly, combined with structured capture of investor and board feedback, is usually sufficient to establish a meaningful baseline.

Identifying Underlying Trends

Once a full year of set of data exists, the focus naturally shifts from individual data points to direction of travel. Year-on-year comparison across the seven competitive advantages begins to reveal where IR is strengthening positioning and where expectations remain fragile. Perception studies, repeated at sensible intervals, will help confirm whether confidence and understanding are improving.

Longer-Term Optimization

Over multiple years, measurement becomes a strategic tool rather than a reporting exercise. Trends can be assessed across cycles, resource allocation refined based on tangible facts, and positioning benchmarked more systematically against peers. At this stage, the value of IR is most visible in resilience, optionality, and preparedness.

Interpreting IR Measurement: Timing, Judgment, and Limits

Measurement adds value only when it supports strategic judgment. Indicators are most useful when they reflect the company's capital markets priorities, are reviewed over time rather than as isolated data points, and are interpreted in a comparative context, against prior periods or competitors. Absolute outcomes matter less than positioning relative to peers.

It won't come as a surprise that progress in Investor Relations rarely appears all at once. Improvements in tone, confidence, and the quality of investor dialogue typically emerge first. Greater stability in expectations and positioning follows. Structural effects on valuation, liquidity, and access to capital tend to materialize later and unevenly across market cycles. Measurement frameworks need to reflect this sequence. Demanding immediate proof of value encourages short-term behavior and undermines the credibility and trust that IR is designed to build.

Quantitative indicators gain meaning only when combined with structured qualitative insight. Systematic capture of investor feedback, recurring questions, and board-level discussion provides essential context that neither quantitative indicators nor share price movements alone can convey.

Measurement also has clear limits. Investor Relations does not control markets, sector rotations, or macroeconomic conditions. Over-attributing outcomes to IR distorts incentives. Equally, forcing inherently strategic and relational work into narrow numerical KPIs risks obscuring real progress. A credible measurement approach acknowledges these boundaries explicitly.

IR is accountable for disclosure quality, engagement discipline, expectation alignment, and the effective use of scarce management time. Over time, it can demonstrate whether these efforts are strengthening the company's valuation and its position in capital markets. That standard—disciplined, contextual, and honest—is what this framework is designed to support.

Properly applied, measurement should not be seen as a constraint imposed on Investor Relations. On the contrary, it offers the legitimacy it needs to function optimally—globally, across governance cultures, and across market cycles.

Practical Implications

- Measure Investor Relations deliberately
- Assess IR through a return-on-investment lens

- Let capital-market priorities and company maturity determine what is measured
- Combine quantitative indicators with structured qualitative assessment
- Interpret market-based indicators comparatively and over time, recognizing external influences
- Focus measurement on interpretation and identification of improvement areas
- Apply realistic time horizons when assessing progress
- Review and adapt the framework as strategy, ownership, leadership and market conditions evolve.

The frameworks presented in this chapter affirm that Investor Relations effectiveness and value must be measured through strategic outcomes rather than activity counts, but measurement does not conclude the discussion.

Investor Relations operates within an evolving capital-market environment, and the final chapter examines what will endure, what may be reshaped, and what capabilities the profession will require as expectations, tools, and market structures continue to develop.

8

Investor Relations: Continuity and Change

Investor Relations evolves continuously—but not in a straight line. Some forces change tools. Others reshape the operating model. A few redefine what boards, CEOs, and IROs are expected to deliver.

This chapter is not a futurist forecast. Its purpose is practical: to help IR leaders distinguish what will endure, what is already changing, and what could reshape the field faster than organizations are prepared to absorb.

8.1 What Will Not Change in IR

The Structural Constants of IR

Despite technological acceleration and evolving regulatory frameworks, three foundations of effective Investor Relations remain stable.

- **The competition for capital**

Capital markets will remain a global competition—crowded, comparative, and unforgiving. Companies with similar fundamentals will continue to be differentiated by the quality of their Investor Relations. That advantage cannot be automated, outsourced, or regulated away.

- **Trust, transparency, and consistency**

Formats will change. The market's requirements will continue to demand:

A. Guimard, *Investor Relations Strategy*, https://doi.org/10.1007/978-3-032-21679-3_8

- timely, accurate, comparable information;
- explanations that link performance to strategy;
- credible outlook communication;
- disciplined disclosure.

Technology may change distribution, facilitate narrative development, and refine investor targeting. It does not diminish the market's demand for—or pricing of—trust.

- **The human element**

Investor Relations will always require judgment: interpreting signals, managing expectations, negotiating constraints, and building relationships. The IRO's advisory role to the CEO and the board becomes more—not less—valuable as complexity rises. No algorithm replaces seasoned judgment in a crisis, a profit warning, or a hostile approach.

8.2 What Will Change in IR

One of IR's enduring strengths is adaptability. That will remain true—but the pace of change will test operating discipline.

- **Technology and the digital IR ecosystem**

AI, automation, data platforms, and digital channels are changing how IR is executed—without changing its purpose.

This evolution is not limited to the IRO or the Investor Relations function. It reflects the maturation of a broader Investor Relations ecosystem—one that includes technology providers, data platforms, analytics firms, perception specialists, and advisory services. Far from displacing the profession, this ecosystem has become an essential enabler of modern IR practice. The relationship is not adversarial, but interdependent.

A critical structural shift underpins this evolution. There was a time when issuers typically possessed more information than investors. While companies still control material non-public information, many institutional investors, asset managers, proxy advisors, and financial intermediaries now possess analytical capabilities that exceed those of most corporate IR functions. They have invested earlier and more aggressively in technology, data science, and analytics than most listed companies themselves. As a result, the asymmetry increasingly lies not in access to information alone, but in the ability to process data, benchmark performance, identify patterns, and translate fragmented signals into investment conclusions at scale and speed. Markets increasingly analyze companies through tools and lenses that issuers themselves do not fully control—or even replicate internally.

This creates a strategic paradox for Investor Relations. IROs are pushed into a perpetual catch-up race: expected to match the analytical sophistication of markets while operating with fewer internal resources, tighter governance constraints, and higher regulatory risk. The danger is not falling behind technologically per se, but reacting tactically—chasing tools rather than clarifying meaning.

Used well, however, technology offers a decisive opportunity rather than a threat. AI and advanced analytics can help IR functions:

- measure the return on Investor Relations activity with greater precision, linking engagement, perception, and outcomes more rigorously than before;
- design genuinely differentiated shareholder engagement strategies, informed by behavior, patterns, and feedback rather than generic targeting;
- empower IROs with an additional analytical dimension in an already multipolar market environment, where capital, narratives, and influence are globally dispersed.

These benefits are real—but so are the risks. Poor data quality, flawed assumptions, manipulated information, fake news, or over-reliance on automated outputs can lead to false confidence. Technology can amplify noise as easily as insight, obscure what truly matters, or introduce new vulnerabilities through cyber risk and data manipulation. AI does not eliminate judgment; it raises the cost of getting judgment wrong.

The strategic task for Investor Relations is therefore not to "keep up" with markets technologically, but to harness the evolving ecosystem intelligently—using tools to sharpen insight. Technology becomes an extension of IR judgment, not a substitute for it.

What fundamentally changes in the age of AI is not only how companies communicate, but how investors read. Advanced analytics increasingly extract insight from language, tone, sequencing, and peripheral signals that were never intended as disclosure in the traditional sense. In this environment, meaning is inferred as much as it is stated, as algorithms and machine-driven analysis increasingly shape both disclosure and investment decision-making.

The IRO's role therefore shifts further toward:

- curating insights (what matters);
- providing interpretation (what it implies);
- guarding narrative coherence over time and across channels;
- integrating technology with disclosure discipline, ensuring that tools serve communication goals rather than the reverse.

- **Reporting and regulatory requirements**

Three forces will continue to reshape disclosure:

- ESG disclosure becoming mandatory, more standardized, and more assurance-driven;
- convergence toward integrated reporting;
- conflicting pressures between more continuous disclosure, as real-time data capabilities mature, and reduced formal reporting frequency, as exemplified by periodic debates over allowing public companies to replace quarterly reporting with semiannual interim disclosures.

The primary disclosure risk is no longer what is said, but what is unintentionally revealed through inconsistency. Divergence between strategy narratives, operational execution, capital allocation, governance behavior, and leadership tone is increasingly detectable—and priced—by markets. AI does not create this risk; it accelerates its visibility and consequences.

At the same time, the reporting cadence debate remains unresolved. Whatever direction it ultimately takes, the implication for Investor Relations is consistent: fewer formal anchors increase the cost of imprecision, thereby strengthening the case for greater transparency, more granular disclosure, and clearer contextual communication.

ESG, in particular, has moved from a communications topic to a matter of governance and data architecture. This shift will continue to shape—and in some organizations determine—the position and authority of IR within the enterprise.

- **The redefinition of engagement**

Engagement is no longer confined to roadshows, conferences, earnings calls, and one-on-one meetings. The boundaries of the "IR audience" keep widening.

Key shifts include:

- hybrid and virtual engagement becoming permanent;
- targeting and outreach becoming increasingly data-driven;
- stakeholder groups consuming information through the same ecosystem;
- non-traditional distribution channels—social media and "finfluencers"—shaping perception even where they are not formally regulated.

Extended and 24-hour trading will add pressure, as most companies will not staff IR around the clock. The challenge—already familiar to companies dual-listed across multiple time zones— concentrates in three areas:

1. Timing: when to disclose and when to communicate for actual comprehension;
2. Resourcing: monitoring and escalation without building a 24/7 function;
3. Expectations: global investors increasingly expecting responsiveness across time zones.

The companies that cope best will be those that define clear thresholds, disciplined escalation, and well-understood decision authority.

- **Proxy advisors and activist investors**

Proxy advisory firms and activist investors have evolved from exceptional disruptors into permanent market infrastructure. Activism and proxy dynamics are now a structural feature of modern capital markets and a visible mechanism through which dissatisfaction is expressed.

Proxy advisors increasingly function as *de facto* standard-setters. Their governance frameworks influence voting outcomes across thousands of companies and are applied systematically by many institutional investors, particularly on routine matters. Governance approaches that diverge from these frameworks—even when strategically justified—therefore face higher voting friction.

Companies need to recognize that no capital structure or governance design is immune to activism. Activist campaigns typically emerge where investors perceive persistent gaps between stated strategy and observable outcomes, inconsistent capital allocation, or governance insufficient to discipline decision-making.

The most consequential campaigns succeed when activism and proxy advisor influence reinforce one another. Activists appeal to mainstream investors by highlighting strategic inconsistency, governance weaknesses, or misaligned incentives. When proxy advisors validate those claims, activist positions gain disproportionate influence.

In an environment where activists and proxy advisors increasingly shape outcomes together, Investor Relations becomes a critical point of alignment between strategy, disclosure, governance, and market expectations. Activism rarely succeeds by uncovering new information but by exposing gaps between what a company says, what it does, and how it governs itself. In the age of AI-assisted analysis, those gaps are detected faster, amplified more widely, and reframed more persuasively than ever before.

- **The impact of generational change on expectations from Boards and the C-Suite**

Investor behavior is evolving as younger professionals shape capital allocation. Expectations shift in four predictable ways:

- consumption: digital-first;
- values: ESG treated as embedded risk analysis, no longer as a separate topic;
- engagement: virtual by default;
- tone: authenticity increasingly valued over manufactured precision.

Investor Relations must serve diverse preferences simultaneously without fragmenting the message. This is not either/or. It is both/and: written depth alongside short-form clarity; in-person access alongside high-quality virtual alternatives; financial fundamentals alongside credible ESG linkage.

Internally, boards and executives increasingly expect IR to deliver sharper analysis, stronger valuation literacy, proactive perception intelligence, and fluency in AI-enabled workflows. Investor Relations' "seat at the table" should become standard. It remains too often treated as discretionary rather than integral to decision-making.

8.3 What Could Change in IR

Investor Relations' preparedness is not in doubt. What remains uncertain is how quickly specific forces will crystallize.

Market Structure

Possible shifts include:

- tokenization and fractional ownership;
- a larger retail role in price formation, often accompanied by greater volatility;
- continued growth of AI-driven and passive strategies, reducing the influence of traditional active management.

These developments could reshape targeting and engagement norms. IR should monitor them closely—without over-investing ahead of proof.

Cross-Border Convergence vs Divergence

Regulatory regimes may converge around global standards—or diverge as geopolitics and domestic priorities pull in different directions. Both outcomes demand global literacy: the same disclosure can be interpreted very differently in Riyadh, London, Paris, Singapore, or New York. In particular, it will be interesting to watch whether emerging and frontier markets will adopt certain disclosure practices as the earnings release that is the standard in more developed markets.

A globally effective IRO adapts context without compromising message consistency.

Information Integrity

Cyber risk, deepfakes, and rapid misinformation already exist. The likelihood is that they intensify.

A paradox is emerging. AI-assisted drafting can improve clarity and efficiency, yet excessive polish risks suppressing the authentic signals that sophisticated investors rely on to assess credibility. In a market where every signal is algorithmically readable, sounding perfect can be as risky as sounding unprepared.

This elevates IR's role as a guardian of verified information and demands tighter internal protocols, faster verification paths, and clearer crisis-prevention mechanics. Information integrity becomes an IR competency—not a problem delegated to IT. Tools will evolve, but governance cannot be outsourced.

Stakeholder Capitalism

Whether stakeholder capitalism represents a paradigm shift or a cyclical rebalancing remains debated. For Investor Relations, the operational reality is clear: investors increasingly assess workforce practices, environmental impact, supply-chain resilience, and societal contribution through the lens of financial relevance and risk.

The IR response require translation:

- linking stakeholder initiatives to performance, resilience, and cost of capital;
- applying rigorous materiality discipline;
- avoiding generic narratives unsupported by measurable relevance.

Boards face growing pressure to articulate capital allocation decisions, particularly restructurings, under multi-stakeholder scrutiny. Investor Relations remains the integrator—connecting ESG disclosure to strategy rather than allowing it to sit as a parallel reporting universe.

8.4 The Investor Relations Officer of the Future

If the foundations of Investor Relations remain constant, the operating environment does not. The appropriate response is anticipatory capability-building—not trend-chasing. While the foundations of Investor Relations remain stable, they do not eliminate the need for ongoing adaptation, capability-building, and operational readiness.

Skills that Will Matter Most

The future IRO sill require a broader range of core capabilities, including:

- valuation fluency and scenario thinking;
- crisis execution and reputation-risk management;
- ESG literacy anchored in governance and data;
- geopolitical and macro awareness;
- AI and analytics proficiency as decision support.

The objective is not to master everything. Capability-building in Investor Relations should reflect the company's context, priorities, and market realities.

The Operating Model

High-performing IR functions are evolving toward:

- more specialized team composition;
- selective use of external experts and technology partners to amplify capacity;
- tighter integration with finance, strategy, legal, risk, and sustainability;
- more structured workflows for monitoring, disclosure, and Board engagement.

The trend favors smaller, agile core teams with deeper expertise, augmented by systems and partners, rather than large in-house departments attempting to do everything themselves.

8.5 Conclusion: The Enduring Role of Investor Relations

The fundamentals endure: truthfulness, accuracy, completeness, objectivity, timeliness, and clarity. They also require authenticity—authenticity that allows investors to distinguish between communication that is produced and communication that is owned. In an environment where technology makes it easier than ever to generate messages, authenticity becomes the signal that demonstrates accountability. These are not principles to be modernized; they are the foundation on which effective Investor Relations has always been built, and will continue to rest.

ESG, AI, and digital transformation are real forces reshaping execution models, but they are tools, not purposes. As AI-generated content becomes ubiquitous, investors will increasingly distinguish between companies that use technology to support transparent decision-making and those that use it to mask weak judgment or avoid accountability. Authenticity—the discipline of ensuring that communication reflects genuine management judgment and accountability—becomes a source of competitive differentiation. In increasingly automated communication environments, it signals responsibility, authorship, and trustworthiness.

What changes is the context in which IR principles are applied: the speed at which markets interpret information, the complexity of stakeholder expectations, and the technologies that enable scale—and amplify inconsistency. Companies compete for capital, and the quality of communication and transparency continues to influence valuation, access to funding, and strategic freedom. In this sense, Investor Relations strategy remains inseparable from shareholder value creation.

The evolution of IR is about transforming IR's strategic role inside the organization—making the IRO a trusted advisor, a guardian of credibility, and a recognized contributor to long-term value. This elevation should no longer be merely aspirational. Yet too many CEOs and Boards still treat Investor Relations as a necessary evil rather than a competitive asset.

Management teams that view IR as overhead rather than investment, or as communications support rather than strategic discipline, create a measurable disadvantage for themselves in the competition for capital.

Successful adaptation therefore requires two conditions: executive leadership that treats Investor Relations as an investment generating measurable returns, and operational discipline that preserves message integrity even as contexts evolve. That tension—between innovation and stability—is where effective Investor Relations has always operated.

In an environment where information is abundant, signals are amplified, and inconsistencies are priced faster than ever, Investor Relations is not about managing information alone.

It is about managing meaning.

That discipline creates measurable shareholder value. When Investor Relations operates as a strategic capability, it delivers the competitive advantages outlined in this book: enhanced visibility, improved shareholder-base quality, stronger management credibility, valuation resilience, superior access to capital, expanded strategic options, and reinforced reputation. These are the predictable outcomes of treating Investor Relations as a management discipline rather than a communications function.

The companies that understand this distinction, and act on it, will continue to win the competition for capital.

9

Resources

9.1 Shareholder Base Management Execution Checklist

I. **Quarterly shareholder review**

Use this checklist every quarter or following major market moves, against engagement events (such as roadshows, conferences, one-on-one meetings).

Data & analysis

- Identify the full shareholder base (top holders, changes, new entrants, exits).
- Compare against target investor profile and competitor shareholder bases.
- Analyze ownership trends (inflows/outflows) vs. valuation performance.
- Identify concentration risk (over-reliance on one geography, one fund type, one style).
- Assess shareholder stability (average holding period, turnover).

Qualitative review

- Review recent meeting feedback and sentiment reports.
- Identify supportive vs. at-risk shareholders.
- Detect early signs of activism or governance concerns.

Outcome & actions

A. Guimard, *Investor Relations Strategy*, https://doi.org/10.1007/978-3-032-21679-3_9

- Update the target list for next quarter, refine the engagement strategy.
- Flag priority investors for outreach or retention.
- Summarize findings for CFO/CEO/Board.

II. **Investor targeting execution checklist**

Use this when planning a targeting cycle (typically quarterly or semi-annual).

Target definition

- Confirm priority geographies and fund styles aligned with your equity story.
- Define minimum investment thresholds (AUM, typical position size).
- Apply exclusion criteria (sector bias, ESG constraints, turnover).

Target identification

- Build a comprehensive list using:
  - Peer ownership
  - Screening tools
  - Broker input
  - Conferences
  - Prior interactions
- Prioritize 30–50 high-potential institutions.

Engagement preparation

- Prepare tailored materials: 3–4 key messages, slides, Q&A.
- Review account-specific preferences (value/growth, ESG screens, financial focus).
- Align CEO/CFO/IRO roles for meetings.

Execution

- Book roadshows or virtual meetings with brokers or directly.
- Track attendance, questions, sentiment, and follow-up items.

Post-engagement

- Debrief, including logistics and broker's execution if roadshow/meetings were outsourced.
- Update CRM system.
- Evaluate effectiveness: conversion rate, progression along targeting funnel.
- Refine targeting criteria for next cycle.

III. **Investor retention checklist**

Use this semi-annually or after significant inflection points.

Retention risk review

- Identify top 20 shareholders' level of conviction and holding horizon.
- Review recent investor commentary or changes in sentiment.
- Assess whether guidance, strategy, or results align with prior expectations.
- Monitor governance and ESG issues likely to influence retention. Ensure you have the contact at the governance/proxy voting team of the institutional investors.

Retention actions

- Schedule one-on-one updates with at-risk holders.
- Provide transparent explanations for underperformance.
- Share mid-term strategy refresh or progress.
- Offer site visits or deeper engagement on key topics.

Success metrics

- Holding period extension
- Decrease in unexpected exits
- Improved satisfaction scores in perception studies

9.2 Investor Engagement Program Checklist

I. **Pre-engagement preparation**

- Define purpose: targeting, retention, education, and correction of misperceptions.
- Confirm participant roles (CEO, CFO, IRO).

- Create executive summary per institution, including a review of prior interactions, meeting notes, and sentiment. Add LinkedIn profiles of portfolio managers and any media interviews.
- Align messages with latest disclosures.
- Conduct rehearsal and scenario planning.

II. **Meeting execution**

- Begin with a clear narrative refresh (investment case, strategy, catalysts).
- Ask investors' views early to calibrate discussion.
- Avoid selective disclosure; refer to public information only.
- Probe investor priorities (valuation drivers, ESG thresholds, risk tolerance).
- Note all questions, objections, and unresolved issues.

III. **Post-meeting follow-up**

- Send thank you note, follow-up answers within 48 hours.
- Update CRM with sentiment, questions, and potential risks.
- Identify cross-patterns across multiple meetings.
- Schedule next touchpoint (in 3–6 months depending on importance and reporting cycle).

IV. **Execution KPIs**

- Meeting-to-engagement conversion rate
- Target investor penetration
- Sentiment improvement
- Increase in quality of shareholder base.

9.3 Global IR Management Checklist

I. **Time-zone planning**

- Provide two options for earnings calls (home market and largest investor-base abroad).
- Schedule global roadshows to minimize travel strain for top management.
- Use virtual engagement to complement in-person meetings.

II. **Cultural adaptation**

- Adjust meeting styles.

- Tailor presentations to regional investor priorities (value vs. growth focus).
- Understand regional expectations for ESG or governance disclosure.

III. **Regulatory compliance**

- Validate disclosure obligations and expectations in each jurisdiction.
- Use consistent wording to avoid unintentional guidance.
- Ensure materials are filed with the local stock market authorities where required.

IV. **Translation & currency**

- Prepare high-quality translated materials where needed.
- Standardize FX explanations (constant-currency metrics).
- Anticipate currency-driven misunderstandings and address proactively.

9.4 Technology & AI Implementation Template

I. **Technology audit**
Determine current capabilities in:

- CRM and meeting tracking
- Ownership analytics
- ESG data management
- Website and content management
- Sentiment monitoring
- Workflow automation (e.g., emailing, regulatory filings)

II. **AI use case identification**
Select relevant high-impact applications:

- Automated drafting of Q&A or meeting summaries
- Shareholder-movement predictions
- Analyst sentiment clustering
- Risk detection (activism, valuation anomalies)
- CRM enrichment
- Natural-language analysis of earnings transcripts

III. **Implementation steps**

- Define objectives and KPIs
- Leverage insights from IR peers/IR societies to identify and select technology vendors

- Run pilot tests on limited datasets, checking for ease of use and cyber-risks
- Train IR and legal teams on responsible use
- Establish approval workflows for AI-assisted content
- Monitor for accuracy and compliance risks

IV. **KPIs**

- Time and costs saved per reporting cycle
- Reduction of manual errors
- Increased targeting precision
- Faster insight conversion to action

Index

A. Guimard, *Investor Relations Strategy*, https://doi.org/10.1007/978-3-032-21679-3

D

K

L

The manufacturer's authorised representative in the EU is Springer
Nature Customer Service Centre GmbH, Europaplatz 3, 69115 Heidelberg,
Germany. If you have any concerns regarding our products, please
contact ProductSafety@springernature.com

Printed and bound by CPI Group (UK) Ltd, Croydon, CR0 4YY
17/09/2026
02218454-0016